STANISŁAW WYSPIAŃSKI
PORTRAITS

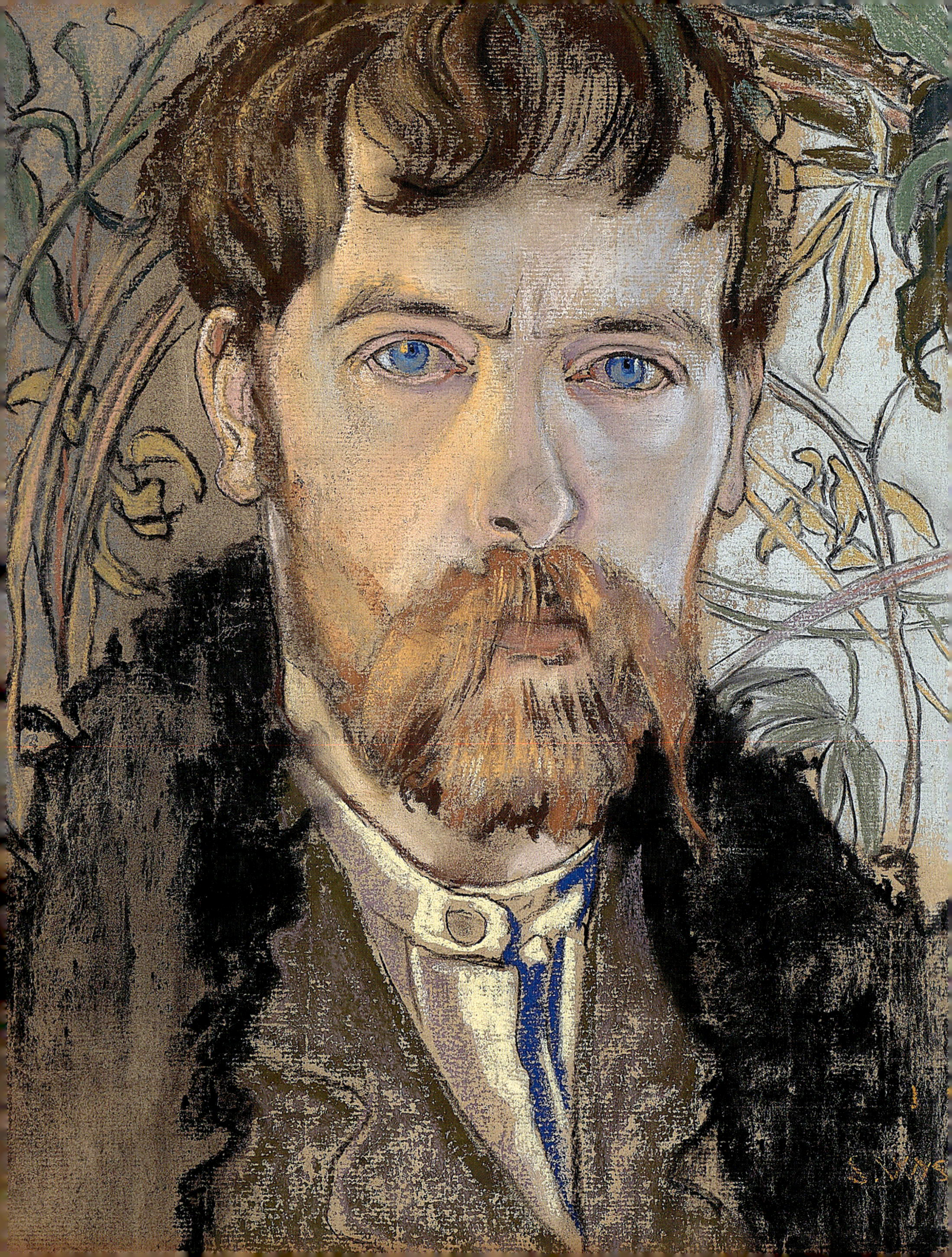

STANISŁAW WYSPIAŃSKI
PORTRAITS

EDITED BY ALISON SMITH WITH JULIA GRIFFIN

WITH CONTRIBUTIONS BY
ANDRZEJ SZCZERSKI, MAGDALENA LASKOWSKA,
AGNIESZKA SKALSKA AND MARIA SKRZYPCZAK-LATZKE

NATIONAL PORTRAIT GALLERY

CONTENTS

TO STANISLAW WYSPIANSKI

From the other side of the world,
From a little island cradled in the giant sea
    bosom,
From a little land with no history,
(Making its own history, slowly and clumsily
Piecing together this and that, finding the pattern,
    solving the problem,
Like a child with a box of bricks),
I, a woman, with the taint of the pioneer in my blood,
Full of a youthful strength that wars with itself and is
    lawless,
I sing your praises, magnificent warrior; I proclaim
    your triumphant battle.
My people have had nought to contend with;
They have worked in the broad light of day and
    handled the clay with rude fingers;
Life – a thing of blood and muscle; Death – a
    shovelling underground of waste material.
What would they know of ghosts and unseen
    presences,
Of shadows that blot out reality, of darkness that
    stultifies morn?
Fine and sweet the water that runs from their
    mountains;
How could they know of poisonous weed, of rotted
    and clogging tendrils?
And the tapestry woven from dreams of your tragic
    childhood

They would tear in their stupid hands,
The sad, pale light of your soul blow out with their
    childish laughter.
But the dead – the old – Oh Master, we belong to you
    there;
Oh Master, there we are children and awed by the
    strength of a giant;
How alive you leapt into the grave and wrestled with
    Death
And found in the veins of Death the red blood
    flowing
And raised Death up in your arms and showed him
    to all the people.
Yours a more personal labor than the Nazarene's
    miracles,
Yours a more forceful encounter than the Nazarene's
    gentle commands.
Stanislaw Wyspianski – Oh man with the name of a
    fighter,
Across these thousands of sea-shattered miles we cry
    and proclaim you;
We say 'He is lying in Poland, and Poland thinks
    he is dead;
But he gave the denial to Death – he is lying there,
    wakeful;
The blood in his giant heart pulls red through his
    veins.'

KATHERINE MANSFIELD
Wörishofen, January 1910

THE LIFE AND ART OF STANISŁAW WYSPIAŃSKI

ALISON SMITH AND JULIA GRIFFIN

In the note that accompanies the first English publication of Katherine Mansfield's stirring paean *To Stanislaw Wyspianski* (1910) – issued posthumously in 1938 – Stanisław Wyspiański (1869–1907) is described as the greatest literary genius produced by modern Poland, an artist with an unconquerable faith in the future of his country.[1] As a result of the partition treaties of 1772, 1793 and 1795, Poland had been divided between Prussia, Russia and Austria-Hungary and was to endure a 123-year-long bitter struggle to regain independence, with a number of uprisings resulting in harsh reprisals. Certainly, during the final years of Poland's political non-existence, Wyspiański was hailed by many Poles to be the voice of the partitioned nation, an artist who envisioned its rebirth not only as a political struggle but, more importantly, as a spiritual quest. This belief must have been uppermost in the mind of the literary critic and translator Floryan Sobieniowski when he introduced Mansfield, then his lover, to the work of Wyspiański in 1909, just two years after the artist's untimely death from syphilis, aged 38. Whether Mansfield actually visited Kraków with Sobieniowski to experience Wyspiański's works first-hand, as is suggested by her poem, is not altogether certain but she was clearly inspired by the artist's vision and example. She was one of the very few English-speaking people to be aware of his achievement in the years immediately following his death. The scant mentions in the British press focused on Wyspiański's remarkable versatility, calling him 'a kind of Polish William Morris, to whom no form of art came amiss'.[2]

Wyspiański was a polymath – an artist, designer, interior decorator, master-craftsman and national bard – who worked across a wide range of disciplines in pursuing his creative goals. In the field of literature, he wrote poems and plays that he directed himself while also devising sets and costumes for his own productions. He designed stained-glass windows, furniture, textiles and wall paintings as well as layouts and covers for his own and others' publications. He produced portraits and landscapes, mainly in pastel, while also practising as a sculptor, architect and urban planner. He was a classical scholar, art historian, botanist and antiquarian with a great knowledge of architecture and particularly of medieval churches. Added to which was his work as a city

FIG.1
Decorative scheme at Kraków's Franciscan Friary, 1895–1904, including the stained-glass of *Blessed Salomea* (left; before 1902) and *St Francis of Assisi* (right; 1897) as well as figurative and ornamental wall paintings

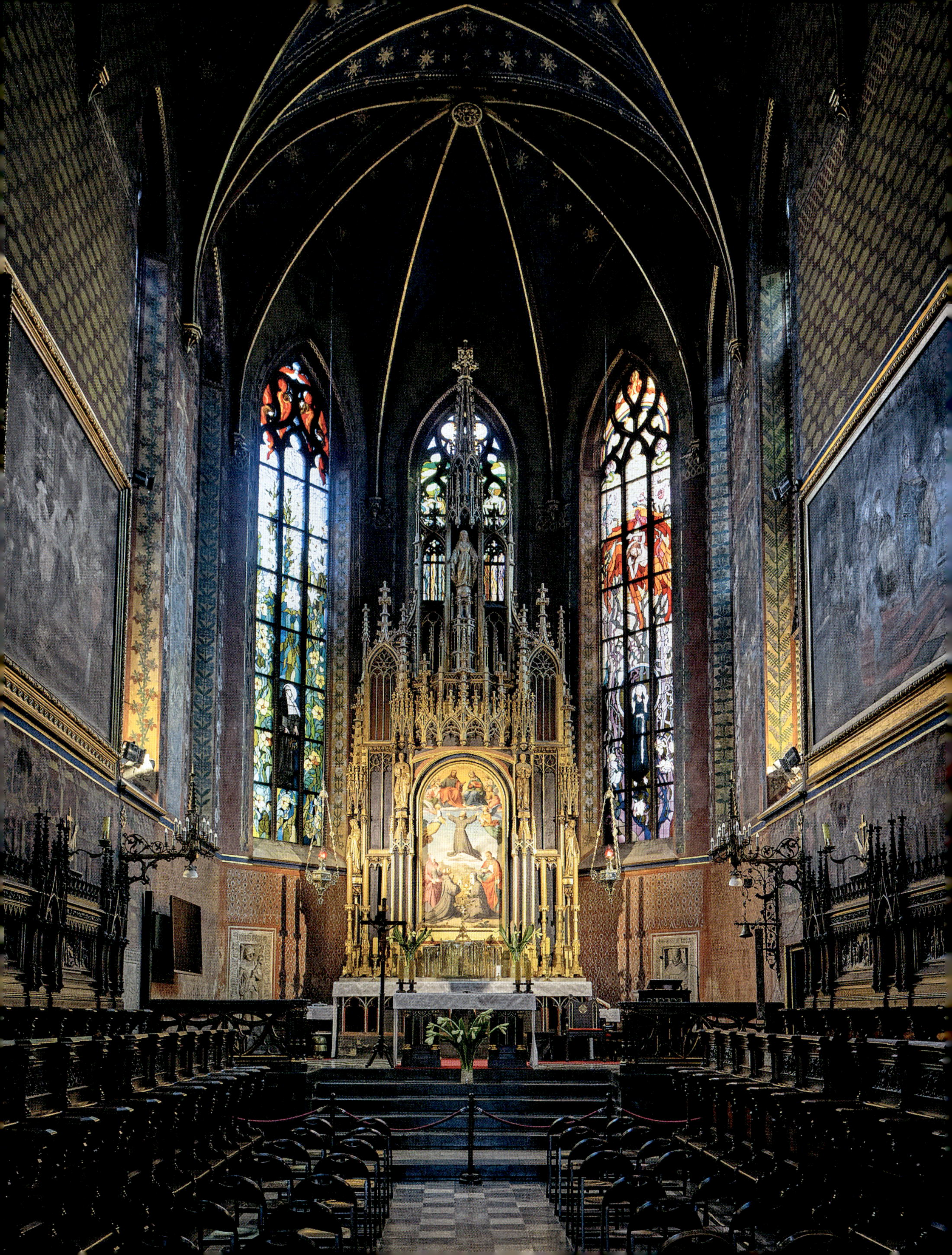

councillor, reformer and teacher at the Academy of Fine Arts in Kraków.
As co-founder of the 'Sztuka' (Art) Society of Polish Artists and the Polish
Applied Arts Society, Wyspiański was an influential force on the art scene,
shaping the development of all visual arts in Poland at what was to prove
a decisive moment in the history of the country.

Crucially, Wyspiański was a key player in Young Poland, part of the
international Arts and Crafts Movement that aimed to create a new national
art based on vernacular traditions interpreted in a distinct, modern way.
The Young Poland movement emerged as an expression of Polish people's
yearning for political independence and as a means of preserving their
cultural identity. It originated under the more liberal Austrian partition in
the south (known as Galicia) and notably in Kraków and the nearby village
of Zakopane in the Podhale region of the Tatra Mountains (part of the
Carpathians). Paintings, household objects, interior decoration schemes
and whole buildings had symbolic meaning, becoming subversive carriers of
Polishness. Artists and designers created a new visual language, simultaneously
inward- and outward-looking, inspired by the history, nature and spirituality
of their lost country. Traditional peasant culture and native handicraft were
seen as authentic repositories of Polish design and antidotes to the influx of
foreign, mass-produced goods imported by the partitioning powers – and
hence by extension an important expression of Polish political resistance.
Young Poland conveyed a spirit of renewal, frequently represented by the
metaphor of spring and youth, and was instrumental in helping to bring about
independence in 1918.[3]

There is a multi-disciplinary aspect to everything Wyspiański created that
gives his work its all-encompassing power and energy, as seen in his greatest
Gesamtkunstwerk creations – the decorative schemes for the Franciscan
Friary (1895–1904; fig.1) and the Medical Society (1904–5; fig.2) in Kraków.
However, his experimental vision and uncompromising manner meant that
his applications to carry out a number of other public arts commissions were
rejected, resulting in ephemeral or fragmentary outputs. His famous stained-
glass design for Lviv Cathedral, *Polonia* (1894; fig.3), for instance, was never
realised and exists only as a pastel drawing but is nonetheless a compelling
piece of theatre in its own right. A pictorial counterpart to the artist's dramatic
1893 verse narrative *Queen of the Polish Crown (Królowa Polskiej Korony)*,
it contains portraits of living people whose expressions of despair are echoed
by the 'rotting tendrils' (to quote Mansfield) that encircle the dying queen.
As a portrait of a nation under duress, it synthesises poetry, stage design,
the applied arts and portraiture to convey its plaintive patriotic message.[4]

Stanisław Wyspiański
*Apollo: Copernicus's
Solar System*, 1904
Stained-glass cartoon for
the decorative scheme at
the Kraków Medical Society
Pastel on paper,
3430 × 1460mm
National Museum
in Kraków

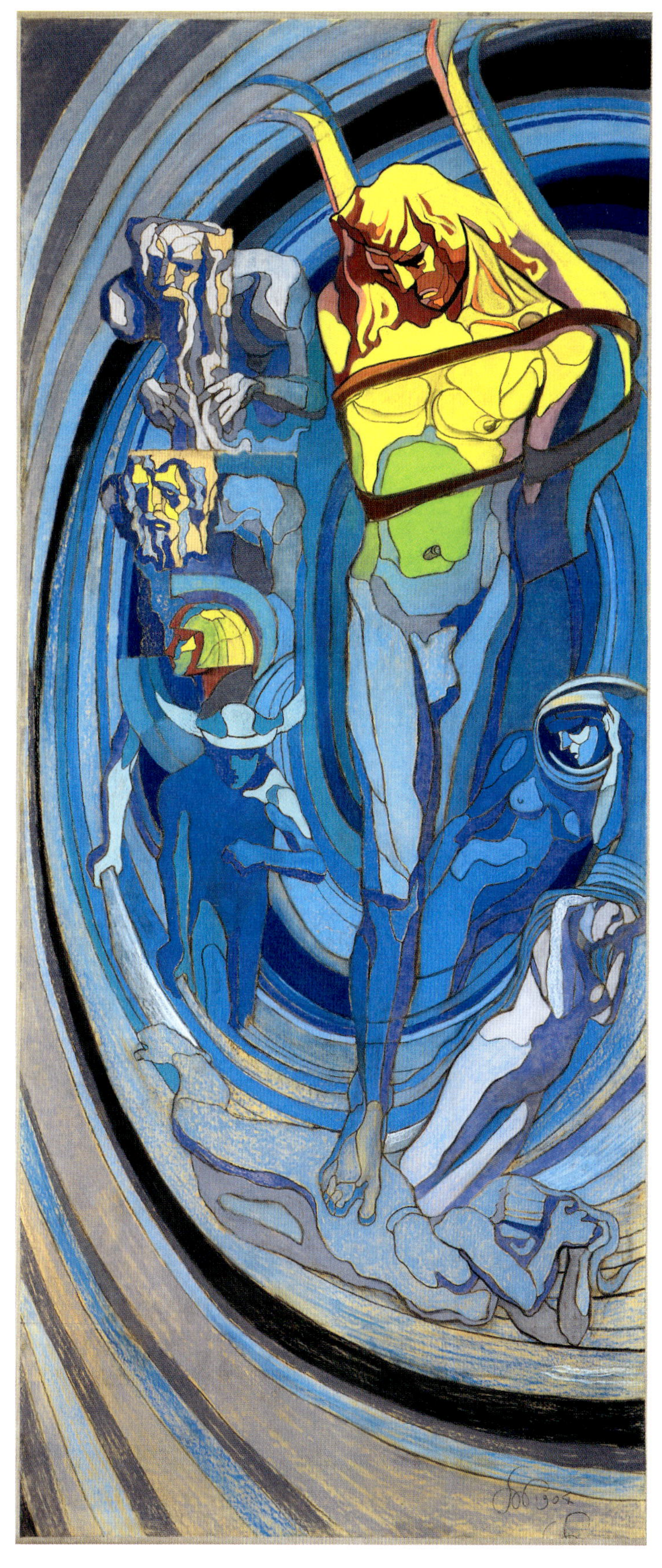

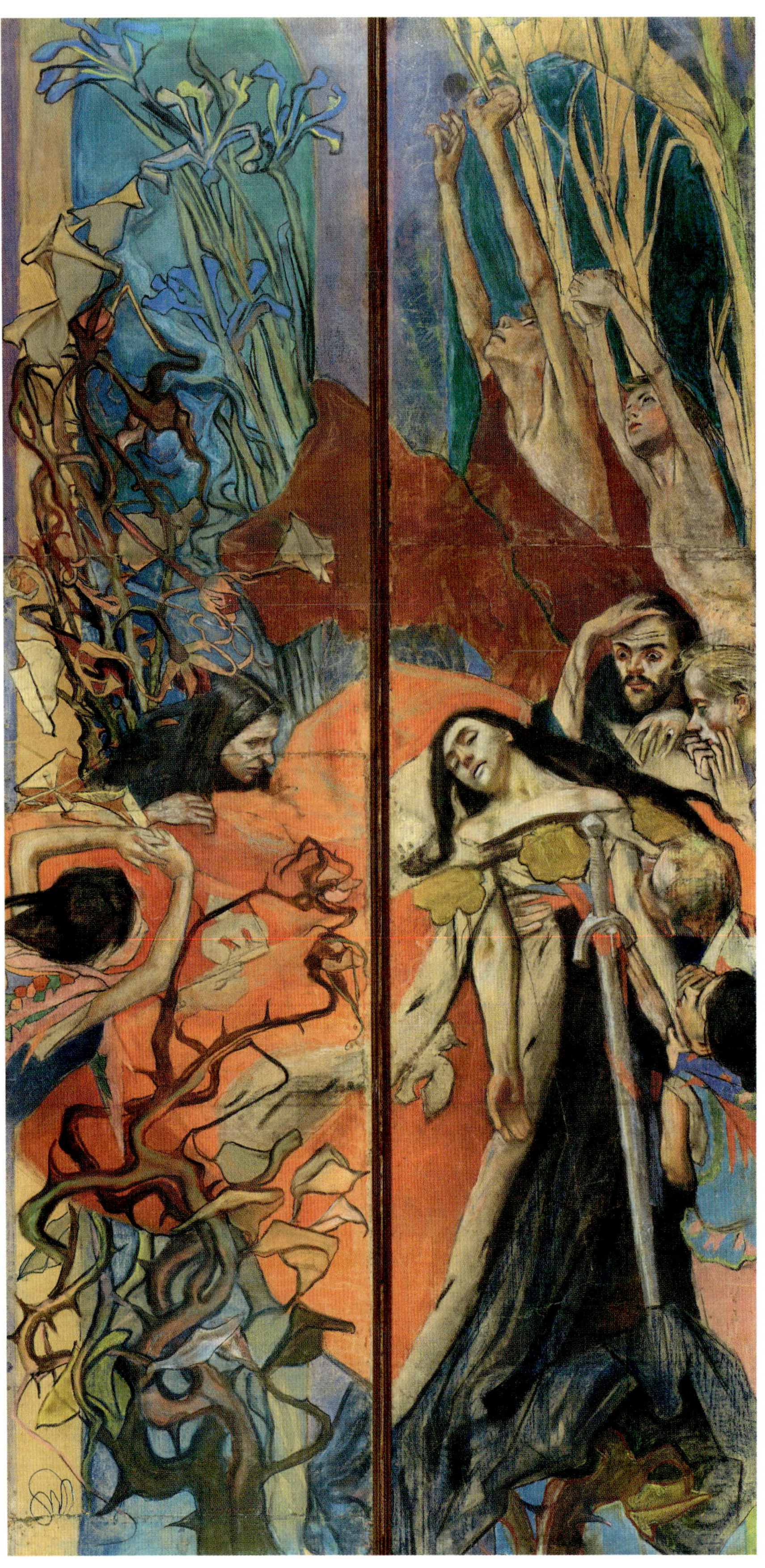

That Wyspiański is only now beginning to be recognised outside of Poland should not be surprising given the country's lack of political autonomy during the years he was active and for a considerable part of the twentieth century. In many respects, Wyspiański was fortunate in being based in the Austrian partition, which allowed greater freedom of expression compared to areas under Russian and Prussian control, but Poland's political oppression impeded recognition in the international arena. Wyspiański was, however, able to travel within Europe and became an exhibitor at the internationalist Vienna Secession, a society of which he was a life member.[5] His works were never accorded a solo exhibition in a mainstream venue further west, either during his lifetime or before the Second World War, despite his strong connections with Paris. During the communist years there were limited opportunities for his work to be seen beyond the Iron Curtain.[6] Most of Wyspiański's creations were site-specific, designed for particular ecclesiastical and institutional settings. They include his plan to reconstruct Wawel Hill as a Polish Acropolis and his highly controversial stained-glass designs for the chancel and transept of Wawel Cathedral, discussed below. Wyspiański's choice of medium also hindered more widespread recognition as pastel is fragile and liable to flake, making it difficult to transport. The hermetic nature of Wyspiański's distinctively Polish subject matter is moreover not easy to understand outside of its immediate context, which helps explain why his plays and other writings are difficult to translate and have only recently been presented in English: *The Wedding* (*Wesele*) first appeared in English translation in 1998, followed by *Acropolis: The Wawel Plays* in 2017, and *Hamlet Study* and *The Death of Ophelia* in 2019.[7]

Because it was impossible for Wyspiański to realise all his monumental interior decoration projects, the portraits he made had to carry the burden of expressing national identity. He had a keen and consistent interest in depicting people throughout his career, with his most outstanding portraits created in the last decade of his life. Encompassing representations of Young Poland personalities, his wife and children, legendary and historical protagonists as well as self-portraits, Wyspiański's portrait practice extended to experimental *kryptoportrety* – concealed (self-) portraits and/or likenesses with a hidden political or biographical message.

It may seem surprising that Wyspiański's portraits were not more highly regarded in his day, but his contemporaries – and indeed the artist himself – believed that monumental decorative schemes and ornamentation were his true forte. The art collector and connoisseur Feliks Jasieński, for one, claimed that Wyspiański's portraits were a case of 'an eagle trapped in a henhouse' – an inadequate outlet of his unfulfilled talent.[8] In fact, Wyspiański's portraits

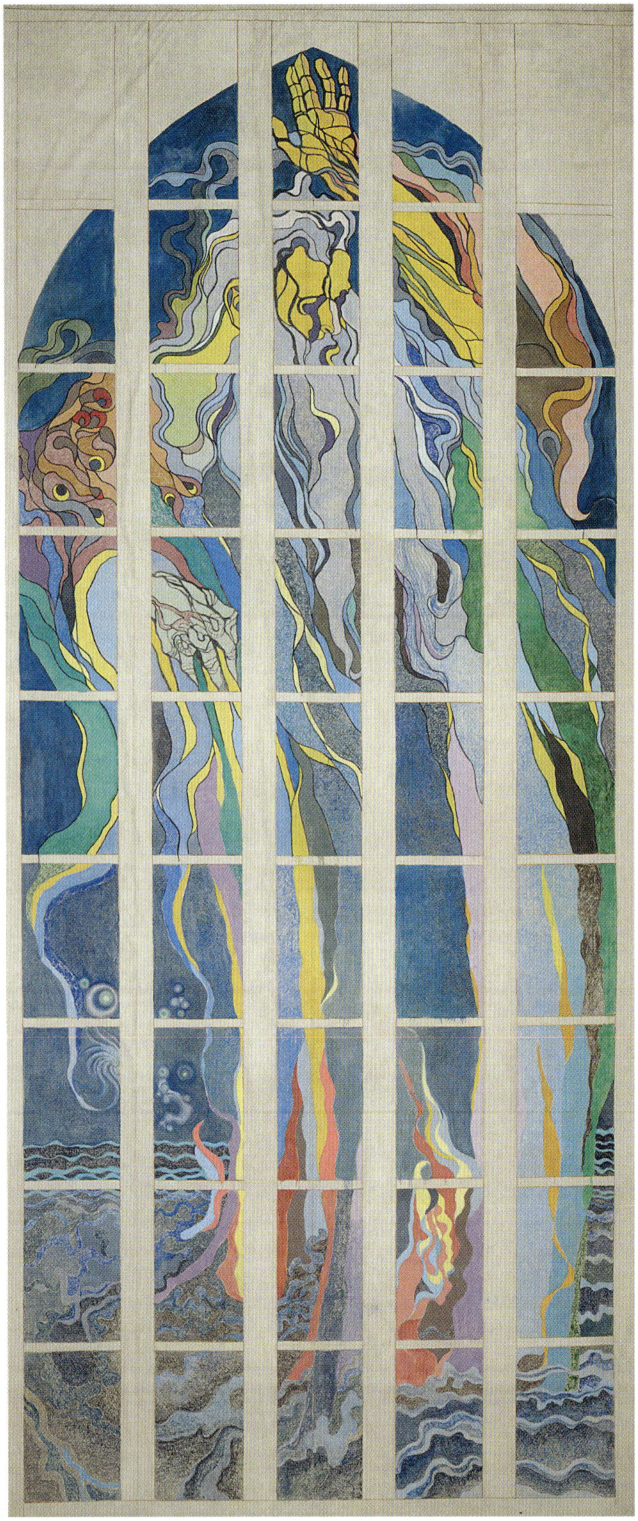

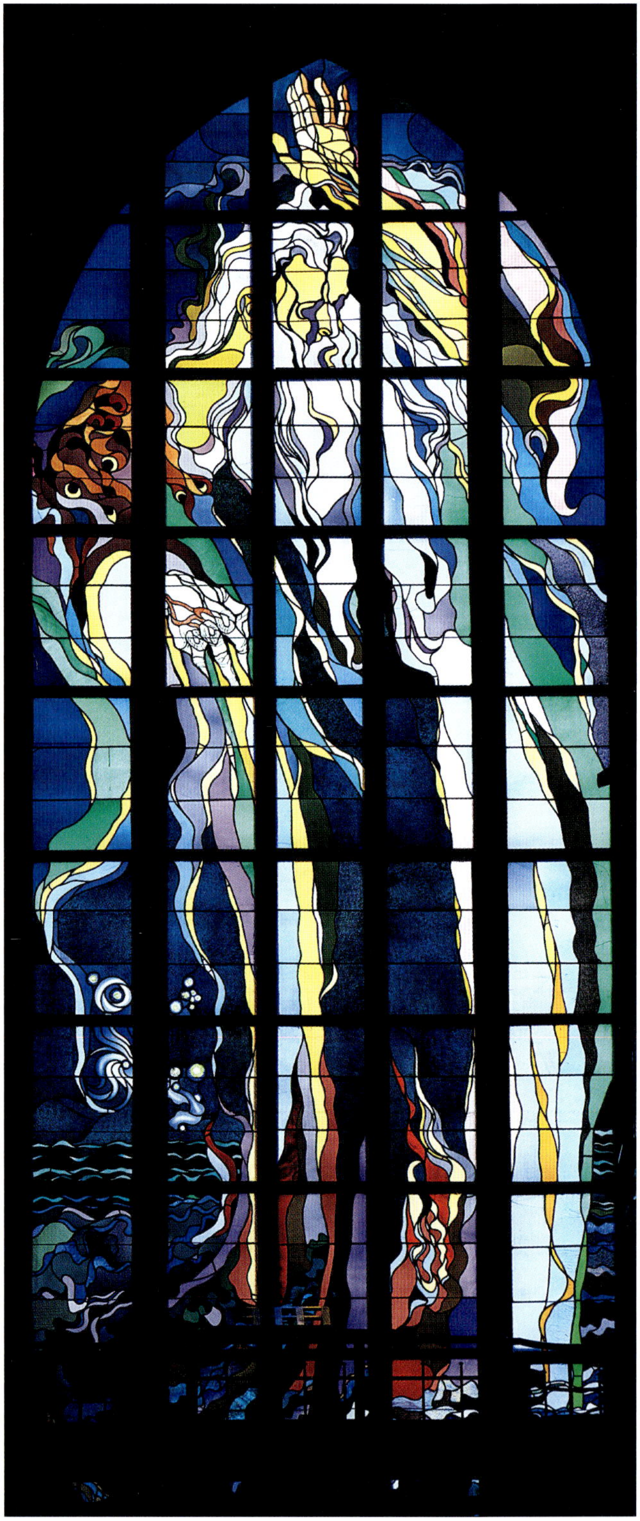

OPPOSITE
FIG.4 (LEFT)
Stanisław Wyspiański
God the Creator
design, 1904
Tempera and crayon
on canvas,
8770 × 3910mm
National Museum
in Kraków

FIG.5 (RIGHT)
Stanisław Wyspiański
God the Creator, 1904
Stained glass,
8770 × 3910mm
The Franciscan Friary,
Kraków

THIS PAGE
FIG.6
Jan Matejko
Wernyhora, 1883–4
Oil on canvas,
2900 × 2040mm
National Museum
in Kraków

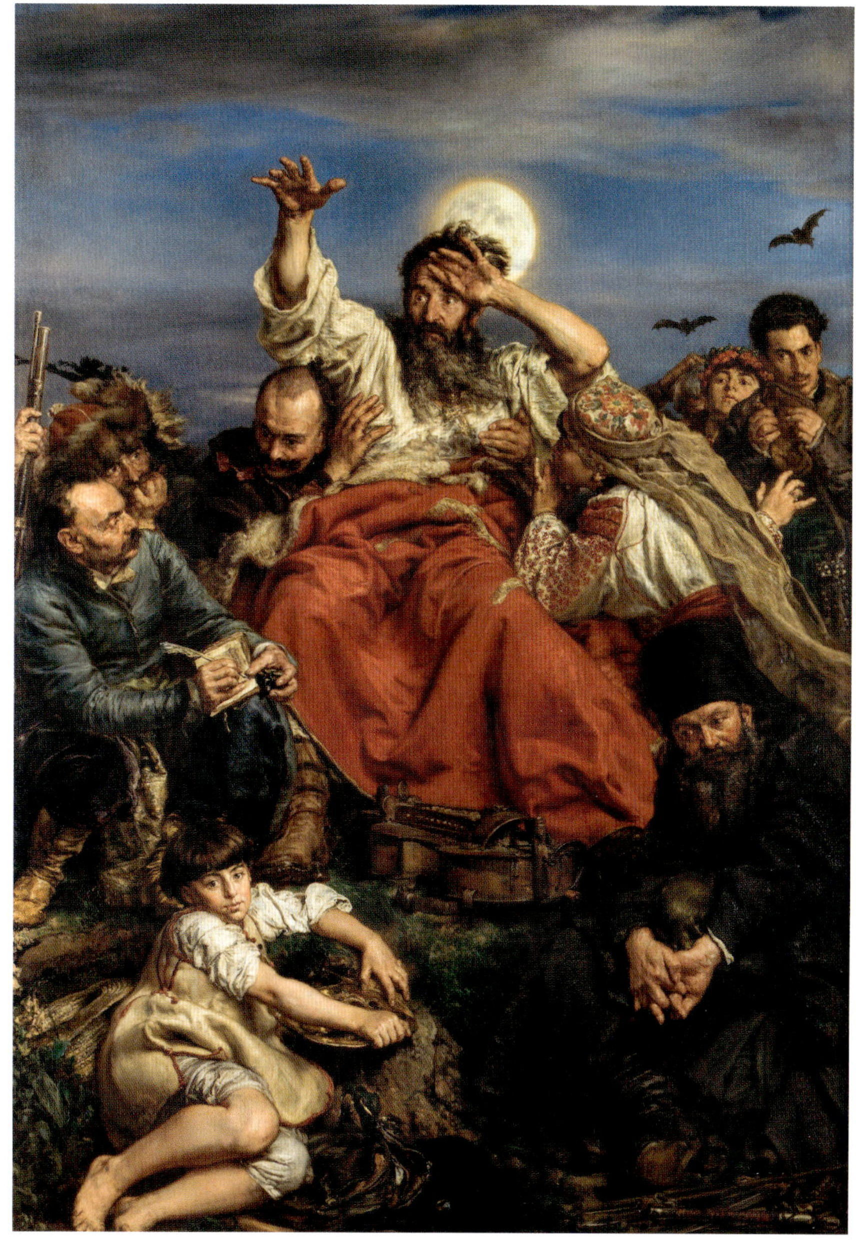

should be seen as part of his aspiration to collapse entrenched boundaries separating the fine and decorative arts, in keeping with his declaration that 'all art is decorative'.[9] It follows that the portraits were intended to bridge the fine and applied arts – with lead-like contours containing an in-filling of bright colour, like stained glass. Similarly, his monumental decorative schemes of stained glass and wall paintings were largely figurative compositions that bordered on portraiture, such as the Franciscan Friary stained-glass cartoons for *St Francis of Assisi*, *Blessed Salomea* and *God the Creator*, the latter modelled from the artist's father (1904; figs 4 and 5).[10] In fact, Wyspiański's acute gift as a portraitist – applied with equal attention to stained glass – became a bone of contention with the Franciscan brothers, who demanded that he revise the faces of *Three Poor Clares* (nuns from the order of Saint Clare) to make them 'prettier' or 'at least without the characteristic asceticism'.[11]

Wyspiański's achievement across all disciplines has to be understood within the context of the medieval city of Kraków where he lived for most of his life. He was born there in 1869, the son of sculptor Franciszek Wyspiański and his wife Maria (née Rogowska) who raised him in their studio house at the foot of Wawel Hill in the historic centre of the city. Due to his mother's death from tuberculosis in 1876 and his father's ongoing alcoholism, Wyspiański was adopted by his mother's younger sister Janina Stankiewiczowa and her husband Kazimierz who instilled in him a spirit of patriotism and love for Polish history. For many centuries Kraków had been the nation's capital and the seat of the Polish monarchs, but by Wyspiański's time it had lost much of its former glory under the administration of the Austrian authorities, who turned Wawel Castle into a military base – a particularly humiliating act for Poles.[12] However, for Wyspiański and his fellow compatriots Kraków remained a place of special significance, filled with monuments testifying to Poland's former glory that inspired hopes for future regeneration. It was a dream Wyspiański also inherited from his mentor, the visionary history painter, portraitist and decorative arts designer Jan Matejko, whose epic canvases depicting pivotal moments in Polish history inspired Wyspiański with a similar sense of purpose. Together, these canvases added up to a national pantheon of historical and legendary figures, which was to serve as a blueprint for Wyspiański's experimental art and theatrical productions for the rest of his life. The works by Matejko included depictions of the fourteenth-century King Casimir III the Great, creator of the modern and powerful state; the Renaissance astronomer Nicolaus Copernicus, who discovered the solar system; the thoughtful sixteenth-century court jester Stańczyk, troubled by the future of his country; and the eighteenth-century prophet Wernyhora, who prophesied Poland's partitions and subsequent liberation (1883–4; fig.6).[13]

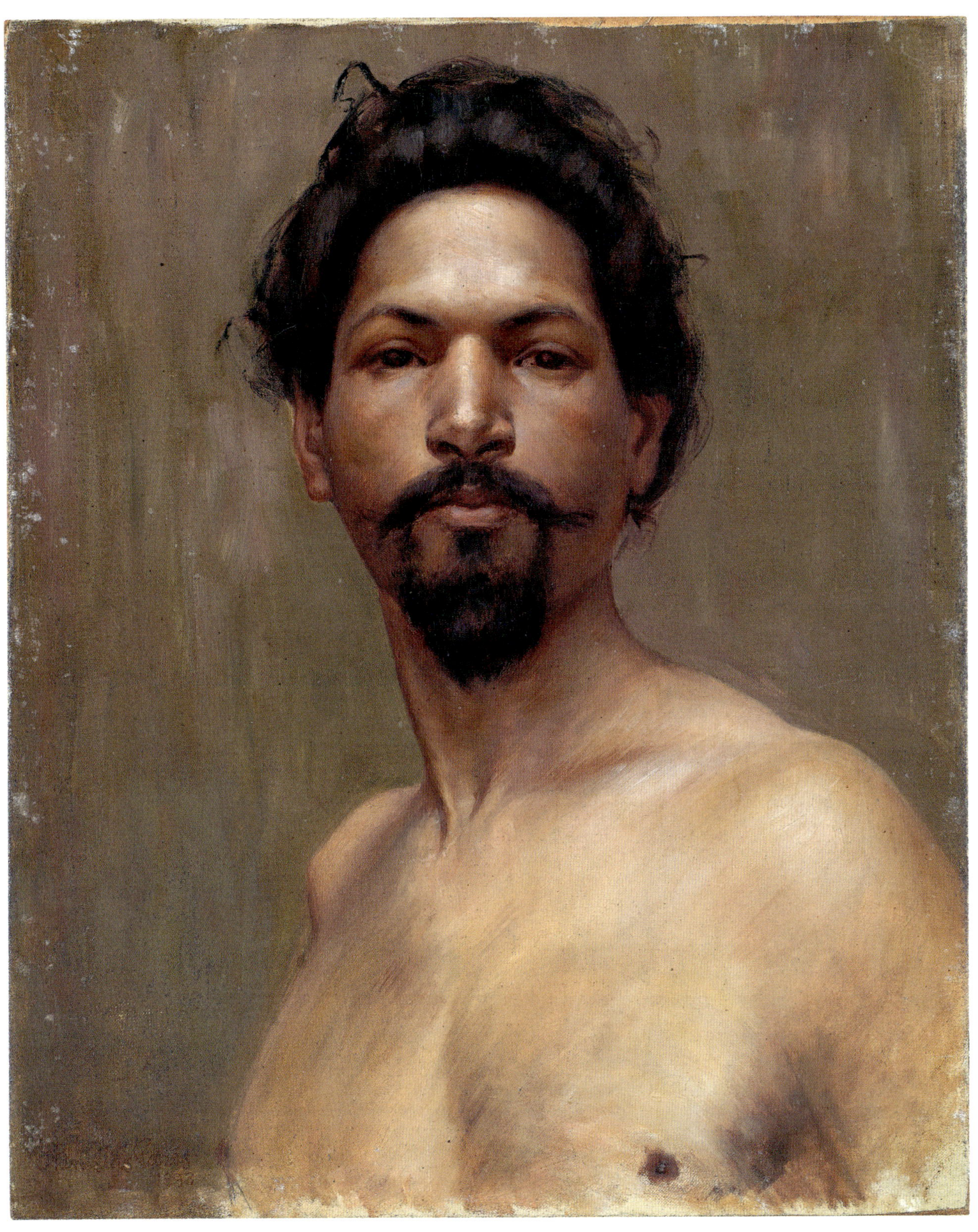

In Matejko's words: 'We must not separate the meaning of art from the meaning of the fatherland in the present times … Art is presently a sort of weapon in our hands.'[14]

After studying art at the School of Fine Arts in Kraków under Matejko, and art history at the Jagiellonian University, Wyspiański spent the years from 1890 to 1894 travelling and furthering his art education in Europe. In 1891 he enrolled at the independent Académie Colarossi in Paris where he produced a number of competent nude studies that reveal a strong interest in the personality of the model, as seen in a study he made there of an unidentified young man probably from French Polynesia (1893; fig.7).[15] It was in Paris that he first started working in pastel, finding he was allergic to oil paint and no doubt influenced by inventive examples of the technique he encountered in the work of artists such as Edgar Degas and Henri de Toulouse-Lautrec.[16] Through his contacts at Madame Charlotte's crémerie in rue de la Grande Chaumière (a meeting place for students and the international artistic and literary avant-garde), Wyspiański became acquainted with Paul Gauguin. It was Gauguin's work that helped shape the future direction of Wyspiański's own portrait style in terms of its bright colour and flat asymmetrical compositions with figures pressed tight against the picture plane or at a sharp angle leaning away from it.

He was most likely introduced to Gauguin by the latter's disciple, Władysław Ślewiński, a Polish associate of the Pont-Aven School. As recalled by another of Wyspiański's friends and fellow art students, Karol Maszkowski, Madame Charlotte's was the place 'where one whole young generation of Polish artists encountered the latest trends in French painting, where we first became familiar with Cézanne and Gauguin'.[17] While abroad, Wyspiański also absorbed influences ranging from ancient Greek art and Japanese prints to Sandro Botticelli, then undergoing a revival, as well as the work of modern French artists such as Gustave Courtois and Pierre Puvis de Chavannes, designers and graphic artists associated with Art Nouveau like Alphonse Mucha and Eugène Samuel Grasset, and representatives of Symbolism and the British Arts and Crafts Movement, notably Edward Burne-Jones. The unique layering and coming together of Kraków and Paris influences helped inform what was to become Wyspiański's distinct linear expressive style. While reflecting on the art collections he was studying in Paris he stated: 'Matejko … was right about everything … It would seem one cannot combine one with the other, namely [contemporary] Paris with Matejko's notions – but in fact, one can – and this is precisely … my philosophy.'[18]

Wyspiański originally envisaged staying in Paris for at least another decade but had to return to Kraków in the autumn of 1894 due to lack of funds. For a long time he remained deeply unsettled, but he eventually found a sense of

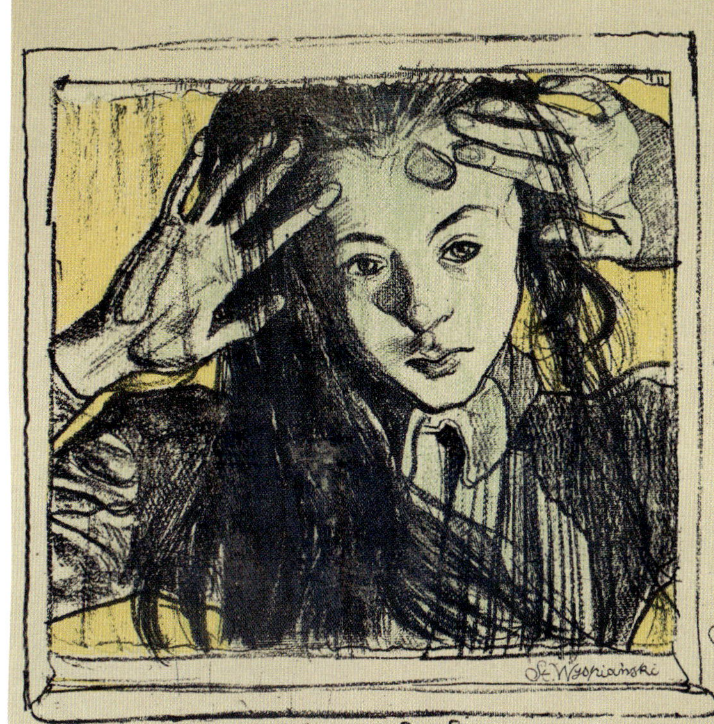

odbito w lit. A. Pruszyńskiego w Krakowie'

W poniedziałek dnia 20ego Lutego
odbędzie się w sali miejskiego teatru
Odczyt
Stanisława Przybyszewskiego
połączony z przedstawieniem dramatycznem
fantazyi
Maurycego Maeterlincka
pod tytułem: „Wnętrze"
w którem wezmą łaskawy współudział
pp. Łapolska, Bednarzewska, Po-
mian, Przybytko, Teodorowicz
pp. Kamiński, Roman, Węgrzyn
prelegent mówić będzie na temat:
Mistyka a Maeterlinck
początek o godzinie 5ej wieczorem..
Ceny miejsc: fotel 3 złr, krzesło 2 złr, parter 1 złr
inne miejsca widowni teatru zamknięte.

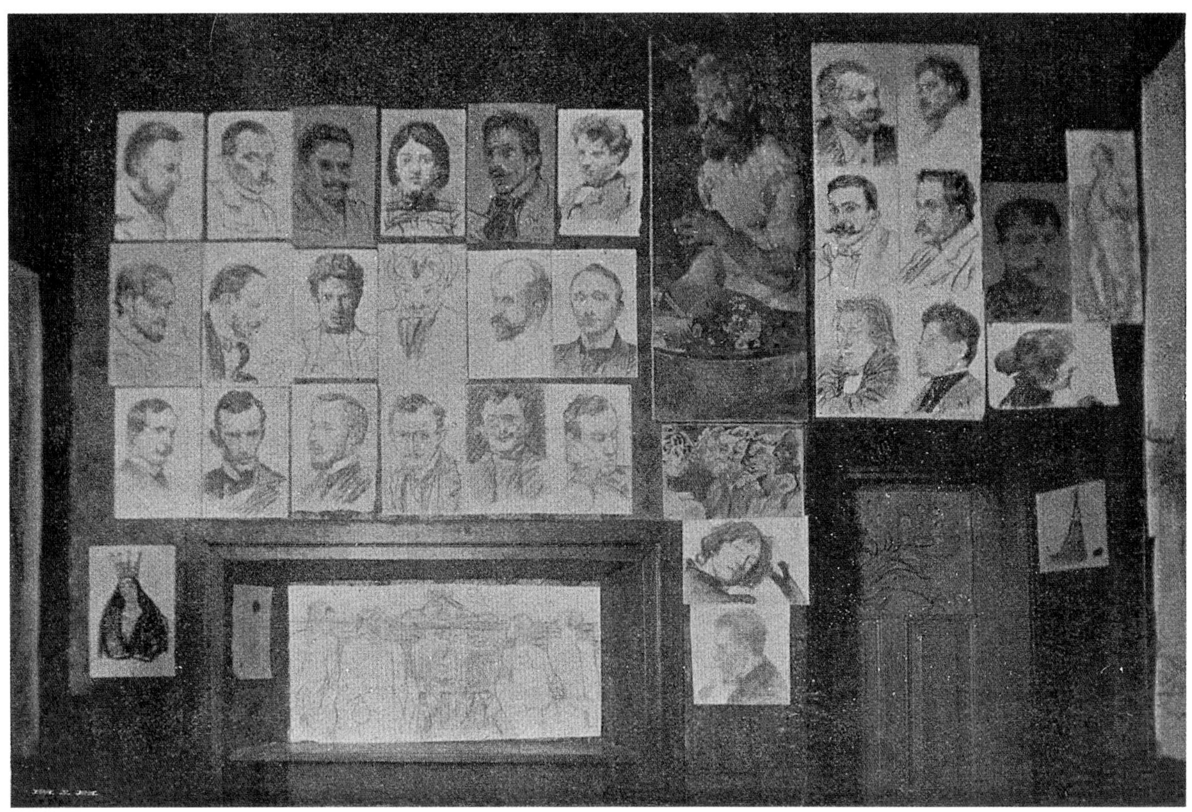

FIG.9
View of Paon café with the
expanded 'Hall of Fame', 1904
from Wilhelm Feldman's
Polish literature 1880–1904
National Library of Poland

OPPOSITE, SELECTED
'HALL OF FAME' SITTERS,
CLOCKWISE FROM TOP LEFT
FIG.10
Stanisław Wyspiański
Kazimierz Lewandowski, 1899
Pastel on paper,
410 × 275mm
National Museum
in Warsaw

FIG.11
Stanisław Wyspiański
Jerzy Żuławski, 1899
Pastel on paper,
410 × 275mm
National Museum
in Wrocław

FIG.12
Stanisław Wyspiański
Ludwik Janikowski, 1899
Pastel on paper,
410 × 275mm
National Museum
in Warsaw

FIG.13
Stanisław Wyspiański
Konrad Rakowski, 1899
Pastel on paper,
410 × 275mm
National Museum
in Warsaw

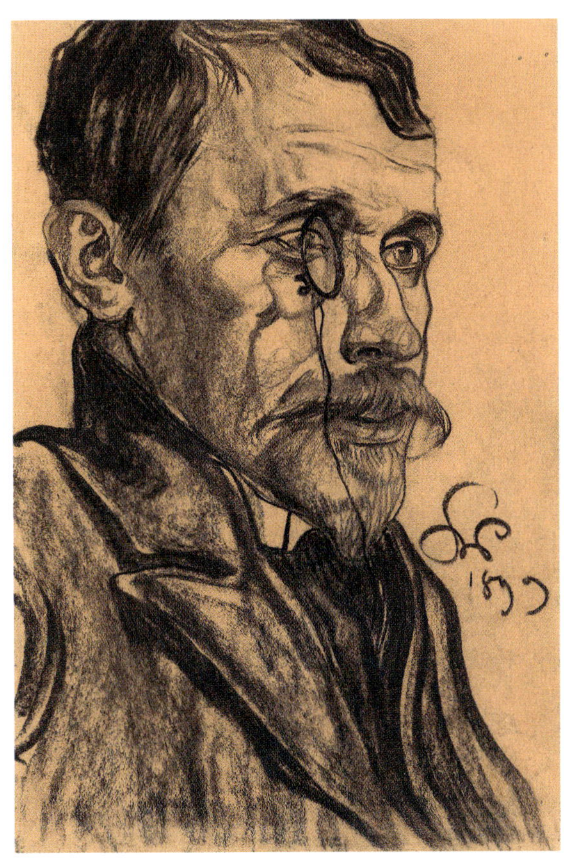
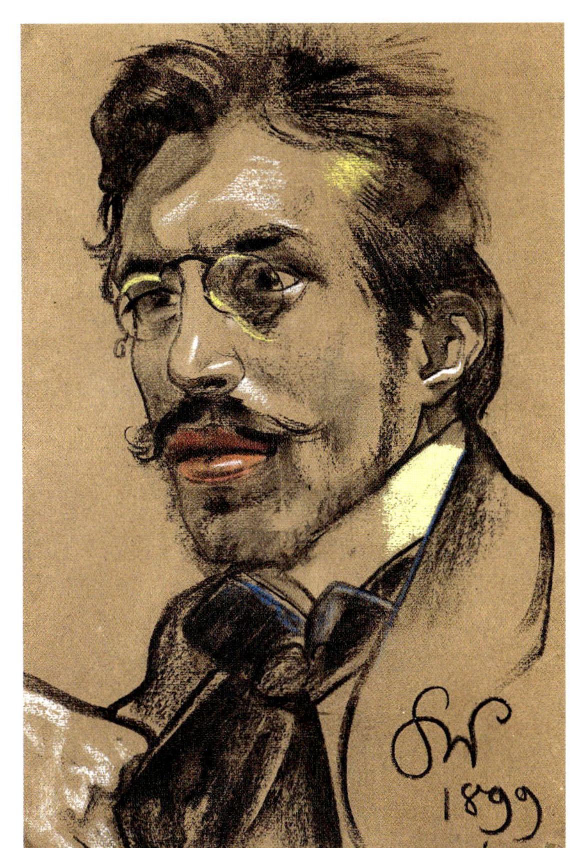
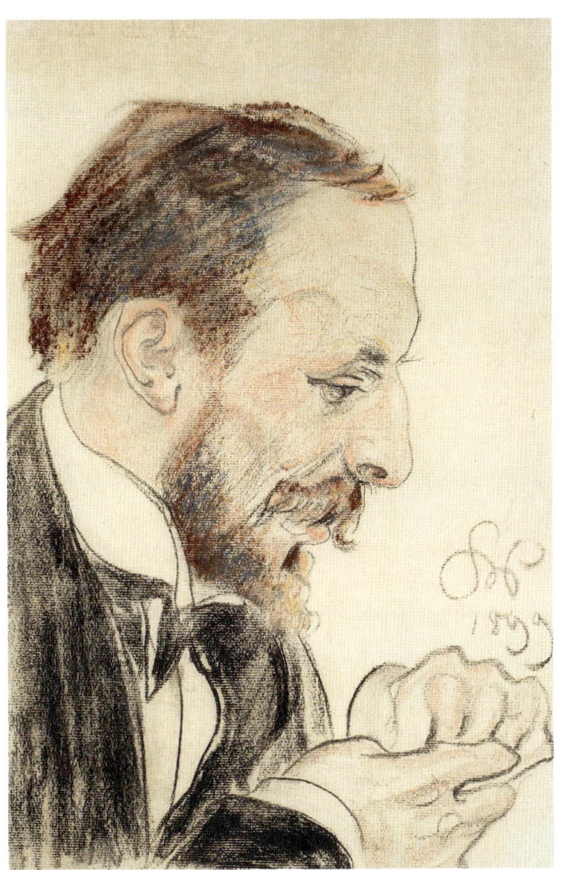
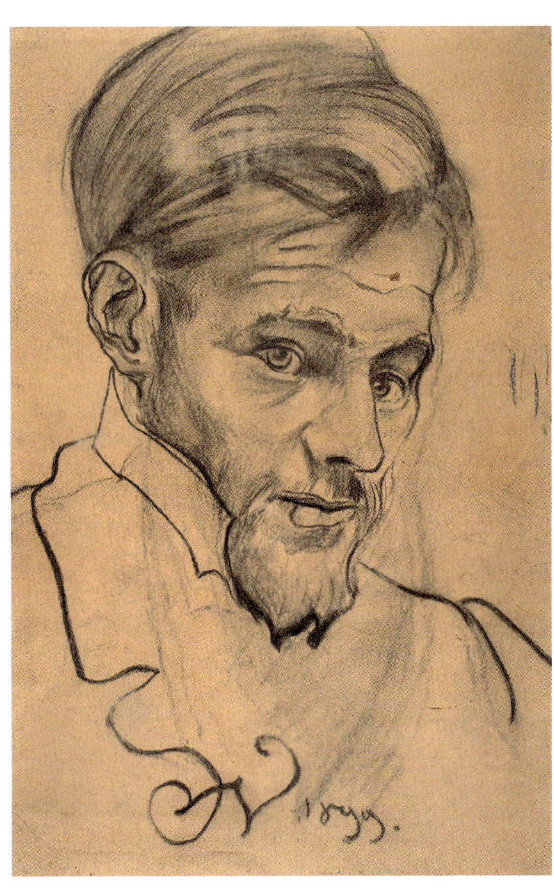

purpose with the establishment of the 'Sztuka' Society in 1897, of which he
was a founding member. The following year he was appointed art director
of the cultural magazine *Życie* (*Life*), on which he collaborated with its editor,
the critic and decadent writer Stanisław Przybyszewski, recently returned from
Berlin with his Norwegian wife Dagny Juel-Przybyszewska, a close friend of
the painter Edvard Munch. Dividing his time between Young Poland's first
artistic club-cum-café, Paon, on Ulica Szpitalna, and *Życie*, Wyspiański started
producing experimental designs for books, magazines and posters. One
notable example was the announcement he made for Przybyszewski's 1899
lecture on Maurice Maeterlinck's mysticism, which takes the form of a portrait
with a symbolic message (fig.8). It shows a girl looking into a room from the
outside with her forehead pressed against a pane of glass as if to suggest
interiority and introspection. Wyspiański also developed a habit of doodling
caricatures of instantly recognisable historical figures such as Henry VIII,
Elizabeth I, Napoleon and Chopin, apparently to entertain Przybyszewski's
wife Dagny, the subject of one of his most penetrating portrait studies of
the period (cat.3).

As a key player within the Young Poland movement, Wyspiański met with
other artists and writers at Paon, where he seems to have first conceived
the ambitious idea to create a composite portrait or 'hall of fame' of
'contemporary Kraków'. A 'gallery of public figures', it was to be made up
of a hundred individual likenesses of established and emerging Young Poland
cultural personalities and of prominent Cracovians.[19] A contemporaneous
photograph of the café shows the evolving shape of the scheme (1904; fig.9).
The surviving Paon drawings are mainly monochromatic, caricature-like
sketches in charcoal, with occasional accents of colour, made on 41 × 27.5 cm
paper and dating to 1899 (figs 10–13), as with the portraits of writers Dagny
Juel-Przybyszewska and Antoni Lange (cats 3 and 4), the former one of the
very few women in the circle. During Paon's existence and after its closure
in 1901, Wyspiański also experimented with alternative paper sizes, media
and styles, including larger and more finished chalk and pastel drawings
of his contemporaries, sometimes created at other settings. These works
demonstrate the working nature of his 'hall of fame' concept and his
continuing desire to find the most suitable format to realise it for posterity.

Wyspiański's portraits provide a fascinating overview of the artists and
people associated with Young Poland and embody the ambivalence of
this whole generation, filled with the spirit of youth and hope for Poland's
eventual liberation, yet despondent and lethargic due to their country's
century-long oppression. Wyspiański's pastel *Straw Men Dancing in the
Planty Park* (1897–9; fig.14) also known as *Chochoły* (literally 'straw-protected

FIG.14
Stanisław Wyspiański
*Straw Men Dancing
in the Planty Park*
(*Chochoły*), 1897–9
Pastel on paper laid on
board, 1000 × 2010mm
National Museum
in Warsaw

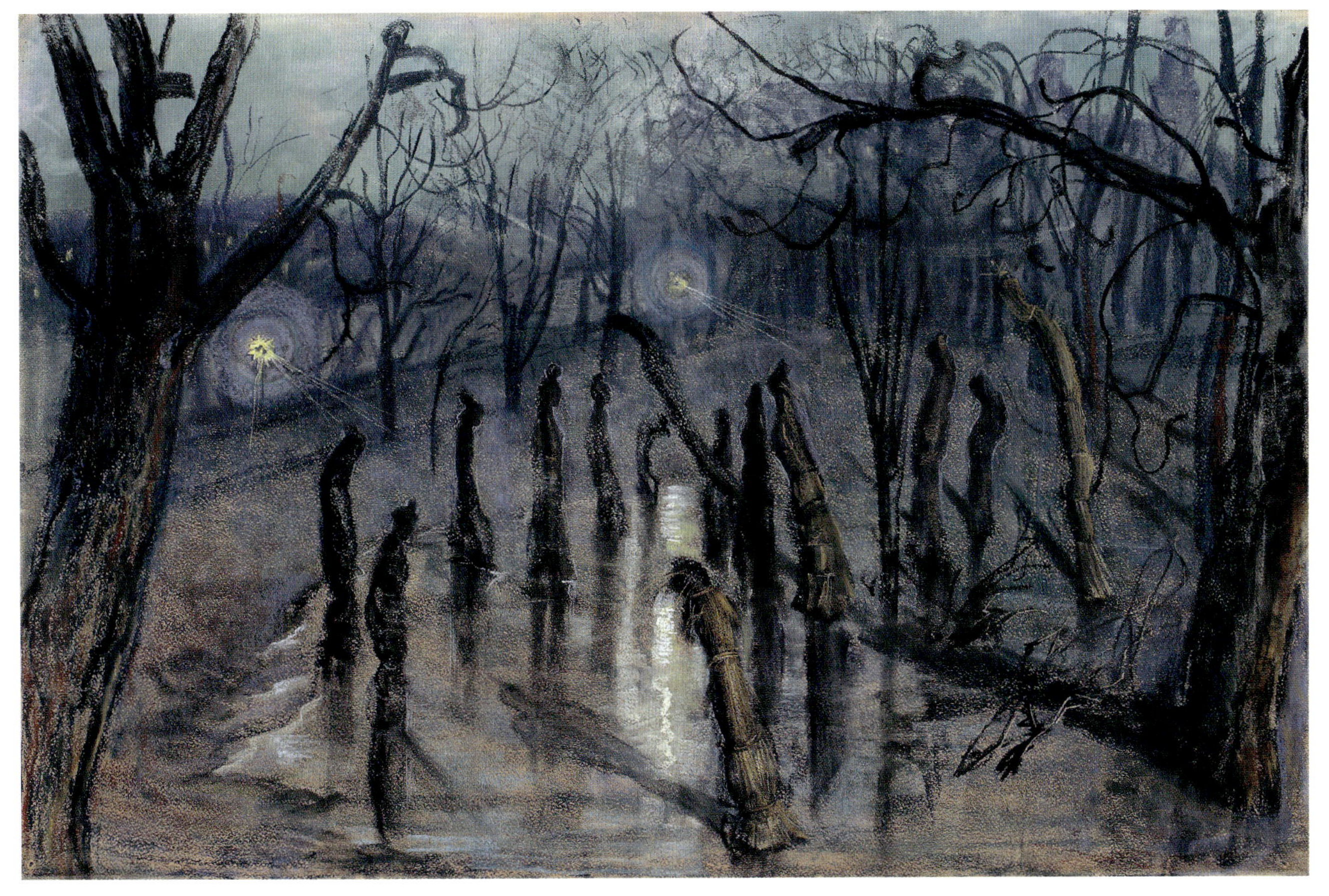

bushes'), is a powerful *kryptoportret* of Polish society from this period.
It shows anthropomorphic rosebushes covered in straw for the winter to
safeguard them against frost – serving as a metaphor of Poles' resilience and
fragility in their struggle to survive as a nation, even while seemingly dormant
during the partitions.[20]

Among Wyspiański's most striking portraits are those he made of his wife,
Teodora Teofila Pytko, and their children, Teodor (Teodora's son from an
earlier relationship), Helenka (diminutive for Helena), Mieczysław or Mietek
and Stanisław or Staś (cats 11–15). Wyspiański first met Teodora, a peasant
woman from the village of Konary near Tarnów, in the mid-1890s and they
had two children out of wedlock. Their marriage in 1900 sent shock waves
through respectable Cracovian society, inviting comparison with the marriages
forged across class boundaries by the English Pre-Raphaelites. Wyspiański's
aunt, Janina, was particularly disapproving. After his death, the District Court
in Kraków deprived Teodora of custody of her children – with various
stakeholders including legal guardians, Wyspiański's executors and the City
Council arranging for the children to be educated at boarding schools away
from their mother. The artist was by no means unique in marrying outside his
class – his friends, painter Włodzimierz Tetmajer and poet Lucjan Rydel had
both married peasant women, and the latter's country wedding at Tetmajer's
residence at Bronowice had inspired Wyspiański's most famous play *The
Wedding*, which premiered a year after Rydel's marriage, in 1901. Such unions
were yet further expression of Young Poland's fascination with folk culture,
symbolising the unification of the divided nation and fuelling its belief that
national revival depended more on the commitment of the peasant class
than on the intelligentsia or bourgeoisie. Teodora herself was a strong woman
who played a key role in deepening her husband's long-time interest in folk
tradition through her storytelling (she spoke in dialect), songs, embroidery
work and traditional folk dress.[21] She informed the subject matter and
style of his writing, painting and applied arts, and is said to have partially
embroidered the costume designed by Wyspiański for the emblematic figure
of Lajkonik, one of the symbols of Kraków (1904; fig.15).

In 1901 the family moved into a tenement house in Ulica Krowoderska
where Wyspiański set up a studio in a corner room with a double aspect,
known as the Blue Studio after he painted it a brilliant blue. This period gave
rise to the affectionate but unsentimental studies he made there, including
Self-Portrait with Wife in folk costume (1904; fig.16). One drawing shows
Helenka contemplating a vase of flowers, another Mietek leaning on a table
in the nursery lost in thought. The most disturbing captures Teodor biting
his hands, terrified by the pistols before him. The family portraits culminate

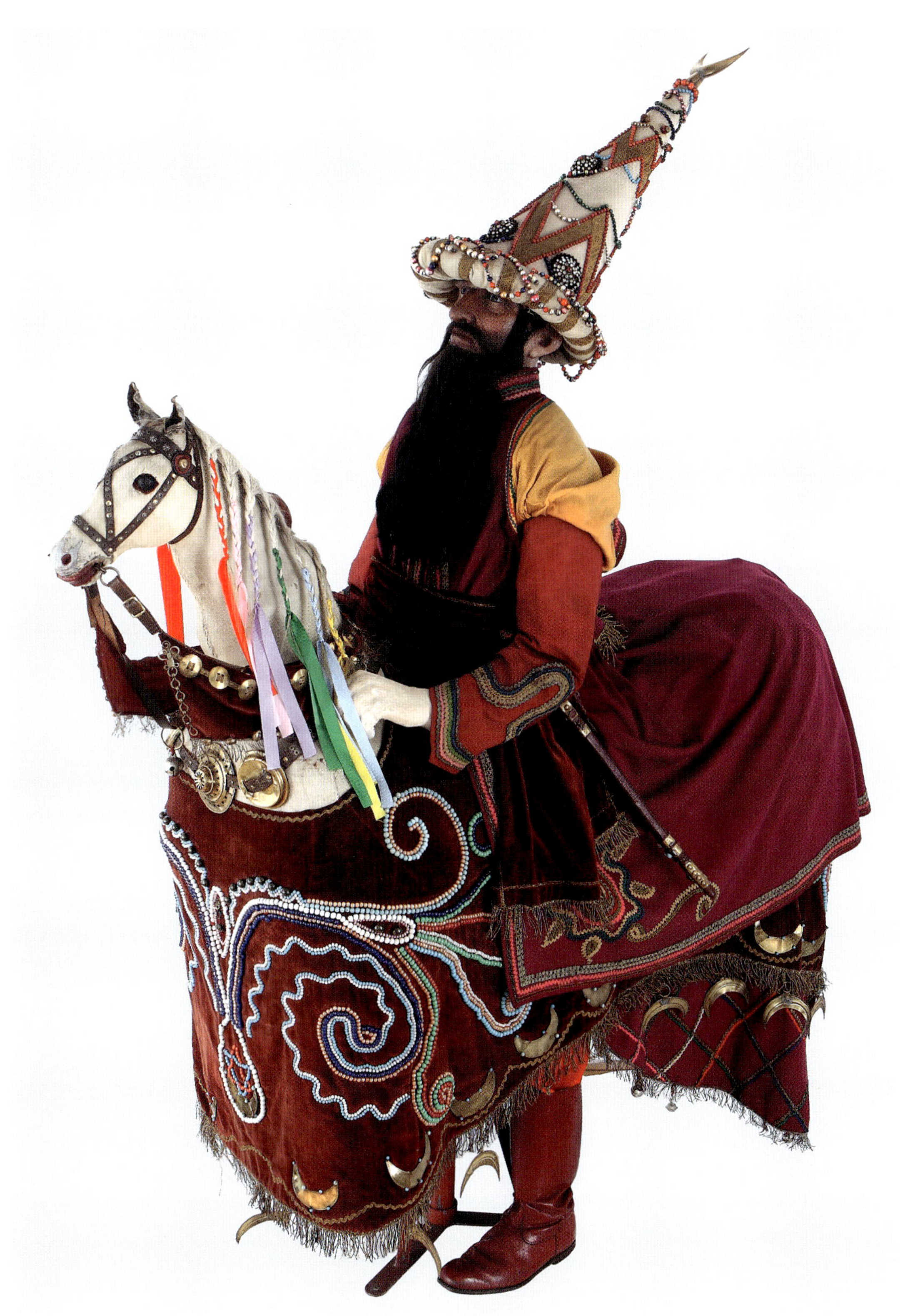

FIG.16
Stanisław Wyspiański
*Self-Portrait
with Wife*, 1904
Pastel on paper,
477 × 622mm
National Museum
in Kraków

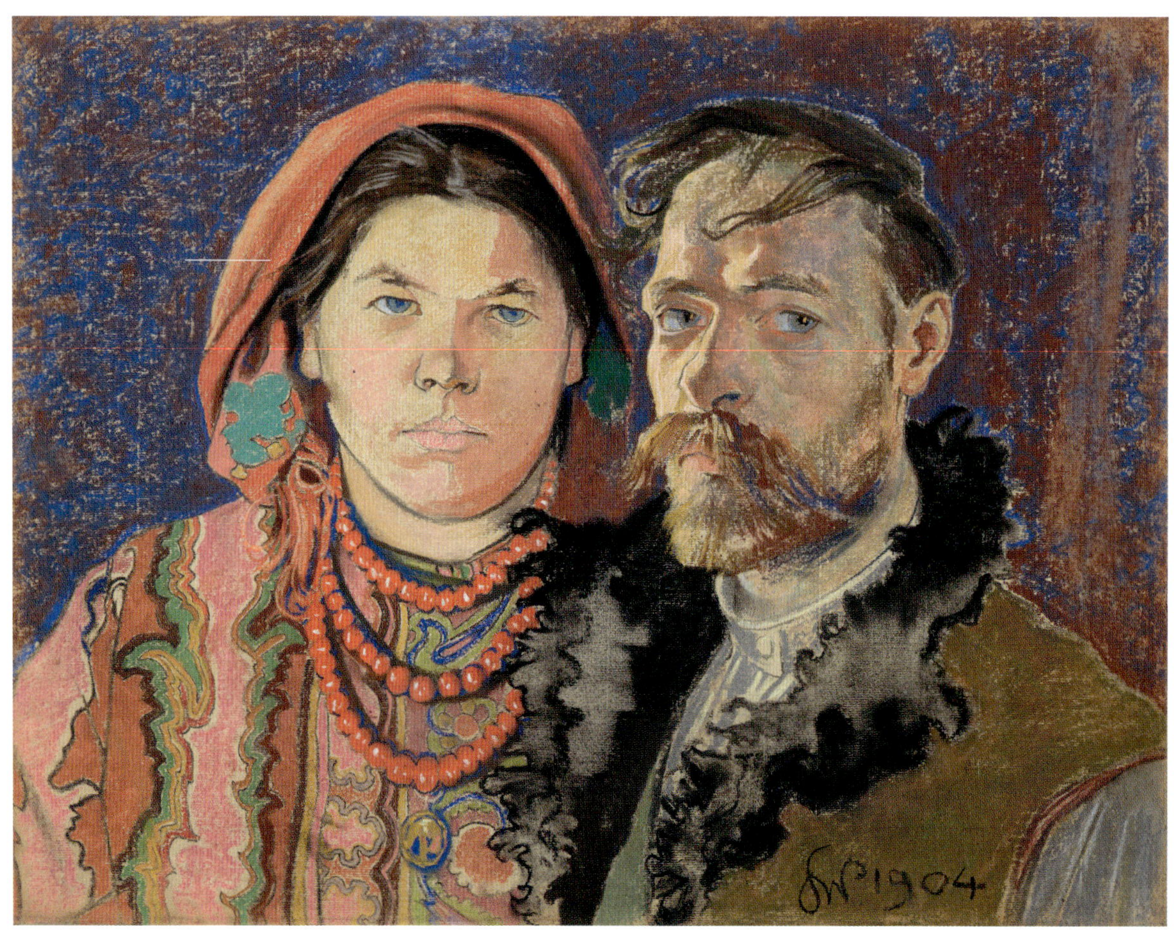

in the large group portrait *Maternity* (cat.15) which Wyspiański started as a design for a floral pattern with fuchsias before working it up as a composite portrait in which Helenka appears twice, watching over her younger brother Staś as he suckles at his mother's breast. It would appear that Wyspiański had wider ambitions for his family portraits, which is why he produced multiple versions and even had plans to display them together as a kind of decorative frieze, as a newly discovered design drawing suggests (1904; fig.17).[22] These pictures also proved to be very popular with patrons, with some purchased by the collector Edward Aleksander Raczyński for his gallery at Rogalin outside Poznań, and *Maternity* bought by Feliks Jasieński and donated by him to the National Museum in Kraków. The family portraits remain the best known and most loved aspect of Wyspiański's art in Poland.

Like a number of bohemian artists, Wyspiański contracted syphilis while he was in Paris, tragically for himself and for his family. Signs of swollen glands, one of the symptoms of syphilis (as well as of tonsillitis), are evident in some of the intimate portraits he made of his children, including the study of Helenka with swollen glands and open mouth (cat.11). By at least 1900 he would have been acutely aware of his own terminal condition, writing to a colleague that he would only take up projects that he found especially meaningful.[23] According to one contemporary account, Teodora transformed Wyspiański's enjoyment of life while also serving as his trusted business advisor and carer.[24] The portraits are an evident expression of his love and tenderness for his family.

Wyspiański's deep interest in the theatre had been encouraged by his foster family, the Stankiewiczs, who had an extensive library complete with the classics, including the first Polish edition of the complete works of Shakespeare. What was to become a lifelong passion for the English playwright intensified during his student years, when he spent much time at the theatre. During this period, he also experienced the operas of Richard Wagner, which left a lasting impression. The years 1901–4 saw the publication and stage adaptations of some of Wyspiański's most celebrated plays, including *The Wedding*, a symbolic portrayal of Poland's predicament in which phantoms from its past, including a number of protagonists from Matejko's paintings, try to engage with the minds of guests at a wedding reception (figs 22 and 23). It caused a sensation, winning Wyspiański a place among the country's literary heroes, and spurred him on to write other dramas including *Liberation* (*Wyzwolenie*, 1903), *Bolesław the Bold* (*Bolesław Śmiały*, 1903), *Achilles: Dramatic Scenes* (*Achilleis: Sceny Dramatyczne*, 1903), *November Night* (*Noc Listopadowa*, 1904) and *Acropolis* (*Akropolis*, 1904), many of which were set at Wawel Hill.

It was while he was working on his plays during the years 1903–4 that Wyspiański envisaged creating a gallery of life-sized (bust-length and

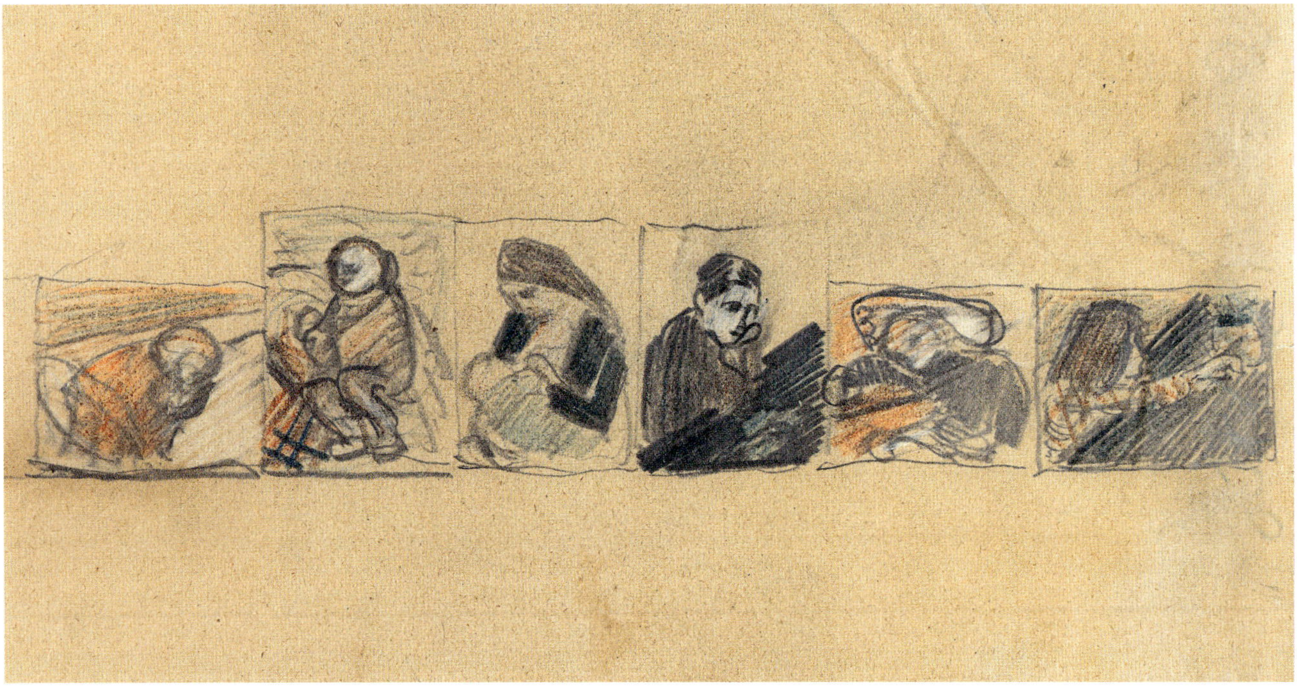

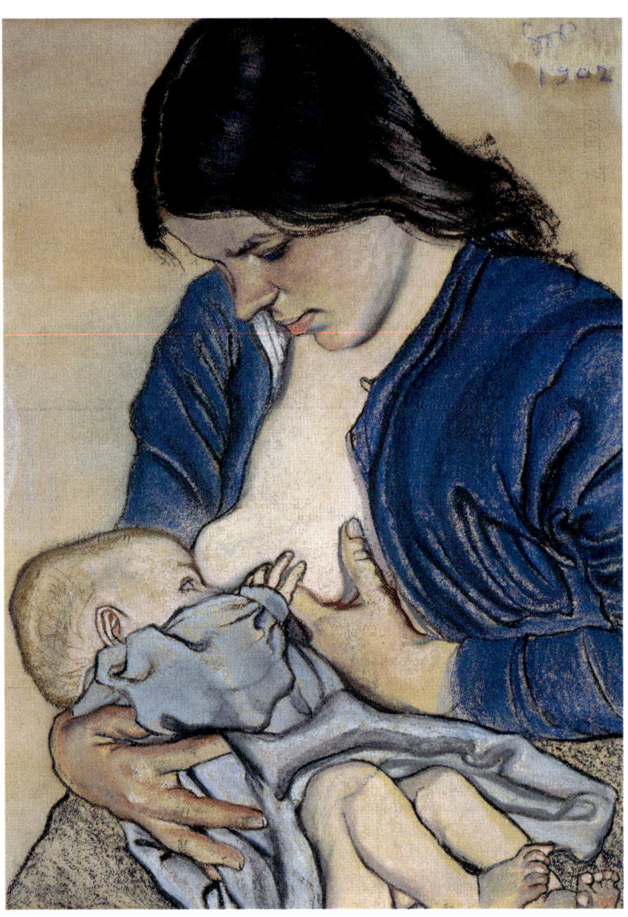

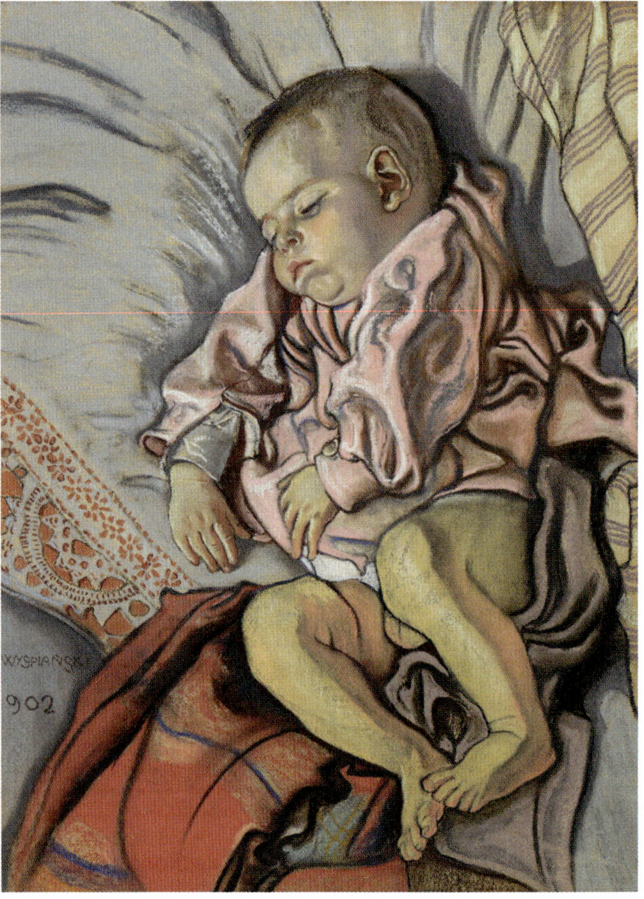

OPPOSITE
FIG.17 (TOP)
Stanisław Wyspiański
Design for a frieze of
family portraits, 1904
Pastel on paper,
170 x 211mm
Collegium Maius
Jagiellonian University
Museum

FIG.18 (BOTTOM LEFT)
Stanisław Wyspiański
Maternity, 1902
Pastel on paper,
640 x 475mm
National Museum
in Warsaw

FIG.19 (BOTTOM RIGHT)
Stanisław Wyspiański
Sleeping Staś, 1902
Crayon on paper,
645 x 475mm
Silesian Museum
in Katowice

THIS PAGE
FIG.20 (TOP)
Stanisław Wyspiański
Sleeping Staś, 1904
Pastel on paper,
471 x 617mm
The Raczyński Foundation
at the National Museum
in Poznań

FIG.21 (BOTTOM)
Stanisław Wyspiański
Sleeping Mietek, 1904
Pastel on paper,
460 x 610mm
Łódź Art Museum

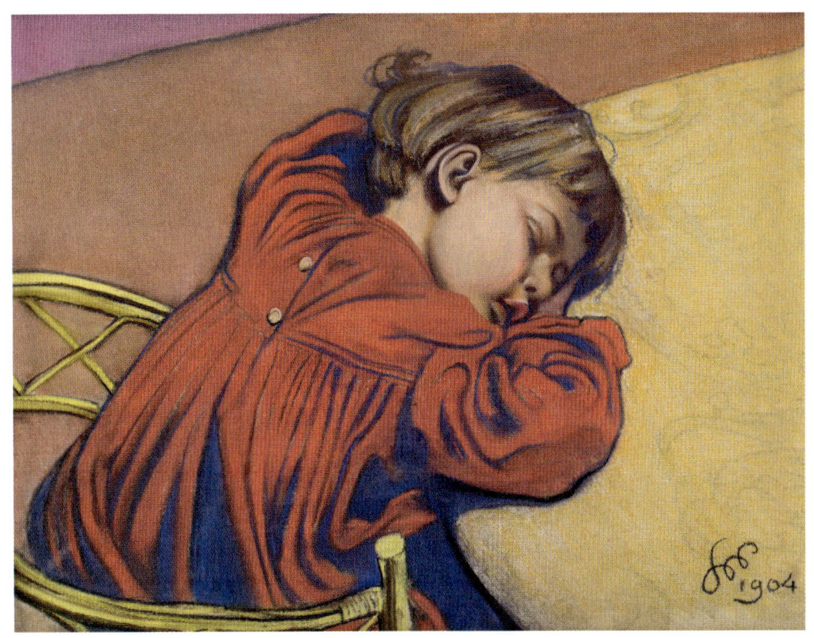

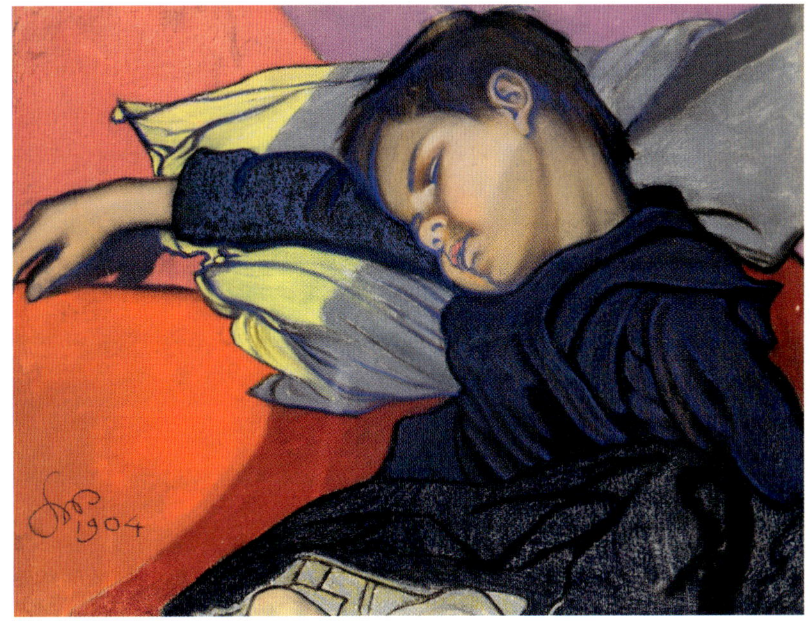

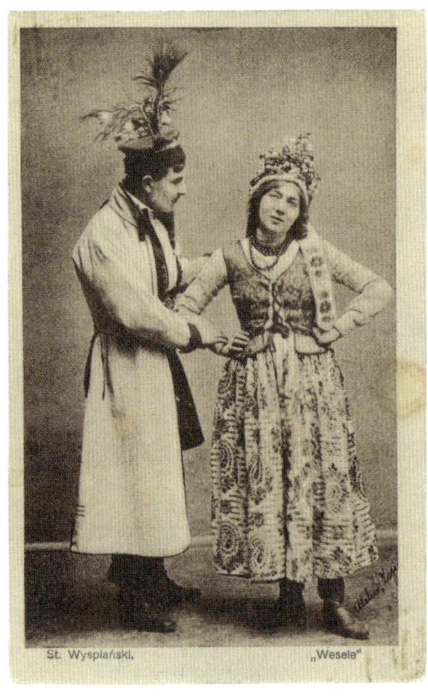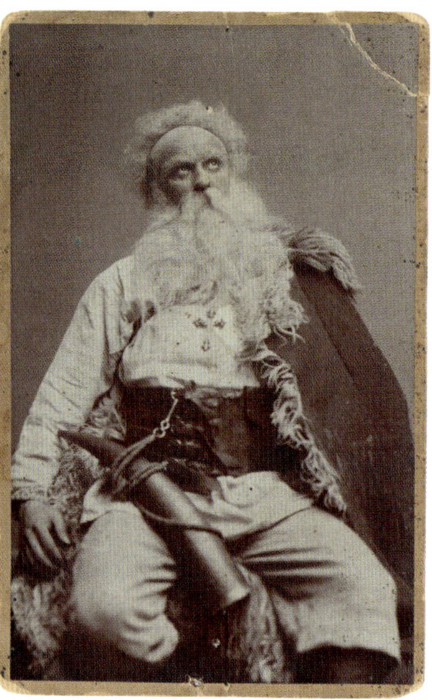

half-length) actors' portraits in character, thus immortalising the cast and
costumes of primarily his own productions. Unfortunately, the project never
materialised, and some works were destroyed during the Second World
War, including portraits of the actor and theatre director Ludwik Solski
in Shakespearean roles, which were lost in the Nazi bombing of Warsaw.
Surviving drawings from his staging of *Bolesław the Bold* are among his
most powerful. The play presented Wyspiański's view that the root cause
of Poland's partitions lay in the power struggle between the Church and
the State, namely the conflict between the eleventh-century king, Bolesław
the Bold and the Kraków bishop Stanislaus of Szczepanów. The latter
excommunicated the king and, in consequence, was murdered while giving
Mass. The stage design was a microcosm of Polish cultural identity, based
on the wooden carvings and dress of Podhale Highlander shepherds, as well
as Cracovian peasants' costume. One likeness from the production is the
portrait of actor Władysława Ordon in the role of Krasawica (Polish for
'beautiful woman'), the king's treacherous lover (cat.8). Dressed in a costume
made up of foliage and flowers, and evoking the figure of Flora in Botticelli's
Primavera, she very much appears as herself as she poses for the artist. One
of Wyspiański's favourite sitters was the actor Irena Solska (wife of Ludwik),
another member of the Young Poland movement who later played a heroic
role rescuing Jewish citizens during the Nazi occupation.[25] Wyspiański was
apparently captivated by her haunting Burne-Jones-like features and long red

hair, leading him to cast her as Rachela, the Jewish innkeeper's daughter in *The Wedding*. His most famous portrait of Irena Solska was most likely drawn in Lviv (a Polish town and a heart of Polish culture prior to the partitions, which became the capital of Galicia, and is now part of western Ukraine), where she was performing the part of Savage in the tragedy *Treasure* (*Skarb*, 1904) by Leopold Staff. Impressed by her performance, Wyspiański captured her offstage in a characteristic gesture of throwing back her hair as she gazes intently at the viewer (cat.9). By 1905 Wyspiański had lost out to Ludwik Solski in a competition for the Directorship of Kraków's City Theatre, which he was hoping to revolutionise. The disappointment likely led him to abandon the theatrical portraits.[26]

Many of Wyspiański's most powerful portraits date from 1904, the year he decided to revive the idea of portraying eminent Cracovians. He explained his aspirations to his friend, the archivist and antiquarian Adam Chmiel:

> I am preoccupied with drawing portraits … Every day someone comes in and I draw them. I intend to carry on until I have filled up my studio to full capacity, so that there's no more space to move in it. Then I will put on an exhibition and create one huge portrait hall.[27]

The project included the portrait of one of his most important patrons, the microbiologist and future Prime Minister of Poland Julian Nowak (cat.7), who came up with the idea of commissioning Wyspiański to decorate the Kraków Medical Society, of which he was chairman. Like many of the artist's male portraits, it is boldly drawn in dark shades of pastel animated with touches of colour. Nowak looks at us with a curious, intelligent expression, the tilt of his body underscored by the empty background. Sketched rapidly, the surviving drawings bear witness to Wyspiański's belief that a portrait had to be set down quickly (like a caricature) in order to seize the essentials of a person:

> You can paint a portrait for fifteen or thirty minutes – or an hour, but no longer than that, because it will not be a portrait any more, only a painting about the person – the person's story. A human on a Tuesday is not the same as on a Monday, we change irreversibly, affected by experiences and thoughts; a portrait is a reflection of the moment, an artistic image of the subject's essence.[28]

Despite the power of the completed works, Wyspiański abandoned his original intention to create a composite portrait of Young Poland in a huge portrait hall, discouraged by what he felt to be the monotony of contemporary dress.[29]

It was also at this time that he returned the Paon portraits to the sitters, disappointed that so few of them had lived up to his expectations (see pp.20–21).[30]

It would appear that Wyspiański spent much of his imaginative life in the past, which perhaps explains why his approach to portraiture encompassed imaginary figures, albeit always based on live models or iconographic sources. This is most clearly seen in the large pastel cartoons he produced in 1900 for Wawel Cathedral, depicting king-spirits, saints and mythical figures from Polish history, which he described as 'witnesses to the past and judges of the present generation'.[31] The monumental designs feature skeletal, revenant apparitions – once again some previously evoked by Matejko (1900; fig.24). Wyspiański's representation of Bishop Stanislaus as the framing device for the scheme was to verge on the blasphemous. As Anna Rudzińska has observed: 'Rather than opposing Stanislaus himself, Wyspiański was taking a stance against the saint's cult ... a destructive force responsible for sending to sleep and de-energising the nation ... whilst awaiting a miracle.'[32] Wyspiański's designs were likely rejected by the church authorities for a combination of reasons, not least the ambivalent representation of the Cathedral's patron saint, and the strange, expressive forms of the figures, which almost anticipate characters from science fiction.[33]

One of Wyspiański's greatest creative disappointments was losing the Wawel stained-glass commission. His powerful *Self-Portrait* of 1902 – in a Renaissance-style frame of his own design, based on ornaments from Wawel Cathedral's Sigismund Chapel – expresses this regret (fig.25). The artist portrays himself in the style of an Old Master, 'capable of bringing about the rebirth of Polish art', posing at the entrance to an arbour, with the drooping passionflower leaves suggesting melancholy.[34] The picture foreshadows another blow – being refused permission to work on the restoration of Wawel Castle after the army began to vacate it in 1904.

Wyspiański's self-portraits offer a summary of his life's journey and evolving identity as an artist, while also projecting his aspirations and disappointments. He only produced a small group of likenesses and increasingly turned to autobiographical *kryptoportrety* in response to his progressing terminal condition. As well as honouring the astronomer Copernicus, the *Apollo: Copernicus's Solar System* stained-glass window for the Medical Society also doubled as a hidden self-portrait – perhaps a reflection of Wyspiański's sense of public responsibility as an artist (1904; fig.2). Apollo is shown with a lyre – a metaphor of creative inspiration – which is not only tied to his back but also binds his hands. At a time when the artist was suffering from the progressive impairment of his hands caused by syphilis, it is possible he also wanted to

FIG.24
Stanisław Wyspiański
Unrealised stained-glass
designs for the chancel of
Wawel Cathedral; from left
to right: *Prince Henry the
Pious*, *King Casimir the Great*,
Saint Stanislaus, 1900
Pastel on paper,
4360 × 1480mm
National Museum
in Kraków

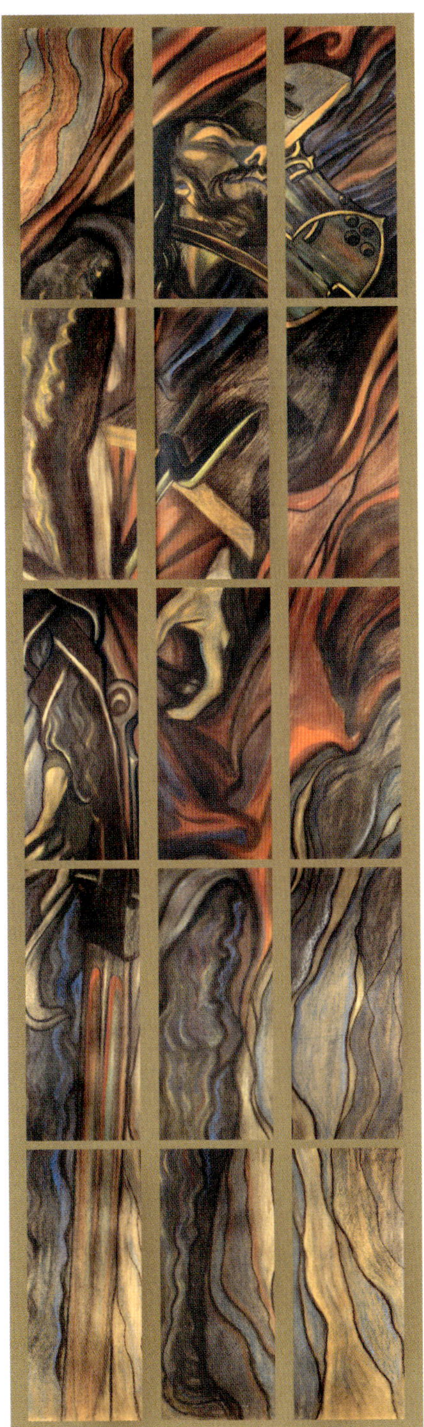
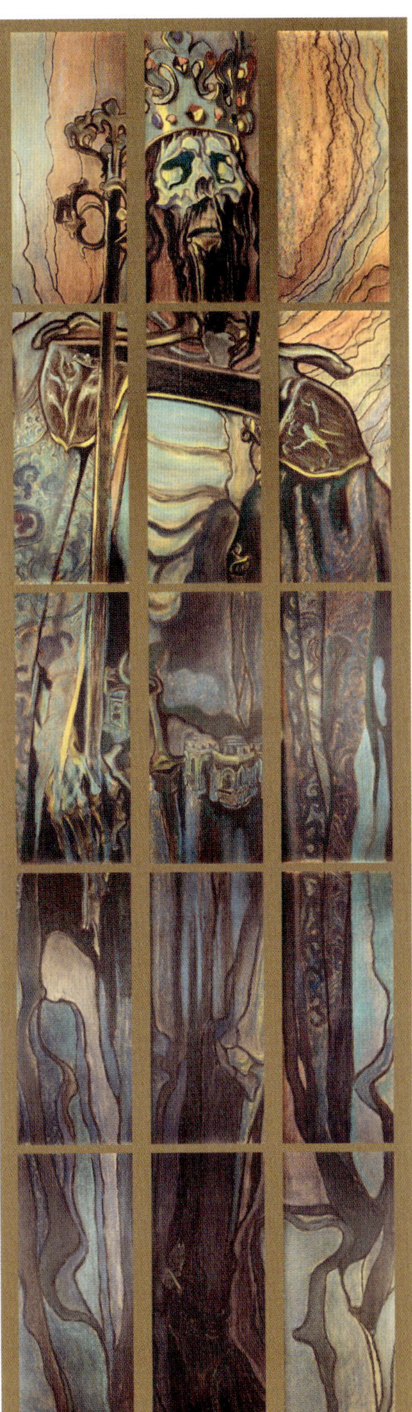
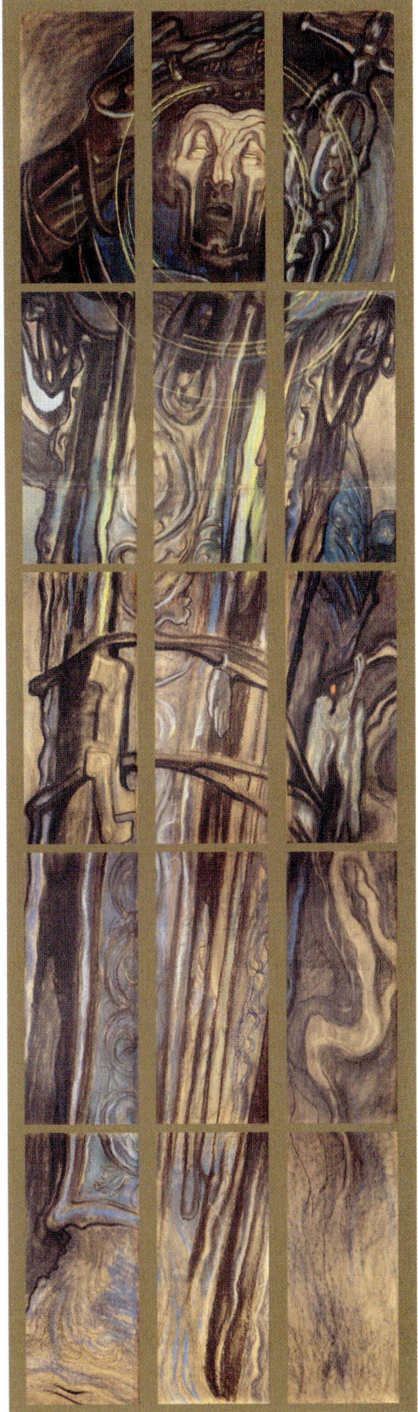

FIG.25
Stanisław Wyspiański
Self-Portrait, 1902
Pastel on lined paper laid on
cardboard, 620 × 620mm
National Museum in Warsaw

FIG.26 (OPPOSITE)
Stanisław Wyspiański
*View out of the Studio
Window on to Kościuszko
Mound*, 1905
Pastel on paper, 910 × 595mm
National Museum in Warsaw

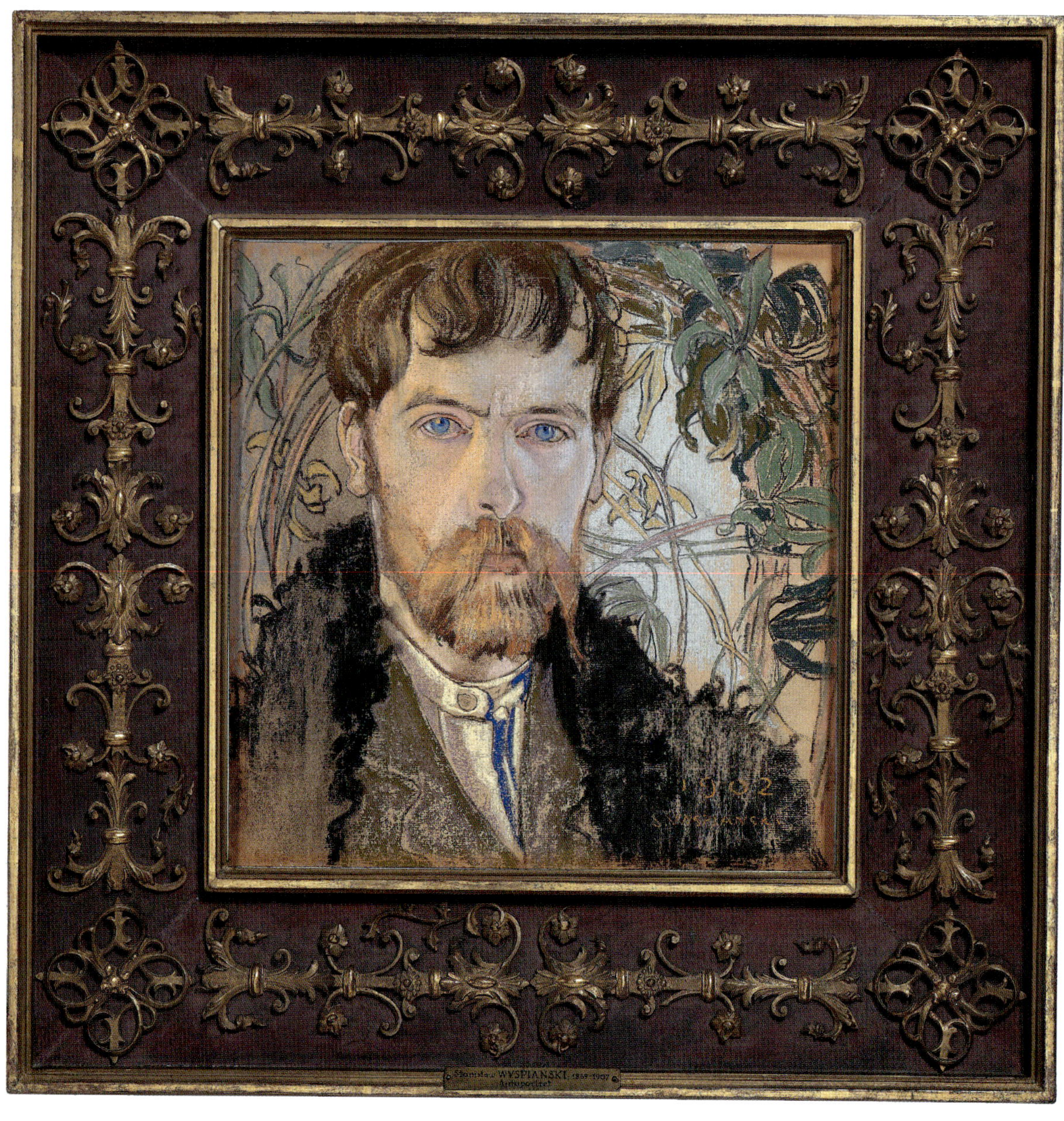

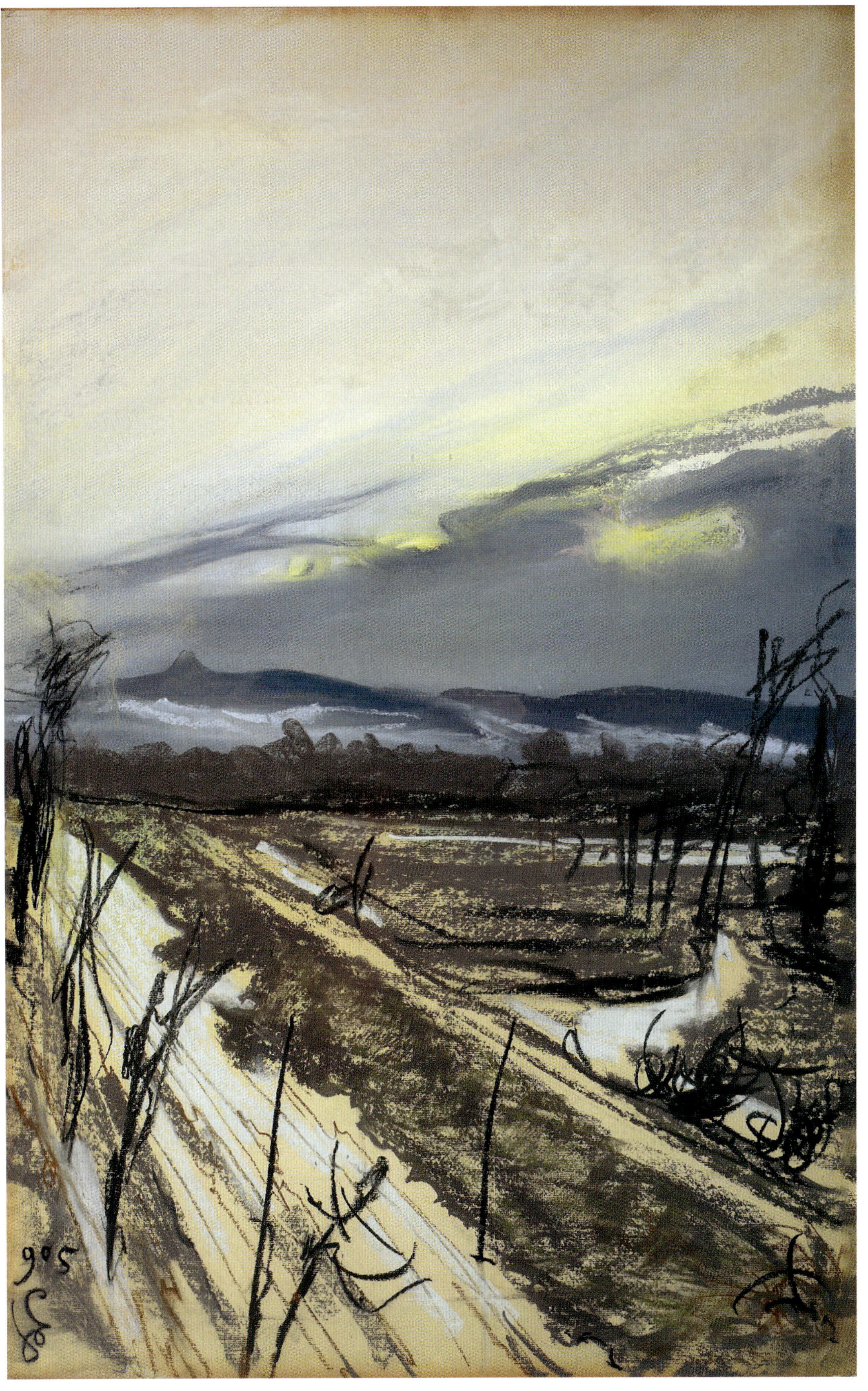

905

FIG.27
Stanisław Wyspiański
*Self-Portrait in Bed with Wife
and Angel of Death*, 1907
Pencil on paper, 170 × 210mm
Private Collection, on long-
term loan to the National
Museum in Kraków

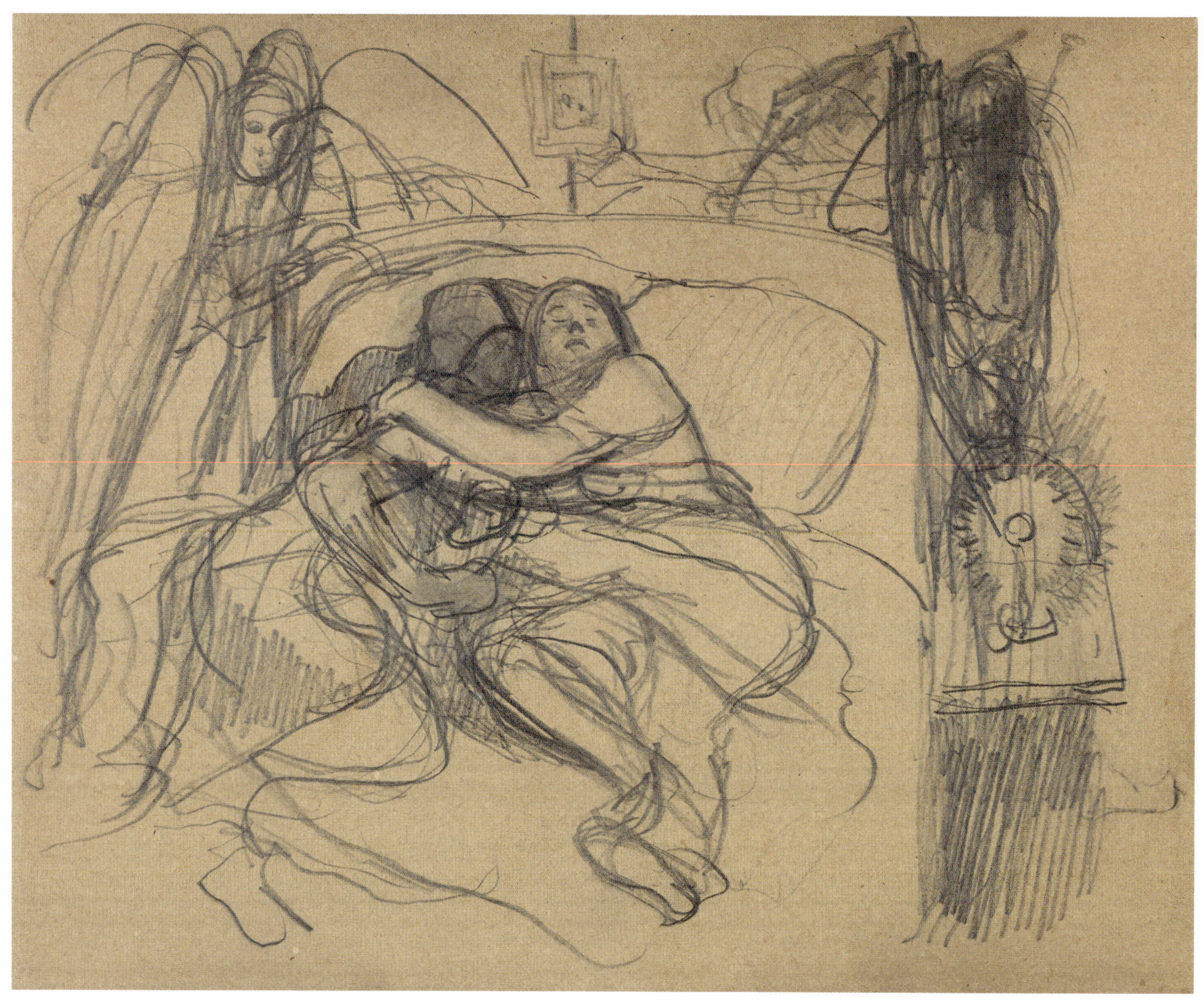

reference his diminishing dexterity. In the advanced stages of his illness, Wyspiański used flowers and landscape to express the state of his soul, as seen in the partially rotting *Irises* of 1904 and *The Kościuszko Mound* landscape series (1904–5).[35] The latter, also known as the 'Chronicle of a Few Days', comprises images of the same view from Wyspiański's Blue Studio created throughout December 1904 and January 1905, at a time he was too unwell to leave the house (fig.26). He was encouraged to undertake the series by Feliks Jasieński, who showed Wyspiański *Thirty-six Views of Mount Fuji* (c.1830–2) by Hokusai from his own collection and drew parallels with Claude Monet's *Rouen Cathedral* series painted in the early 1890s.[36]

By the end of 1905 Wyspiański had lost the capacity to draw or paint, so resorted to writing and dictating his plays. However, he regained manual powers shortly before his death, producing two final self-portraits in 1907. His penultimate self-image – with Death – shows his wife extending a protective embrace around him (fig.27), while his last likeness conveys his disfigurement with unsparing honesty (cat.16).

Wyspiański died young and did not live to see a free Poland. However, despite his short life and numerous setbacks, his art went on to become a steady emblem of Polish cultural identity throughout the country's stormy history. When the avant-garde filmmakers Franciszka and Stefan Themerson produced *Calling Mr Smith* (1943), a dramatic public information film about the Nazi invasion of Poland for the British public, they chose to showcase Wyspiański's portrait of his daughter Helenka as the most potent symbol of Polish culture, alongside Fryderyk Chopin's music.[37]

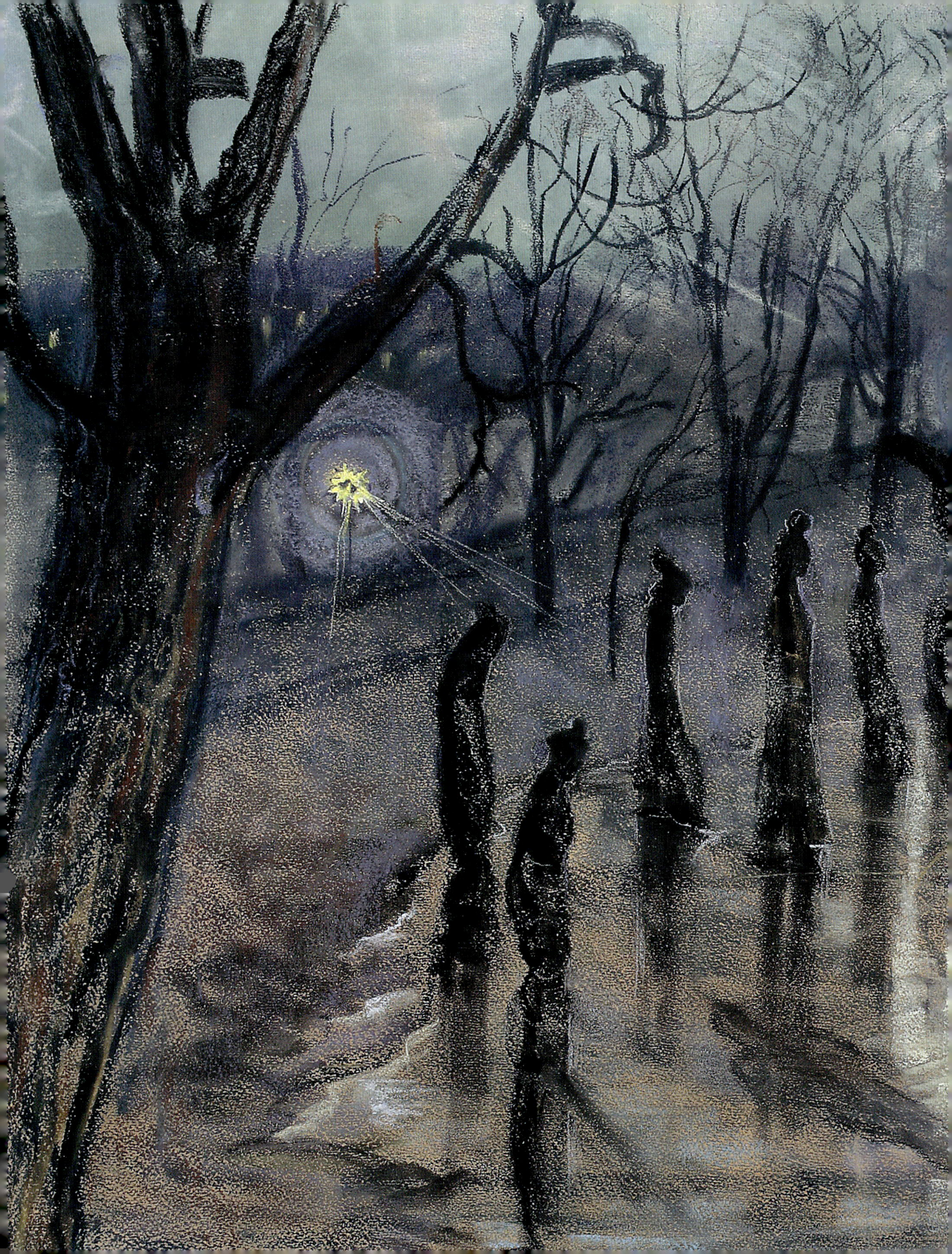

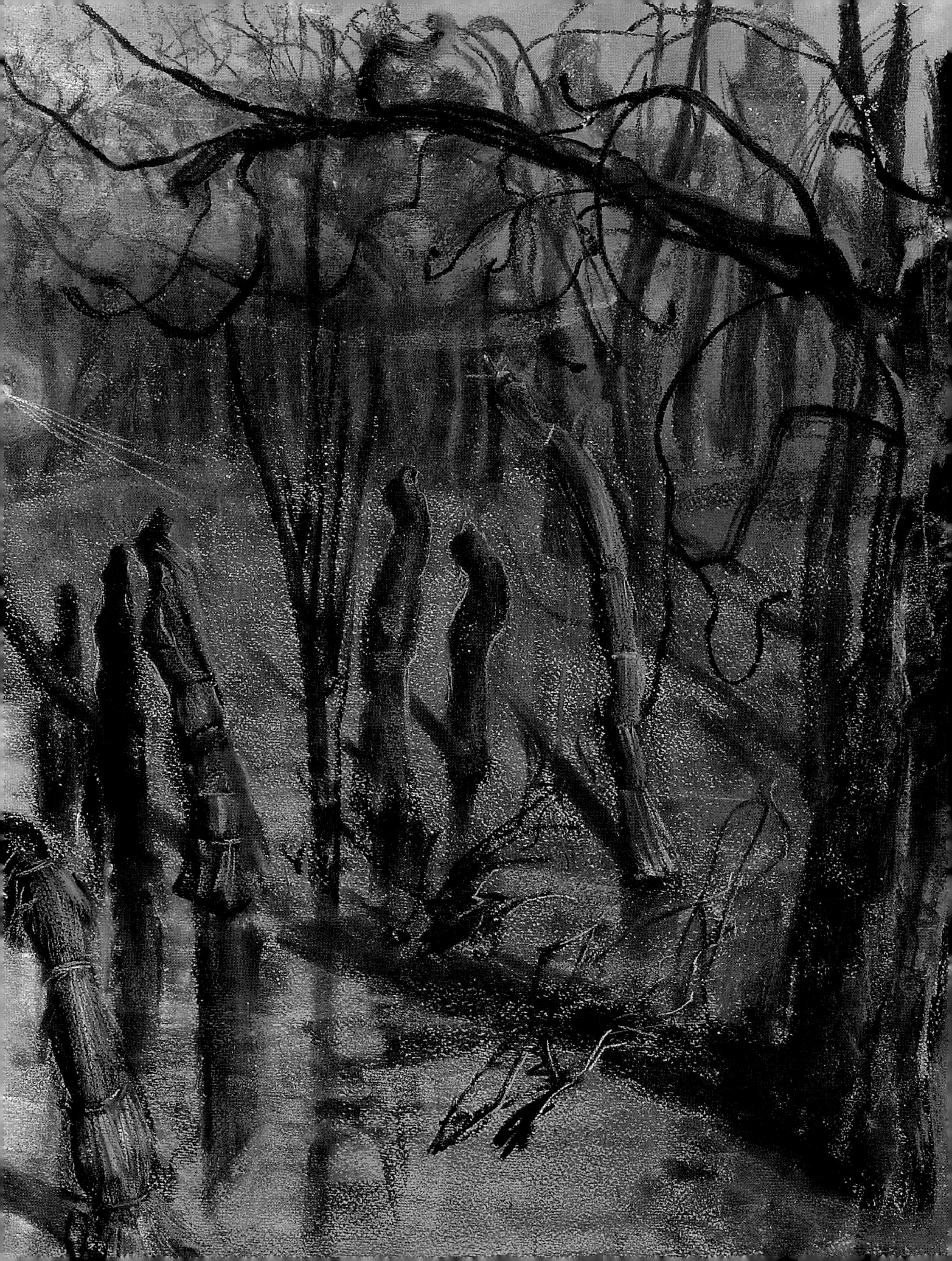

PORTRAITS OF THE YOUNG POLAND MOVEMENT

ANDRZEJ SZCZERSKI

In Stanisław Wyspiański's lifetime, portraiture acquired a new importance, beyond its traditional role as an official representation of sitters or a token of their social status. For artists of the Young Poland movement, portraiture became a means to express the contradictions of an epoch that was immersed in the recognition of people's individualism and subjectivity, yet simultaneously nostalgic about a disappearing sense of obligation towards society. In Poland's case, these tensions were heightened by the political situation of a divided nation deprived of its own statehood. Artists in its different partitions felt compelled to act as agents of change to convey the message of national reawakening. Accordingly, portraiture presented figures as symbols of current social and political change, often with reference to recent history. At the same time, the new generation sought to express a sense of personal freedom, unfettered by imposed social expectations – especially because many of them felt at home in the cosmopolitan art world. These different attitudes to portraiture were not exclusive, and the boundaries between them blurred, even in works by the same artist.[1]

Interest in portraiture echoed the debate about the value of the individual, a topic that occupied a prominent place among the champions of the Young Poland movement. Considered as the manifesto of the new movement, 'Young Poland' – the series of articles by Artur Górski published in the journal *Życie* (*Life*) in 1898 – included an early appraisal of the singular person as opposed to the masses.[2] The author critiqued the rise of a society dependent upon ordinary men and women, whom he called philistines. He contended that due to their lack of understanding of high culture and individuality, they encouraged a uniform society that expressed itself primarily through mass movements. Instead, the Young Poland movement valued the self and the uniqueness of the human soul, believing this should be the basis of a new world created by each individual, governed by their own rules. Such personalisation of attitudes to reality went hand in hand with an emphasis on the spiritual, and the rejection of the materialist approach to the world. The concentration on emotions and tensions within every human being proved crucial, and the purpose of art was to express this. Significantly, as Górski explained, this development coincided with a renewed interest in the national traditions that had been suppressed in the decades prior to the rise of Young Poland. The neglect had been caused by the old social elites who were resigned to the political status quo and the impossibility of regaining independence. Instead, the Young Poland rebellion drew strength from the rediscovered distinctness of Polish culture. Thus, according to Górski, no contradiction existed between the personalist approach to the world and a commitment to national culture, as both opposed the ossified structures that had dominated Polish society before the 1890s.

Stanisław Przybyszewski was a key figure who influenced Young Poland's understanding of individualism. Przybyszewski was a poet and writer whose versatile interests ranged from architecture to medicine and socialist politics.[3] In his lifetime he became popular and widely read, not only among Polish readers but also internationally. He wrote in both Polish and German; his publications were translated into several European languages, gaining significant readership not only in German-speaking countries but also in Scandinavia and East-Central Europe. Przybyszewski's career began in Berlin in the early 1890s, where he won literary acclaim. In 1893 he married Norwegian writer and musician Dagny Juel-Przybyszewska, and the couple lived mostly between Berlin and Dagny's birthplace in Kongsvinger, Norway. They quickly attracted the attention of Norwegian artists, notably Edvard Munch who in 1895 portrayed *'der geniale Pole'* (the great Pole), as August Strindberg referred to the writer (fig.28). In 1898 the Przybyszewskis moved to Kraków, where Stanisław took the position of chief editor of the Young Poland journal *Życie*. Soon afterwards, Dagny sat for a melancholic portrait by Stanisław Wyspiański (cat.3). The marriage was regularly shaken by Przybyszewski's affairs with other women, ultimately leading to the couple's separation in 1900, when Dagny left Kraków and began to travel in Europe. The following year, in Tyfilis (now Tbilisi), she was murdered by a man she trusted, who then committed suicide. Roughly at the same time of the couple's separation, *Życie* collapsed into bankruptcy and Przybyszewski moved to Warsaw to continue his career as a writer, later relocating to Munich.

The pair's tumultuous life, not least Przybyszewski's rejection of any sense of social or moral obligation, illustrated his own concept of the 'naked soul' as the key driver of human existence. Przybyszewski placed individualism above any social or cultural constraints. The 'naked soul' stood for all hidden and suppressed instincts which needed to be expressed in order to enable a person to develop to the fullest. Art allowed the 'naked soul' to be revealed, and so artists were elevated to a status equal to the Nietzschean *Übermensch* – superhumans able to act in whatever way they desired. Przybyszewski

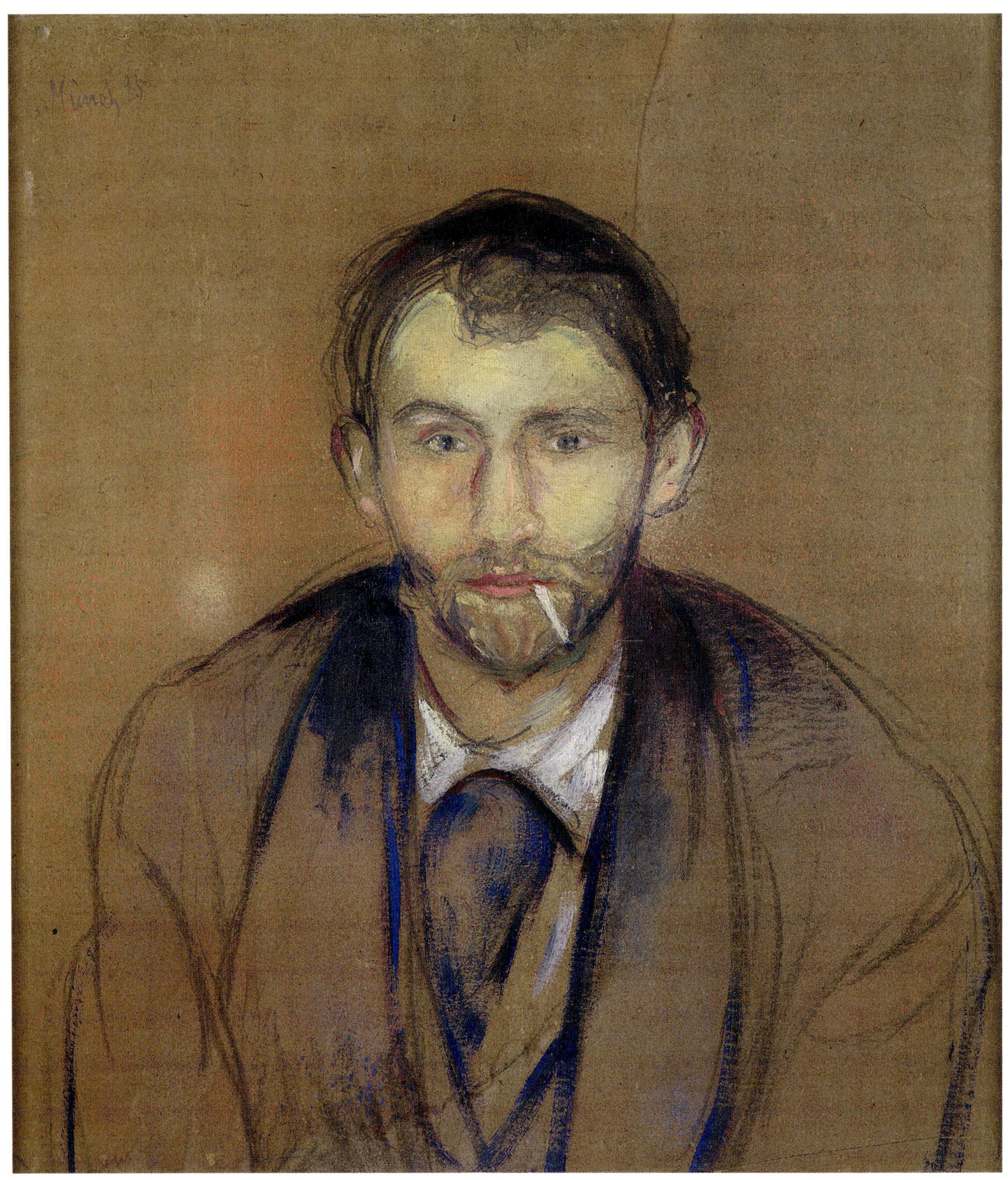

believed in the fundamental unity of the biological and spiritual. He praised individual intuition as a means of unlocking the inner workings of the world, inaccessible through purely intellectual speculations. At the same time, he thought that in order for people to be able to develop freely, their biological forces and drives should not be suppressed, regardless of the moral conflicts they provoked. He also claimed that the irresolvable tensions in the human psyche were caused by the intervention of evil forces and blind fate. Protagonists of Przybyszewski's novels and plays usually turn out to be extraordinary geniuses. Misunderstood by society, they live as outcasts in pathological states caused by alcoholism or wrecked relationships with others. Yet he interpreted these contradictions as the driving force behind personal evolution and necessary steps towards self-realisation and individual perfection. His writings analyse the internal life of his characters, often in the form of monologues that describe their emotions and the reasoning behind their actions in obsessive detail.

Stanisław Brzozowski's book *Legend of Young Poland* (*Legenda Młodej Polski,* 1910) – highly regarded as a literary self-portrait of the epoch – foregrounded contradictions in understanding the value of human individualism.[4] A philosopher and writer, Brzozowski intended his text to be a critical analysis of the main artistic and intellectual tendencies within Young Poland in the wider context of the Polish national character and cultural history. He summarised contradictions that impeded the Polish national reawakening. Amongst them he saw the idea of individualism as a mark of undeserved self-esteem that led to Poland's exclusion from cultural exchange with the external world, in turn leading to its debilitating provincialism and ultimate collapse. Equally, Brzozowski criticised contemporary glorification of the individual self, which further fragmented society and prevented the emergence of the socialism he often praised. Yet, he pointed to the literary work of Stanisław Wyspiański when looking for positive examples of a subjectivity that takes the broader community into account. For Brzozowski, Wyspiański understood and expressed the tensions within Polish society, demonstrating through his plays how it depended upon a moral order rooted in Catholicism, which Brzozowski viewed as the most individualistic of philosophies, yet felt the burden of this order as it limited the autonomous pulse of the national psyche. According to Brzozowski, Wyspiański called for transgression of these limits. While appreciating individualism, he saw it as part and parcel of a national community, which would be able to turn 'the national religion' rooted in the past into a forward-looking 'energy of nationhood' that would allow Poland to rise again.

Crucially, these vivid debates about the values and contradictions of individualism also influenced the art of portraiture. Among the Young Poland artists, Jacek Malczewski painted idiosyncratic portraits that can only be understood in the context in which they were made.[5] In the 1870s he studied at the School of Fine Arts in Kraków under Jan Matejko, who inspired his interest in Polish national history. Further studies in Munich and Paris allowed him to develop a singular interpretation of Symbolist art, extending to portraiture. Although painted in a realistic manner, his sitters were accompanied by allegorical figures that alluded to their personality and role in public life. The image of poet and writer Adam Asnyk (1895–7; fig.29) exemplifies the multilayered significance of such portraits. In his youth, Asnyk had played a prominent role in the Polish military rebellion against Russia of 1863–4, known as the January Uprising, emigrating to the Austrian partition of Poland after its defeat. The uprising's failure cast a shadow on an entire generation of Poles, changing the course of their lives; it stalled Polish military efforts to win back independence for half a century, until the outbreak of the First World War. Asnyk settled in Kraków in 1870 and became a well-known poet and playwright. His work centred on the fight for independence, coupled with a fascination with nature and folk culture as sources of national revival. Malczewski, who became a friend of Asnyk's, portrayed him as inward-looking, sitting in an armchair deep in thought. He is accompanied by a Muse, a young woman dressed in folk costume holding a lyre characteristic of Polish and Ukrainian folk music traditions. She wears a laurel wreath, a traditional attribute of classical muses. In the background, a procession of men and women represent the fighters and victims of the January Uprising. It ended in brutal bloodshed, the deportation of insurgents and their families to Siberia and confiscation of their possessions. A female personification of suffering Poland ('Polonia'), classical satyrs and fauns, as well as angels and the dead are among them. These visionary figures allude to Asnyk's imagination and personality, defined by both the catastrophe of the failed uprising and his commitment to the idea of national revival. Malczewski paints not only the visible sitter but what he sees 'in his mind's eye', thus providing an analysis of his hidden thoughts.

Malczewski's other portraits evoke dreamlike realms in which the sitter plays a particular role, as in the portrait of Aleksander Wielopolski, also known as 'Polish Hamlet' (1903; fig.30). Wielopolski was an aristocrat and amateur painter whose grandfather and namesake was governor of the Russian partition of Poland. Loyal to the Tsarist empire, his decisions were instrumental in sparking the tragic January Uprising. Marked by the grandfather's guilt, the Wielopolski family history was the artist's choice of background for the portrait. The young man is dressed in historical costume and wears a soldier's belt featuring tubes of paint instead of bullets. His art is

FIG.29
Jacek Malczewski
Adam Asnyk, 1895–7
Oil on canvas,
1770 × 1540mm
National Museum
in Poznań

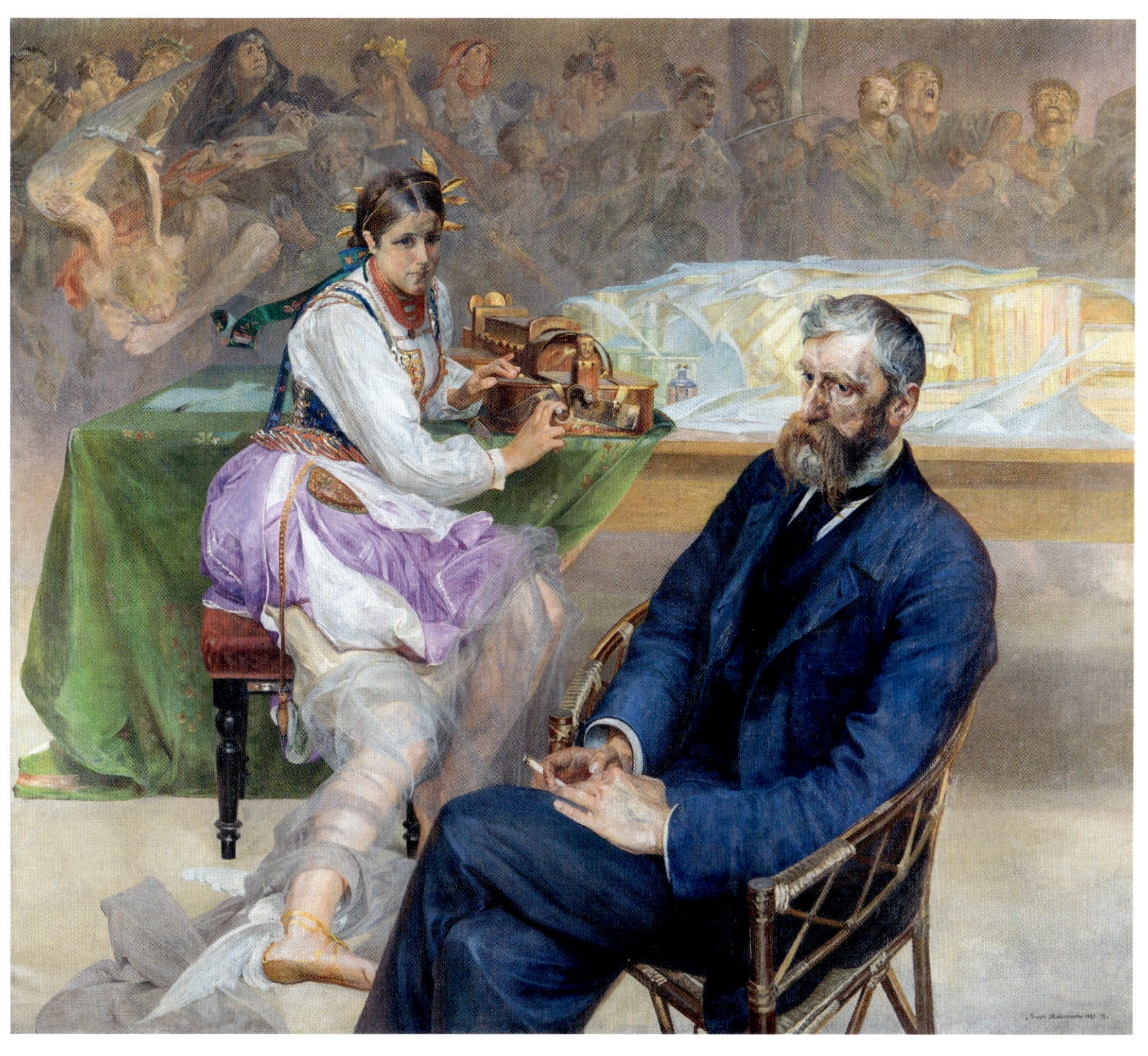

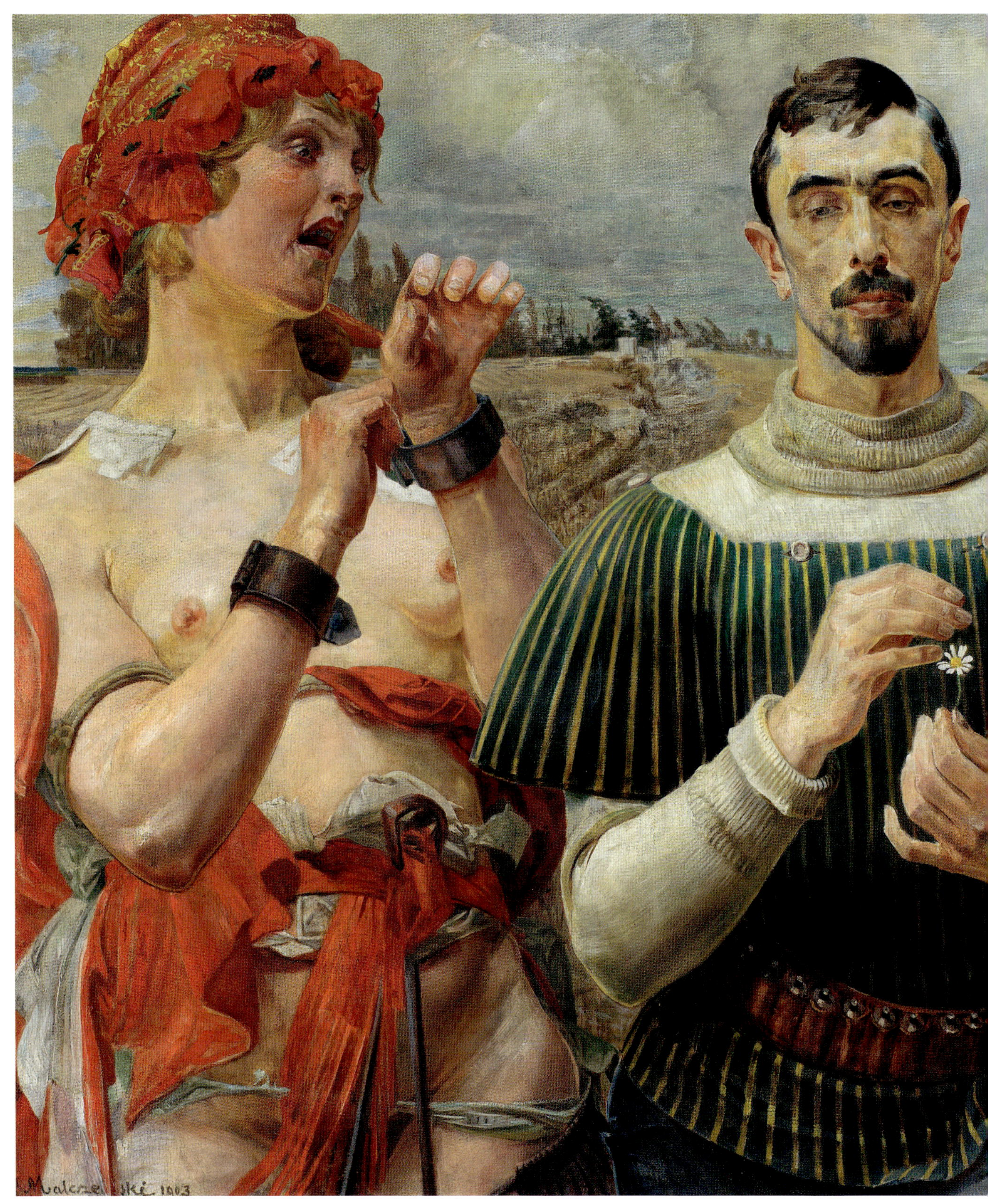

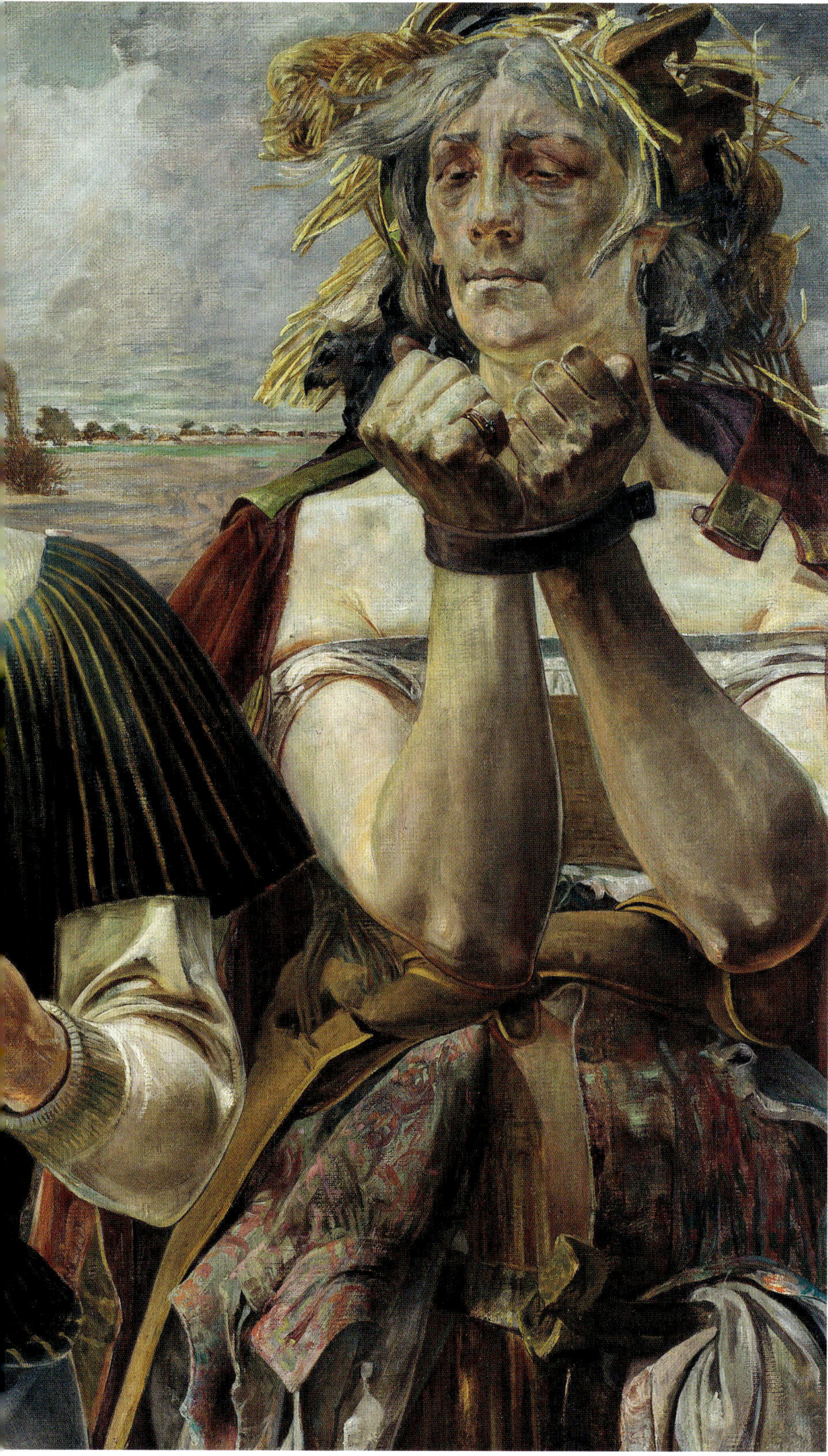

FIG.30
Jacek Malczewski
Aleksander Wielopolski
(*'Polish Hamlet'*), 1903
Oil on canvas,
1000 × 1480mm
National Museum
in Warsaw

his weapon, but his path is undecided. He has to choose between two worlds, represented by two allegorical female figures standing either side of him. One is an old woman in shackles dressed in a simple coat of the type worn by the deportees to Siberia (the latter often featured in Malczewski's paintings). She represents the trauma of the failed uprising, which extinguished all hope and prevented any course of action aimed at regaining freedom. The other is a young woman, mostly naked except for small pieces of red and white cloth – the Polish national colours – who stands for vitality and revival. Her shackles are broken, and she calls out towards the sitter as if to awaken him from his melancholic dreams. A backdrop of the Polish countryside further enhances the meaning of the portrait, with the 'Polish Hamlet' asking himself whether to be or not to be free. The portrait may be seen as an analysis not only of Wielopolski's state of mind but of his generation's, thus epitomising the dilemma of the Young Poland period: whether to fight once again for independence, or whether to opt to live without any national commitments.

The majority of Malczewski's Symbolist portraits refer to Greek and Roman mythology with sitters shown in the company of fauns and chimeras, who stand for Dionysian and Apollonian aspects of the human psyche. Malczewski's backgrounds often feature the characteristic flat countryside of central Poland or important monuments from Polish history. He also included Biblical figures in his portraits, such as in his depiction of his religious mentor, the Reverend Jan Jasiak, the background of which features angels with a fishing net – a clear reference to Biblical metaphors of priestly life and work. In his self-portraits, which he painted regularly, Malczewski assumed various roles, dressing as a medieval knight, St Francis of Assisi and Jesus Christ, and also as a participant in allegorical scenes that refer to the recent history of partitioned Poland. However, most of his self-portraits present him either as a dandy or solitary figure in the studio, accompanied by young voluptuous women as muses, often holding musical instruments. These works illustrate the tensions of the epoch, between an untamed Dionysian lust for life on the one hand and obligations towards the nation and history on the other. Significantly Malczewski never saw them as contradictory. During the First World War he eagerly supported the Polish national cause through numerous paintings on the subject of the Polish military units, as well as a portrait of their leader Józef Piłsudski (1916). In 1921 he completed one of his most elaborate self-portraits, titled *Polish Victory 1920* (fig.31). It was inspired by the Polish Army's victory over the Bolshevik Army at the Battle of Warsaw, which secured the survival of the Polish state. The work is permeated with symbols of Polishness such as the Polish manor house and the royal crown worn by the female allegory of Poland. The other female figure wears a red

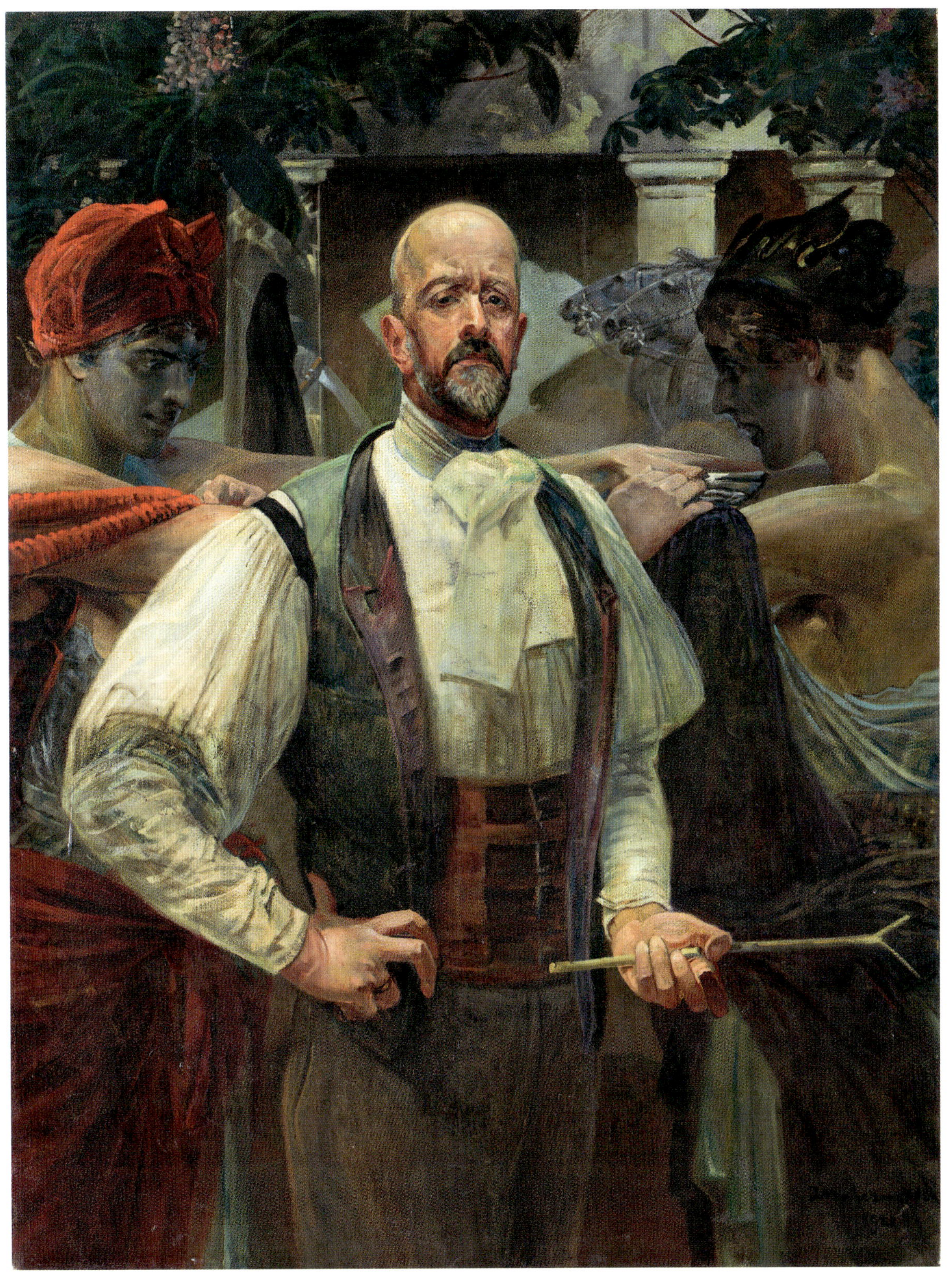

cap with horns, a clear reference to what the artist took to be the devil-like appearance of Red Army soldiers. The artist stands in the foreground, in sophisticated dress, celebrating the victory without taking part in the actual fight. His own weapon is a mahlstick – a simple tool used by painters. With this Malczewski praises the artist as the most effective agent of change.

A different approach to portraiture emerged in the works of painter Olga Boznańska.[6] In contrast to Malczewski she concentrated on the sitters themselves, analysing their personalities without detailed rendition of their appearance. As a woman she was not allowed to study at art academies, so was educated in private schools, first in Kraków and subsequently in Munich. In 1898 she moved to Paris, where she lived for the rest of her life. Boznańska's work achieved international recognition, including in Britain, where she exhibited at the New Gallery in London's Regent Street and became a member of the International Society of Sculptors, Painters and Gravers. By the early 1890s she had gained renown as a portraitist, receiving commissions and awards, such as a gold medal at the third International Art Exhibition in Vienna, in 1894, for her portrait of Paul Nauen, a fellow painter from Munich. While this portrait was largely conventional, subsequent works reveal more of her own distinct approach. Boznańska developed an original painterly style based on blurred details and subdued colours, which allow her sitters to be seen as if covered by a subtle veil, in a misty atmosphere. Consequently, instead of realistic representations, the viewer encounters psychoanalytical portrayals of particular personalities as conveyed by the artist's selective treatment of their features. A key work is *Girl with Chrysanthemums* (1894; fig.32), a portrait of an unknown teenage model painted in Munich. Boznańska concentrated on the child's face, with a particularly dramatic rendition of her dark eyes, which appear inward-looking despite being open. The artist captures an intense moment of self-reflection, with great insight into children's emotions, which were only beginning to be understood as decisive factors in the development of human personality. The white chrysanthemum may be seen as a symbol of the child's innocence, contrasting with her dramatic and mesmerising look, which expresses a psychological awareness of approaching adulthood. The girl's red hair stands out against the Whistlerian colour palette of white and grey, the bare setting and cast shadow further enhancing the power of her gaze.

While living in Paris, Boznańska painted numerous portrait commissions, which won her great acclaim. Her sitters included Poles resident in Paris – mostly prominent artists and intellectuals, as well as members of Parisian artistic society. The majority of these portraits avoid detailed representation

FIG.32
Olga Boznańska
*Girl with
Chrysanthemums*, 1894
Oil on cardboard,
885 x 690mm
National Museum
in Kraków

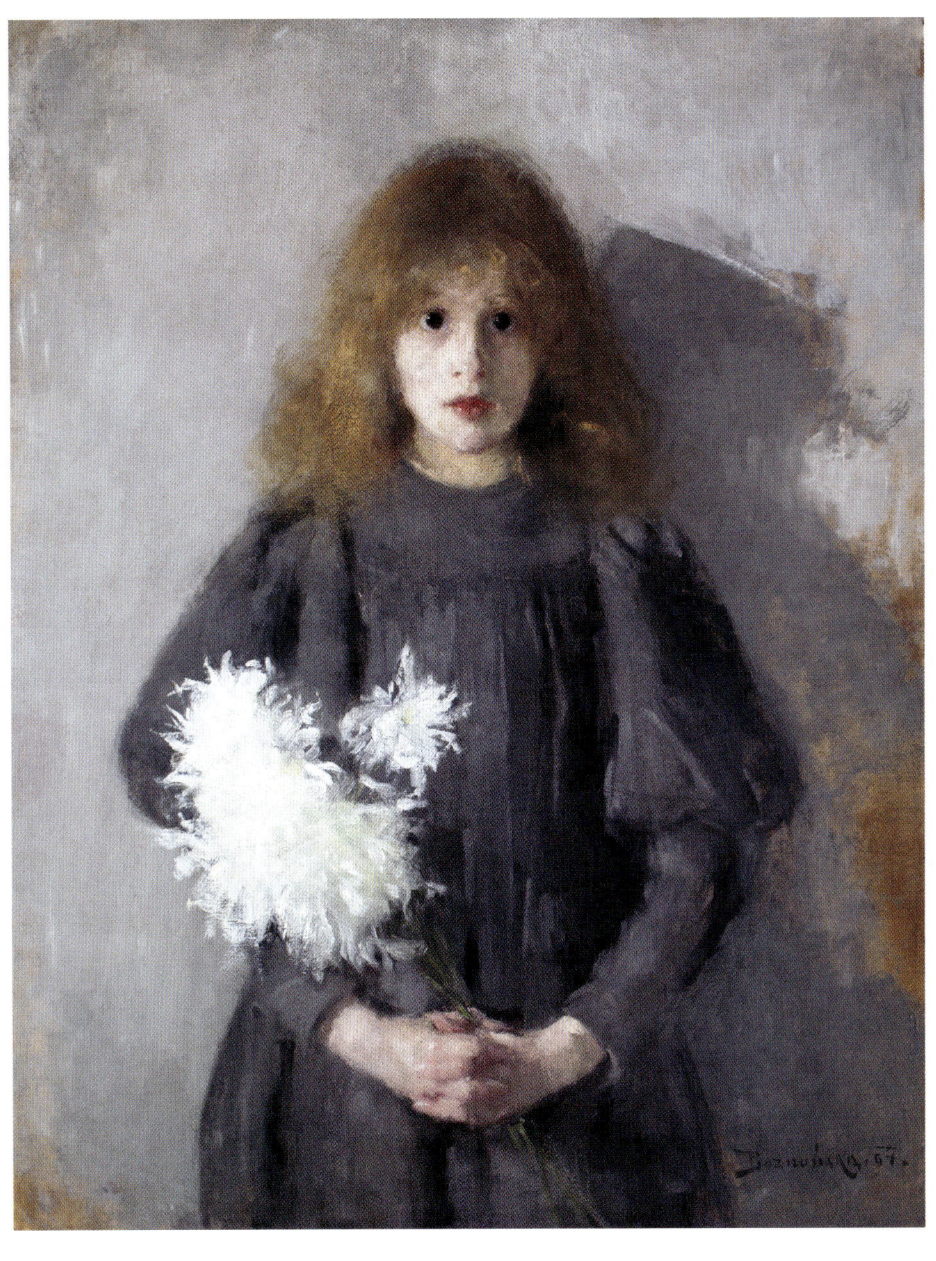

and have an almost dream-like character. In Boznańska's paintings, people do not perform any social or political role, rather the focus is on their uniqueness, fragility and intimacy. Her portrait of Henryk Sienkiewicz (1913) – the Polish winner of the 1905 Nobel Prize in Literature – is a case in point. It shows the writer as a gentlemanly figure absorbed in his own thoughts, caught in a moment of personal reflection, without any hint of international glorification. Similarly, the portrait of Jadwiga Sapieżyna (1910) prioritises the dignity of the elderly woman over her aristocratic status. In her portrayal of a Romany woman painted in Munich (1888; fig.33), Boznańska avoids clichéd representation and instead focuses on the personal emotion of the model. When painting female sitters Boznańska carefully studied their beauty but also gave them a sense of pride and independence. Throughout her life, the artist often painted self-portraits that became insightful studies of her own evolution as an artist and woman; they documented her successes, growing recognition and self-esteem, but also ageing and self-imposed isolation.

These portraits and self-portraits by other Young Poland artists offer a fascinating insight into the changing understanding of human personality at the time, which also relates to the development of psychology and psychiatry, including psychoanalysis around 1900.[7] Thanks to the influential teaching and publications of Kazimierz Twardowski, the capital of the Austrian partition Lviv (then known as Lemberg) became a particularly important centre of Polish modern psychology. Twardowski's works focused on the psychological aspect of human decisions, while his pupil Władysław Witwicki studied individual ambitions and the will to rule as sources of human creativity. At the same time Freud's understanding of the subconscious was promoted by his Polish students who worked as psychiatrists, for example, Ludwik Jekels and Ludwika Karpińska. The impact of their work on the artistic scene was limited however, and can be mostly discerned in literature, especially in the writings of Karol Irzykowski. He frequently analysed the internal life of his novels' protagonists in Freudian terms, and in 1913 wrote a pioneering popular study about Freud and his followers.[8]

The interest in hidden human emotions also found expression in the portraits painted by Young Poland artists. An example is Wojciech Weiss's *Self-Portrait with Masks* (1900; fig.34), in which the artist portrayed himself as a dandy cradling an array of theatrical masks. These symbolise the various and often contradictory elements of his personality hidden behind the restrained smile on his face, as well as the archetypes that govern his behaviours. This self-portrait can be seen as a reflection of Weiss's stay in Paris and his enchantment with the dynamism of the modern metropolis. Weiss wrote that he wanted to reject the ossified model of Renaissance portraiture, and

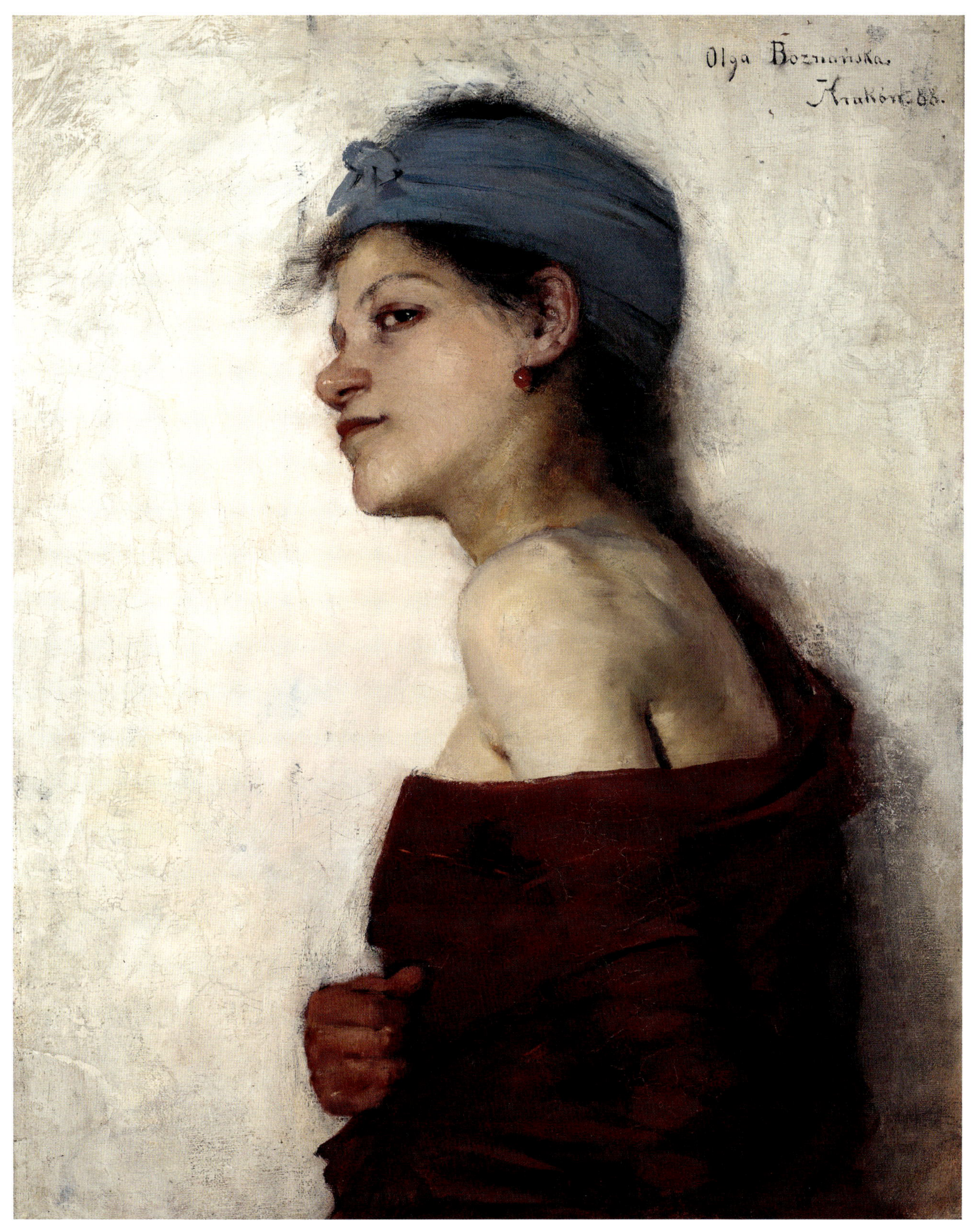

Olga Boznańska.
Kraków 88.

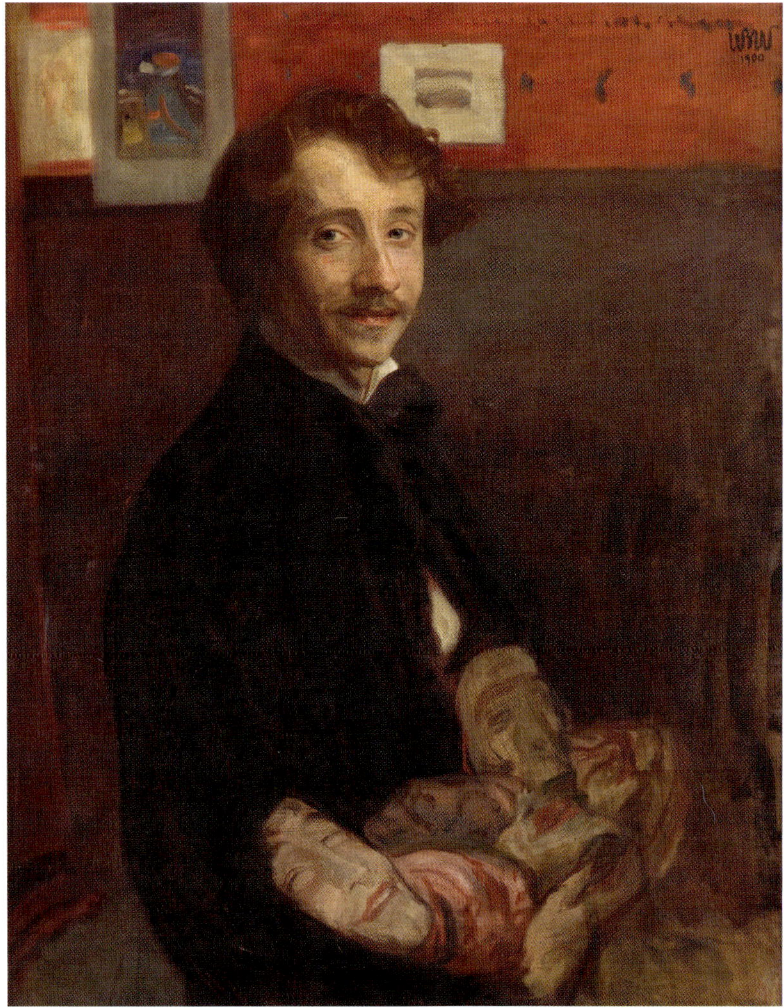

show the ever-changing and uncontrollable life of contemporary people, who
perform an ongoing masquerade.

The idea of masquerade and life-as-performance also fascinated Kazimierz
Stabrowski, who produced several portraits of students from the Warsaw
School of Fine Arts wearing fancy dress for their 'Ball of Young Art' in 1908.
In one portrait (fig.35) Bronisław Brykner wears a costume made of crêpe
paper that represents an evil spirit. Glamorously decadent, he contemplates
the world he is ready to govern with his symbolic sceptre. In another
portrait of Emilia Auszpitz, the sitter appears as a princess of ethereal beauty,
posed against sea waves and holding pearls – allusions to melancholy as a
source of creativity but also a psychological burden that distracts from the
surrounding world.

Kazimierz Stabrowski
Bronisław Brykner, 1908
Oil on canvas,
1820 x 1070mm
National Museum
in Warsaw

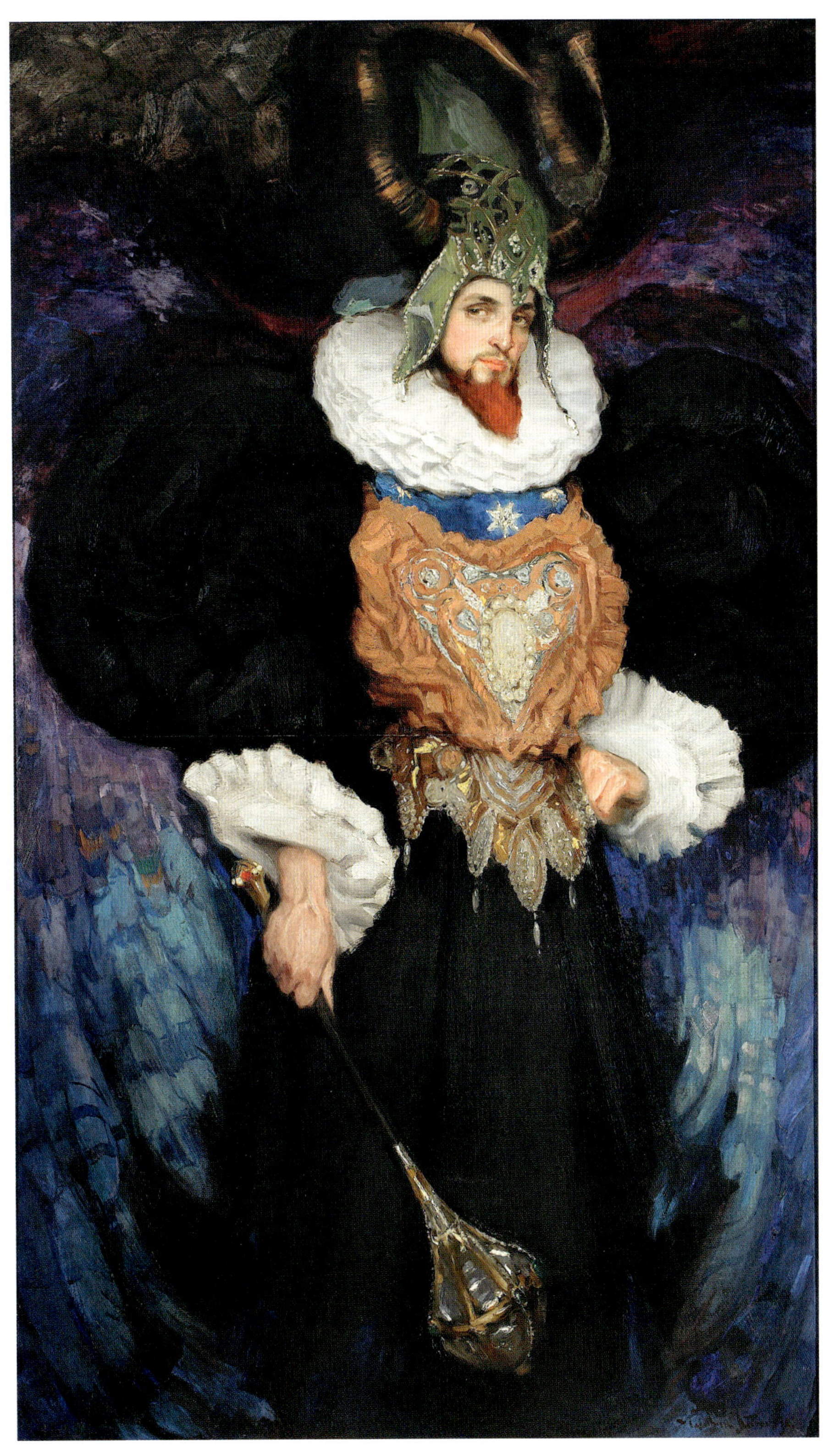

FIG.36
Witold Wojtkiewicz
Bolesław Raczyński, 1905
Oil on canvas glued
to cardboard,
900 × 720mm
National Museum
in Kraków

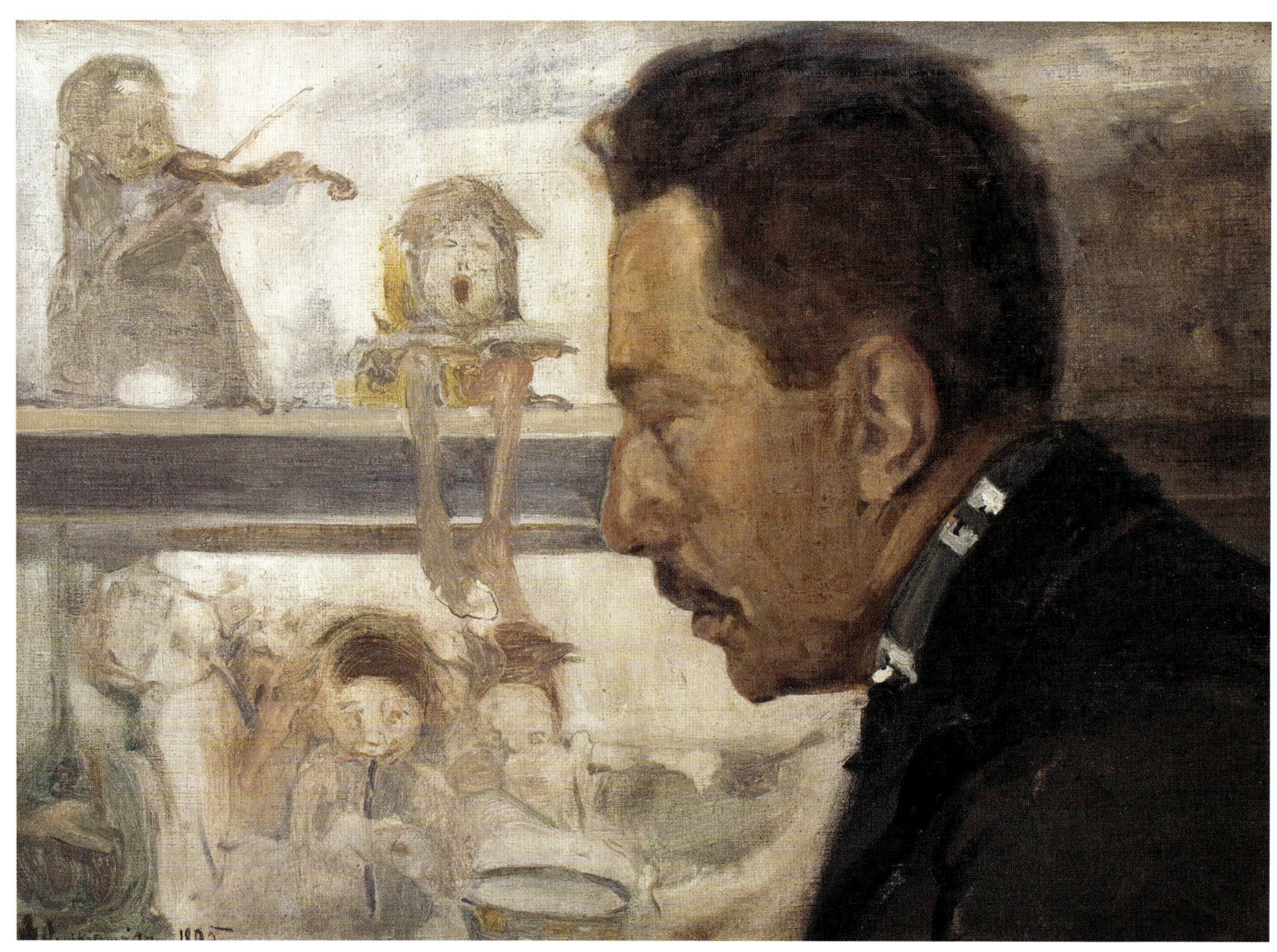

Melancholy, interpreted by Freud as a consequence of traumatic loss that cannot be comprehended, often features in Young Poland painting. Wojciech Weiss painted his fellow painter Antoni Procjałowicz in his *Melancholic* (*Totenmesse, Portrait of Antoni Procjałowicz,* 1898), sitting in a state of inertia, with his eyes open but paying no attention to the surrounding world. In the upper left Weiss quotes the title of Przybyszewski's popular poem 'Funeral Mass' ('*Totenmesse*'), which describes an artist undergoing self-imposed seclusion and self-reflection in order to locate the source of his creativity. Melancholy also permeates the portraits painted by Witold Wojtkiewicz. In Wojtkiewicz's interpretation it becomes the attribute of a creative spirit, as in his portrait of composer Bolesław Raczyński (1905; fig.36). Seemingly composing music in his mind, Raczyński appears detached from grotesque reality symbolised here by two childish figures playing a violin and singing in the background.

The interest in psychology and new theories concerning the subconscious can also be detected in portraits by Konrad Krzyżanowski where sitters are shown in interiors that are homely yet have an unsettling quality (1912; fig.37). In these apparently everyday scenes, Krzyżanowski employs dimmed light and intense colour to reveal hidden aspects of his subjects: their loneliness, beauty, mutual affection or fear of illness and death. Józef Mehoffer's *Strange Garden* (1902–3; fig.38) must surely be one of the most extraordinary portraits of the Young Poland era, filled with archetypal symbols of happiness and creativity. The painting depicts the artist's wife Jadwiga (also an artist) and their little son Zbigniew in an enchanting summer orchard. Fashionably dressed and subtly smiling, Jadwiga reaches out to the apple tree, as though innocently repeating the gesture of Eve. The naked child holds exuberant hollyhocks up as sceptres while in the distance a peasant woman looks in on the scene as if supervising it. The composition is crowned by an enormous gold dragonfly that eschews the logic of the picture and gives the scene an almost surreal character – like an unexplained riddle with a hidden meaning. The dragonfly may symbolise the sun, but also eternity and immortality, as if Mehoffer understood that all earthly beauty is transient and through his art he could make it permanent.

Stanisław Wyspiański's portraits also stand out in terms of their artistic form and intense psychological content, inspiring artists of the next generation, who interpreted his artistic legacy in their own manner. This is evident in the output of Stanisław Ignacy Witkiewicz – known as 'Witkacy' – especially in his pioneering photographic works.[9] Witkacy was the son of the prominent writer and art critic Stanisław Witkiewicz, who became famous in the 1890s for his idea of the Zakopane Style. Based on the wooden architecture and

FIG.37
Konrad Krzyżanowski
The Artist's Wife with a Cat, 1912
Oil on canvas, 1140 × 1240mm
Museum of Opole Silesia

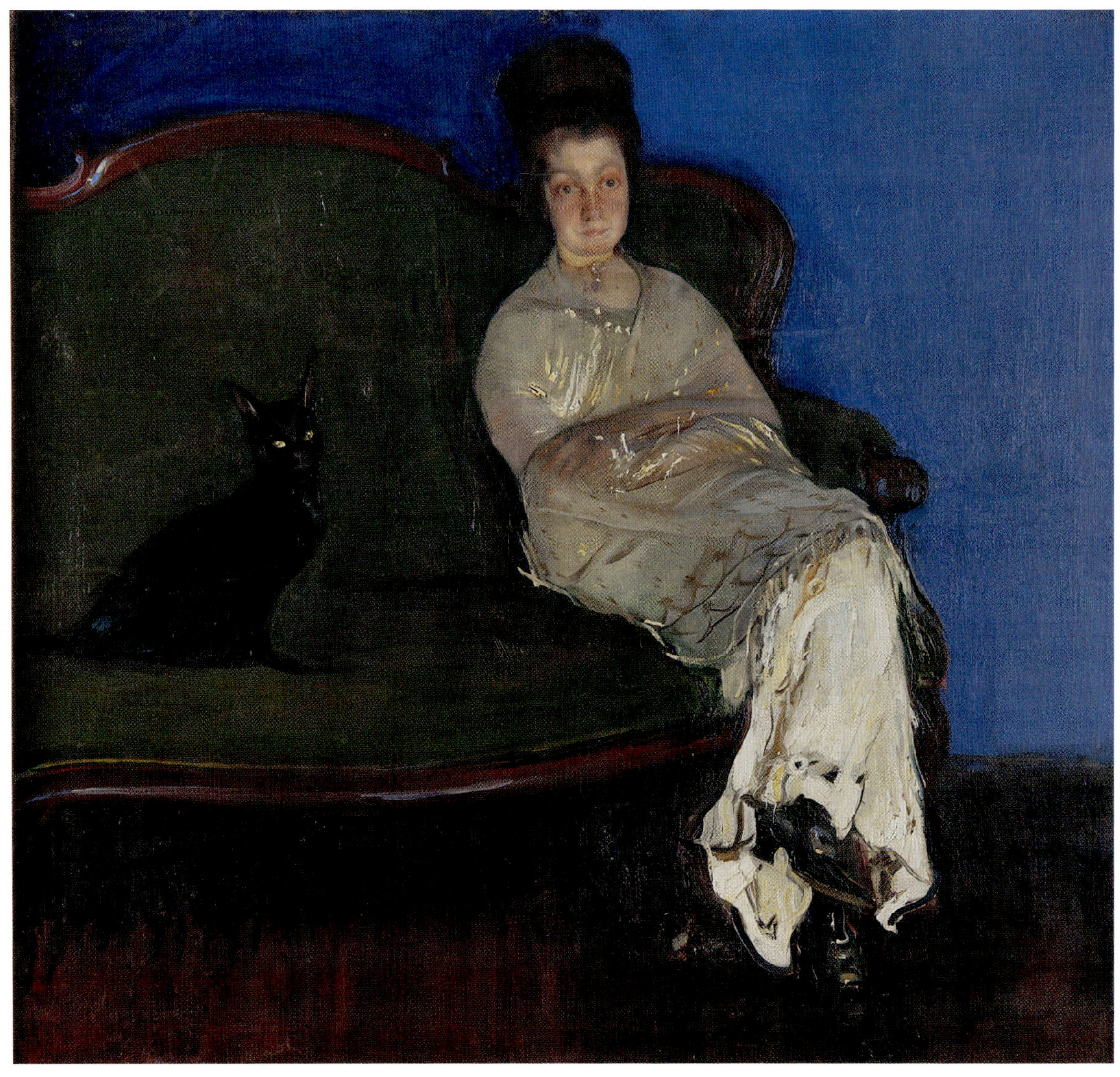

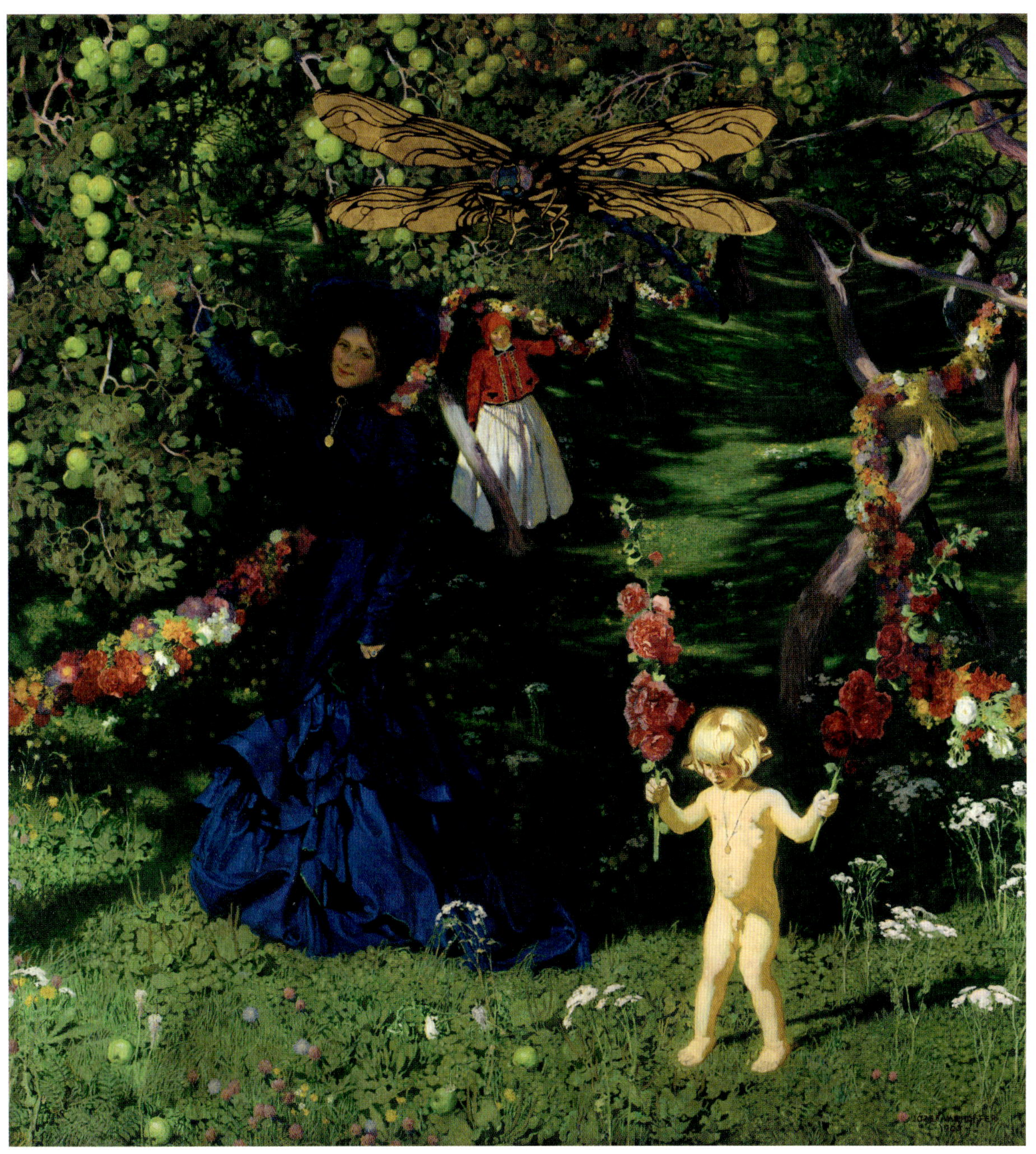

FIG.38
Józef Mehoffer
Strange Garden, 1902–3
Oil on canvas,
2225 × 2085mm
National Museum
in Warsaw

FIG.39
Stanisław Ignacy Witkiewicz
*Irena Solska with
daughter Hania*, 1912
Photograph, 130 × 180mm
Tatra Museum in Zakopane

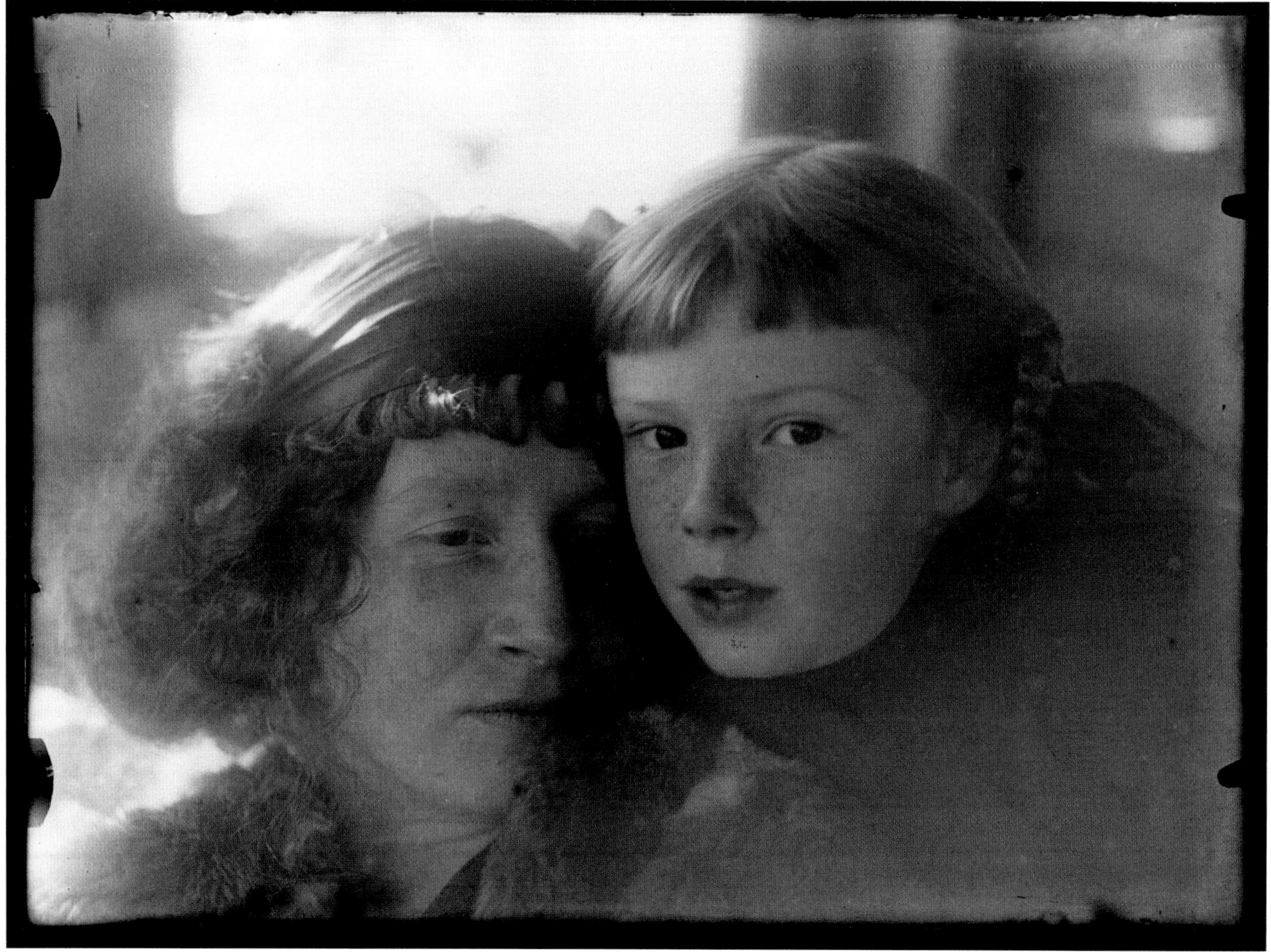

decoration of Highlanders' huts and crafts from the village of Zakopane and the Podhale region of the Tatra Mountains, the Zakopane Style was to become Poland's national style in architecture and design. Witkiewicz Senior believed that the Highlanders' vernacular traditions were an authentic repository of the partitioned nation's culture. As such they could be the basis for the national style, capable of strengthening Polish hopes and aspirations for regaining independence. Witkacy's father and his followers also painted portraits of Highlander men and women, endowing them with a sense of dignity and glorifying their costumes and customs. Similar portraits of Highlanders and Cracovian peasants were painted by other Young Poland artists, too. During this time, the notion of reviving national art through folk models was well propagated across Poland and more widely in East-Central Europe. Despite his appreciation for Highlander culture and long-time residence in Zakopane, Witkacy did not follow his father's path. Instead, he focused on the uniqueness of the human being, which he saw as the basis of civilisation. It eventually led to an interest in psychoanalysis, encouraging him to undergo experimental treatment under the supervision of his friend Karol de Beaurain in 1912.

Witkacy's fascination with the human psyche inspired a series of photographic portraits of his friends as well as self-portraits, executed in the 1910s. He focused on the fragmentation and linear qualities of the figure, intensified by contrasts of light and shade, in order to reveal the inner self in all its complexity. The shots were taken in profile and face-on, but most were also – unusually – from close proximity, with the lens held exceptionally near to the sitter. In effect, the photographs give a sense of intimacy and rejection of conventional representation, achieving almost theatrical drama. In one self-portrait (1910) Witkacy positioned his head against the black background and lit it from beneath, thus achieving a haunting expression of an individual conscious of his virtues and vices. His portraits of his fiancée Jadwiga Janczewska visualised the emotional stress and tensions that characterised their uneasy relationship. Occasionally Witkacy photographed her in semi-intimate situations, lying in her bed or reading a book, but also in the artist's family house in Zakopane, including a double portrait with his mother. Several portraits have a more lyrical and melancholic quality, such as those of fellow artists like Arthur Rubinstein or Leon Chwistek, scholar Bronisław Malinowski or actress Irena Solska (fig.39), the latter also portrayed by Wyspiański (cat.9). In these works, Witkacy showed unique creative personalities, detached from everyday reality as revealed by their faces, and especially their eyes. Photographs of Witkacy's father show an elderly man suffering from lung disease but retaining the inner strength of the artist-prophet despite his failing health.

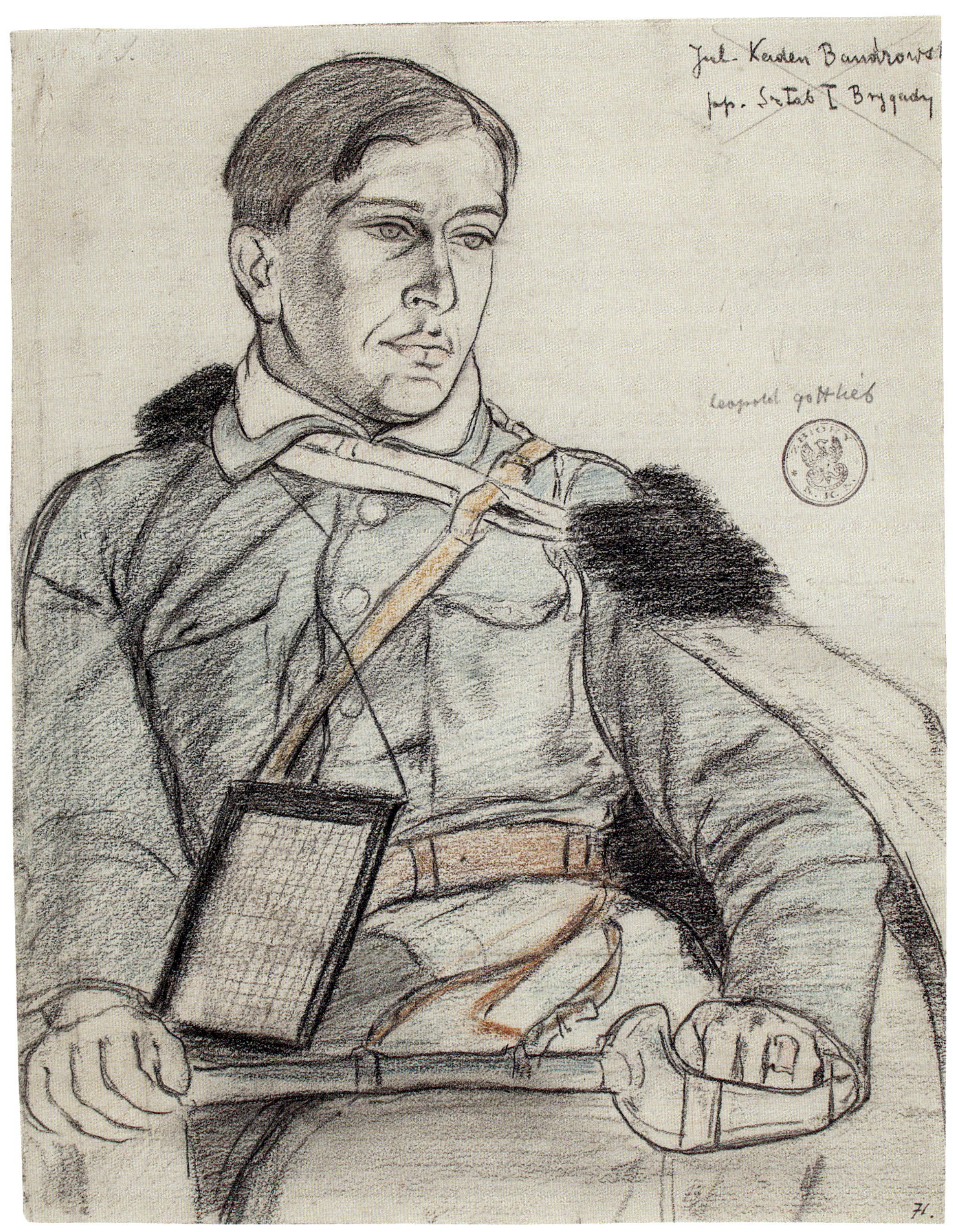

Jul. Kaden Bandrowsk
pp. Sztab I Brygady
leopold gottlieb

During the Young Poland period Wyspiański's art received acclaim on account of its artistic quality, and as a call for action to revive the long-abandoned dreams of independence. The next generation of artists followed this call. When the First World War broke out, Polish pro-independence organisations under Józef Piłsudski founded military units in Kraków known as the Polish Legions. Although formally instituted under Austrian command, the Polish Legions fought for the Polish cause. They attracted many writers, intellectuals and artists. Driven by national feelings, they wanted to bring about a new world, not with easels or pens but with arms. They included Leopold Gottlieb, who painted numerous battle scenes and hundreds of portraits of his fellow legionnaires, pausing between battles or in the trenches, such as his portrait of writer and journalist Juliusz Kaden Bandrowski (1914–15; fig.40).[10] His drawings and prints show his indebtedness to Young Poland portraiture and illustration by focusing on the psychology of his models, using a distinctive linear idiom. The soldiers, many of whom were Gottlieb's friends, are presented with sincerity, showing their chivalric manners and dedication to military service. Some portraits focus exclusively on their faces, while others are full- or half-length, depicting soldiers carrying out everyday duties, mourning their dead colleagues or preparing for battle. As portraits, they also document the historical events of the war, which brought about an end to the Polish partitions with the country regaining independence in 1918. Presenting individuals who consciously sacrificed their lives to the common good, and transgressing the anxieties and contradictions of the epoch, Gottlieb's pictures mark the end of Young Poland portraiture. In serving a greater cause, they sought to reconcile individual and collective freedoms; the struggle for the nation's liberty also entailed battling for the liberation of the individual.

The portraits of the Young Poland movement are among the most popular works of the period in Poland. They include Wyspiański's works, which are showcased not only in museums but are also widely reproduced in school books, murals, posters, advertisements and postmarks. Their fame is not accidental, as they present diverse approaches to human dignity and the complexity of the inner self. These notions remain inspiring today, not only in their country of origin but internationally. They fly in the face of uniformity and of any levelling of differences imposed in the name of standardisation. Above all, they stand for the appreciation of personal freedoms whilst simultaneously emphasising the importance of each individual's cultural roots.

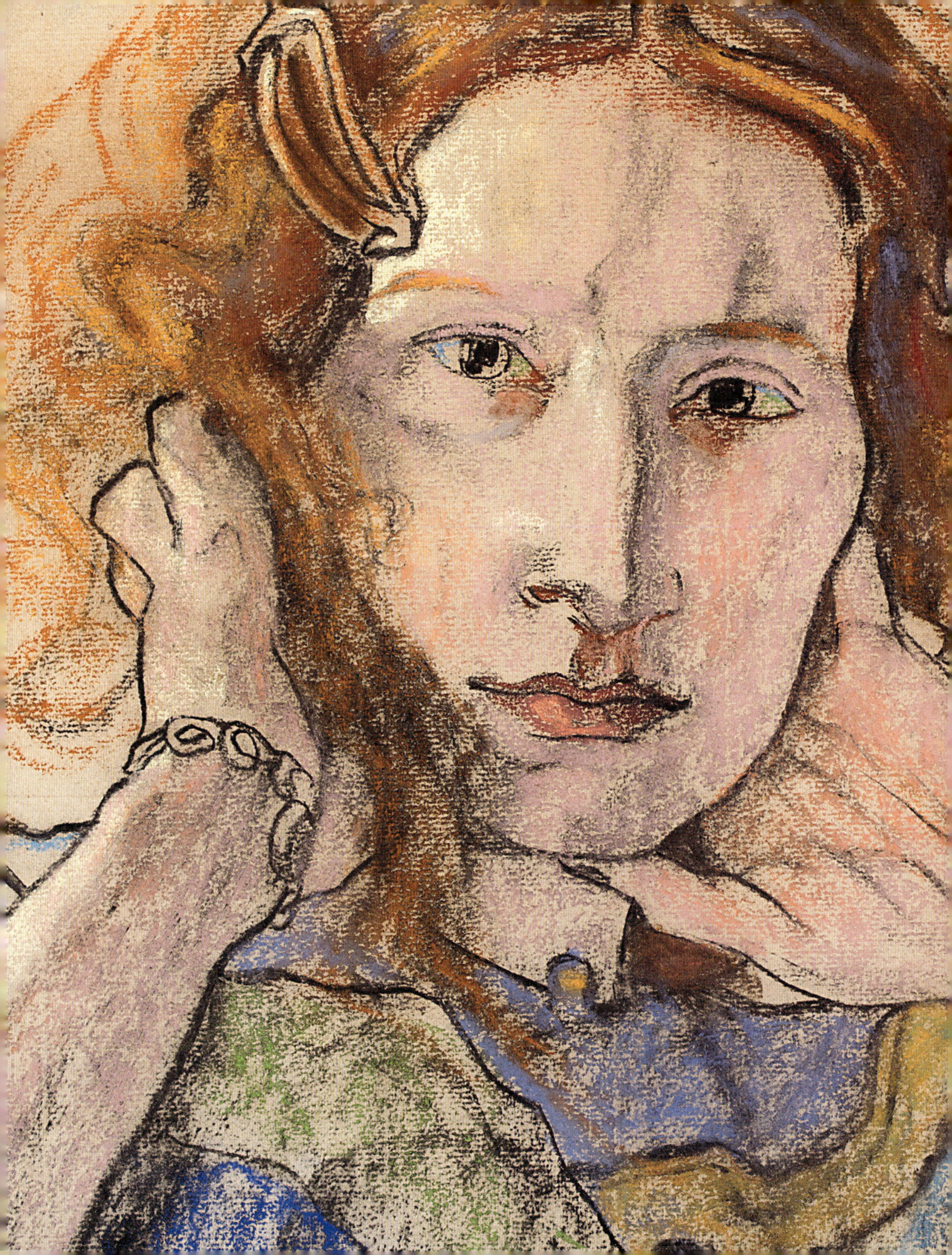

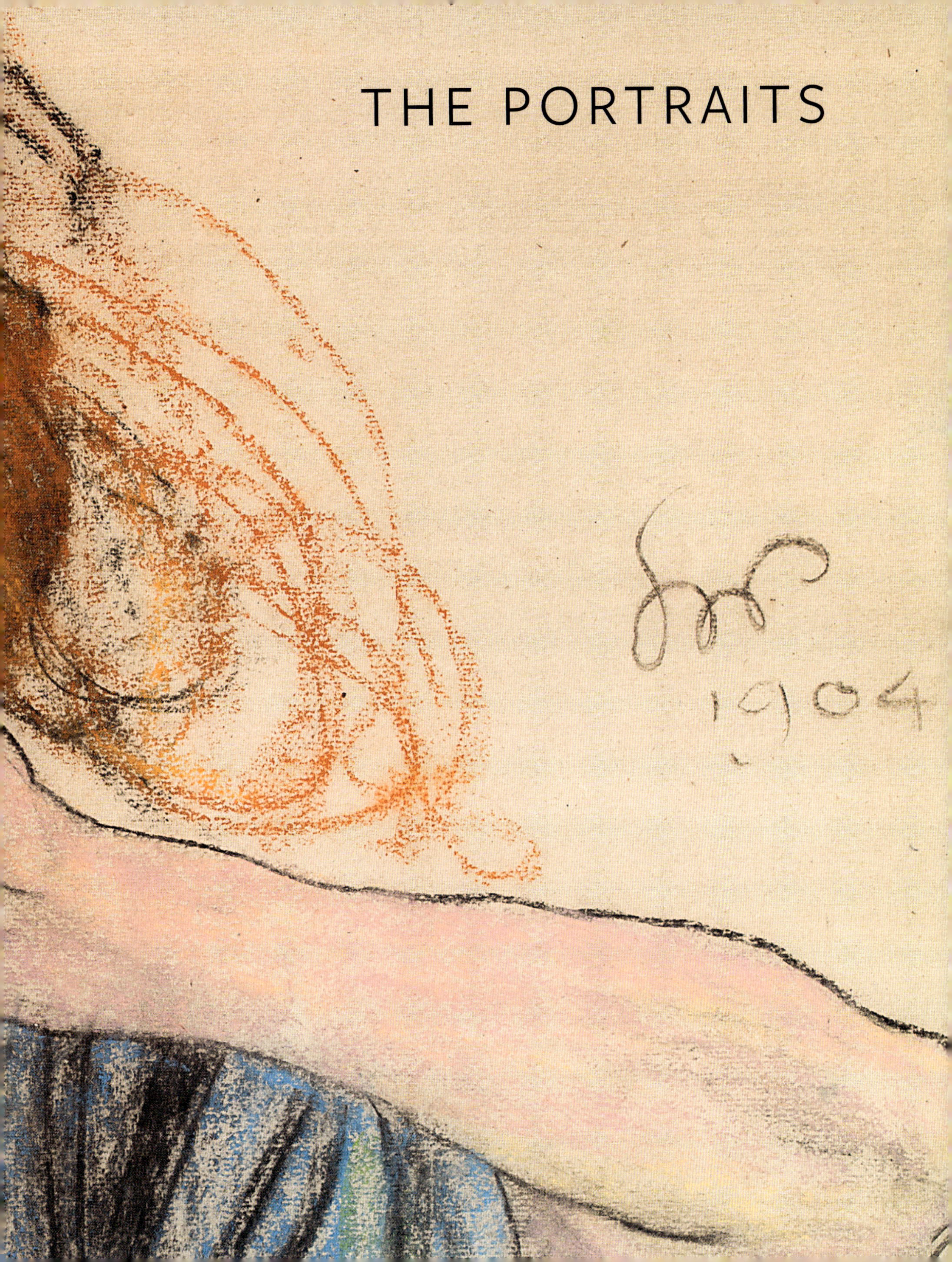

THE PORTRAITS
1904

SELF-PORTRAIT –
PAGE FROM A SKETCHBOOK

1890

This small pencil study presents the artist at the outset of his career. It is dated 17 February 1890, at which time Wyspiański was a student at the Kraków School of Fine Arts and the Jagiellonian University. From September 1889 he had also been working on wall paintings at St Mary's Basilica as part of a renovation and redecoration scheme supervised by his teacher Jan Matejko and the architect Tadeusz Stryjeński, arguably the first project in the spirit of the Arts and Crafts Movement on Polish lands and a vital training ground for Wyspiański. In March 1890 he set out on his first trip around Western Europe exploring 'masterpieces of architecture and church decoration',[1] returning to Kraków in September, only to relocate to Paris for over three years to further his arts training.

The artist produced few self-portraits, usually at key moments of his life. This study comes from one of Wyspiański's many sketchbooks, filled with portraits, landscapes and copies of artworks, as well as architectural sketches made in situ during his travels.[2] Taking this portrait from his reflection in a mirror, he paid special attention to his gaze, with his eyes simultaneously looking straight on at the world and at his own self, in a bold yet curious manner. The portrait is made with academic precision but with the aim of capturing what Wyspiański described in a note of the time as 'the psychological aspect' beyond 'the external mask'.[3] The barely indicated collar, complete with distinctive embroidery, further focuses attention on his face.

At some point the drawing was extracted from the sketchbook, and by at least 1911 had entered the collection of the art critic and writer Wilhelm Feldman and his wife Maria. Wilhelm was closely associated with Wyspiański, lecturing about his art and publishing his literary works as well as acting as a dealer on the artist's behalf.[4] He was also a regular guest at Wyspiański's home, and wrote reminiscences of their meetings after the artist's death.[5] Maria shared their literary interests, being a prolific translator of works by British writers such as Oscar Wilde, John Ruskin, William Morris, Charles Dickens, Thomas Hardy and Rudyard Kipling; she also translated books on figures from British history, such as Henry VIII and Oliver Cromwell.[6] The couple owned other works by Wyspiański, including a portrait of Wilhelm (1904) and one of their son Józef (cat.10), all of which were bequeathed by Maria to the National Museum in Kraków. **ML**

St. Wyspiański

Dnia 17ego Lutego 1890r.

KAZIMIERZ LEWANDOWSKI

1898

This portrait represents Kazimierz Lewandowski (1869–1938), a medical doctor and dentist by training, and an aspiring writer with a considerable literary and journalistic output.[7] He wrote poetry and plays and published *Early Spring of Young Poland* (*Przedwiośnie Młodej Polski,* 1935), a book of reminiscences about Cracovian bohemian circles around 1900. Towards the end of his life Lewandowski developed links with Galicia's capital Lviv, where he published the magazine *Lviv's Culture* (*Kultura Lwowa*) and where he died and is buried.

Lewandowski and Wyspiański knew each other from their school days in Kraków. However, by the time he produced this portrait, Wyspiański found his friend 'colossally conceited'.[8] Something of this feeling comes across in Wyspiański's portrait of the lounging Lewandowski, who is cast as a Cracovian *flâneur*, or man about town, in a tightly fastened coat with stand-up collar and fob watch dangling from a button, and a top hat almost covering his eyes. The portrait was executed on watercolour paper, allowing the texture of the paper to double up as the cloth of Lewandowski's coat and hatband. It is drawn in a bold stylised manner, with accents of colour animating Lewandowski's expression and a patch of white masking some error or underdrawing.

Tytus Czyżewski, a painter from a younger generation, summarised Wyspiański's likenesses of this type:

> Wyspiański's painting, or to be precise coloured pastel drawing, does not in fact constitute painting. It comprises stylised, decorative silhouettes in sharp, creased contour lines. Figures ... in his portraits are made up of stylised contour lines or blocks of colour (as if aspirational designs for unrealised stained-glass windows), solitary among the backdrop of plain paper, frequently against a blank background, without depth, as if cut out from some grand unrealised composition.[9]

A year later Wyspiański completed another portrait of the doctor, this time in the form of a head study that was part of a series of charcoal and pastel likenesses created at Young Poland's first artistic café, Paon, on Ulica Szpitalna in Kraków (see cats 3–4 and figs 9–13).[10] **ML**

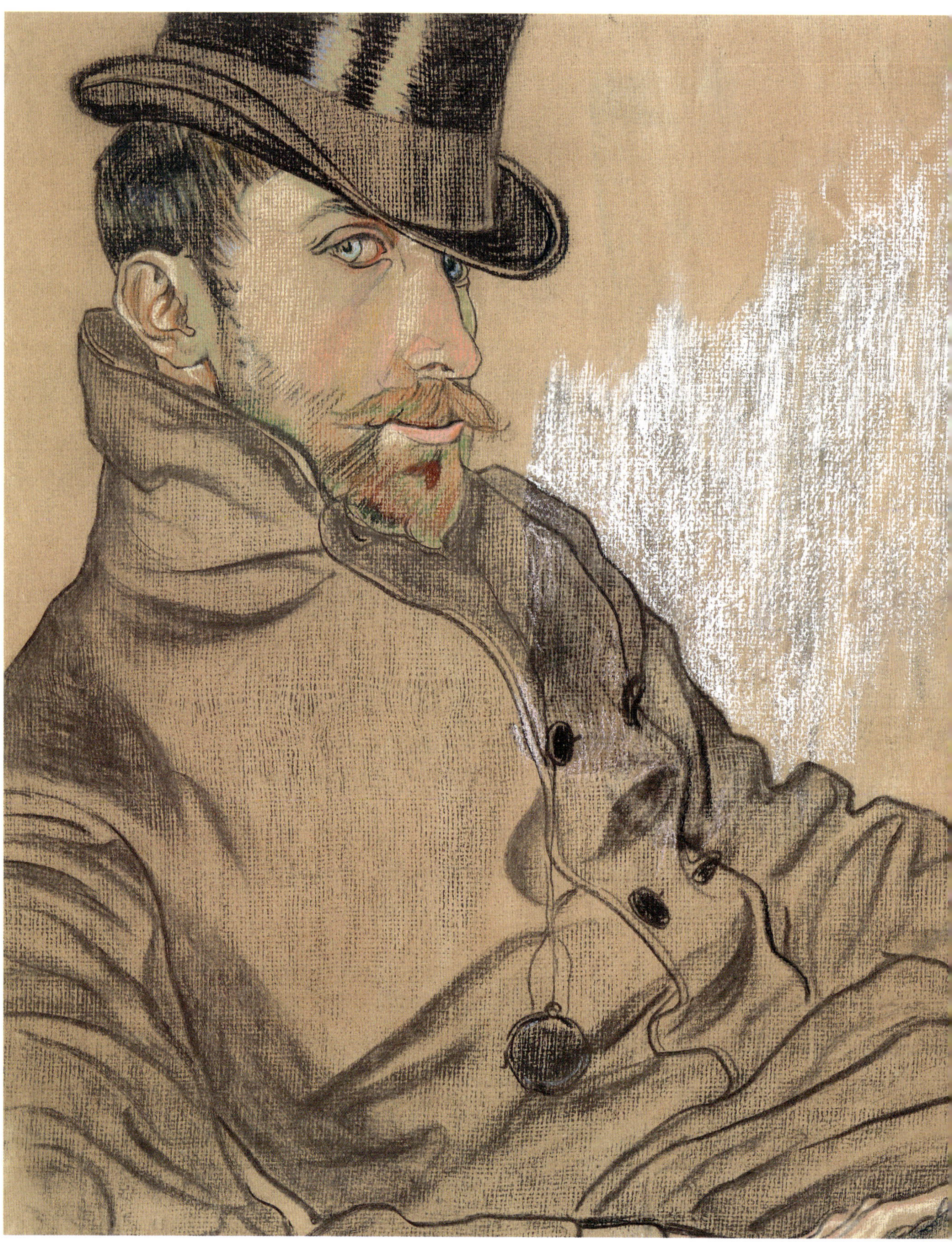

CAT.2
Stanisław Wyspiański
Kazimierz Lewandowski, 1898
Pastel on paper, 608 × 600mm
National Museum in Kraków

DAGNY JUEL-PRZYBYSZEWSKA

1899

The Norwegian writer and pianist Dagny Juel-Przybyszewska (1867–1901) was a
leading figure among the bohemian group that frequented the Ferkel tavern
in Berlin and a motivating force behind the avant-garde arts journal *Pan*.[11]
With her unconventional behaviour and distinctive appearance she became
a muse for many of the artists who gathered there: 'legend associated
her name with Strindberg's; one could find her facial features in Munch's
drawings and her silhouette in Vigeland's sculptures'.[12] In 1893 she married
the decadent Polish writer Stanisław Przybyszewski and five years later
relocated with him to Kraków with their two children – three-year-old Zeno
and one-year-old Iwi. Here she continued her work as a writer and translator
while acting as an agent for several Norwegian artists. Tadeusz Boy-Żeleński,
writer and member of Cracovian bohemian circles, reminisced about their
life there:

> The Przybyszewskis occupied a pretty little apartment with a tiny garden
> on the ground floor in Ulica Siemiradzkiego … From early afternoon until
> late at night, the home was filled with guests, and appeared to be some
> other planet, where nothing existed apart from art. The walls were covered
> in paintings by Munch and Goya brought with them; and before too
> long with works by Wyspiański, Weiss and others.[13]

Shortly after settling down in Kraków, Przybyszewski was instrumental in
setting up Young Poland's first artistic club-cum-café, Paon, located within
a private room of Ferdynand Turliński's Café Restaurant du Théâtre on
Ulica Szpitalna.[14] Both the Przybyszewskis and Wyspiański were fixtures.
Boy-Żeleński recalled Wyspiański's creativity there: 'He would usually draw
portraits of whoever was present, with no discrimination. They were perhaps
slightly different from his other portraits, leaning towards the "characteristic"
type, close to caricatures'.[15] Archival photographs of Paon's interiors (fig.9)
show the walls covered in over 30 such likenesses by Wyspiański. Arranged
in rows into a sort of gallery of types and personalities, the display features
two portraits of Dagny, including this one.

Wyspiański was one of Dagny's favourite artists; she said of him: 'I love
every line of his.'[16] He doodled caricatures of famous European historical
figures at a Paon café table in order to entertain her. Wyspiański's portraits
of her are characterised by a mood of melancholy contemplation in which
her penetrating gaze appears introspective and elusive.

Dagny was subsequently abandoned by Przybyszewski and tragically shot
dead by Władysław Emeryk, a man she trusted, on 5 June 1901 in Tbilisi.[17] **ML**

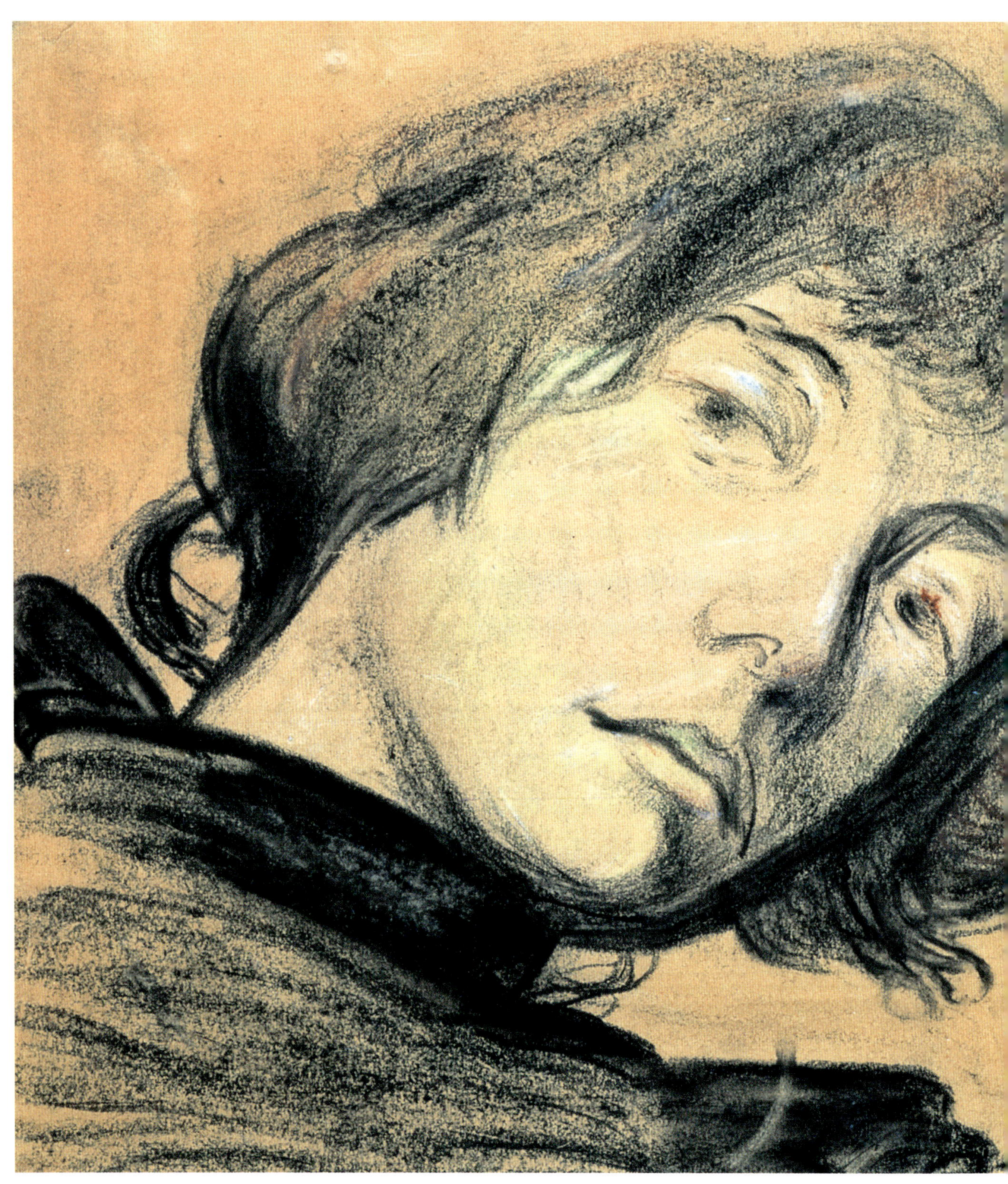

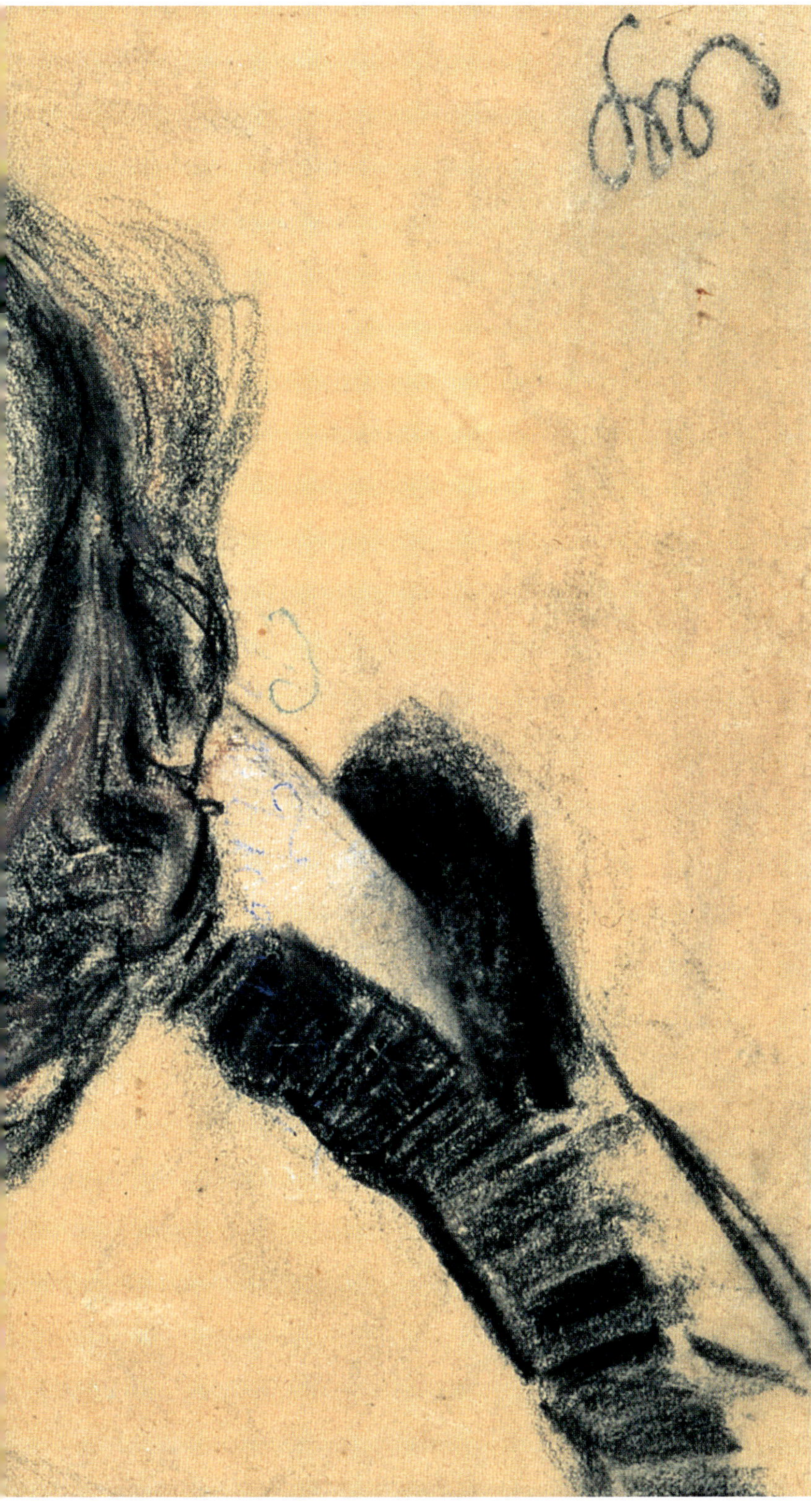

CAT.3
Stanisław Wyspiański
Dagny Juel-Przybyszewska, 1899
Pastel and charcoal on paper,
270 × 400mm
Krzysztof Musiał Collection

ANTONI LANGE

1899

The bearded man wearing pince-nez is Antoni Lange (1862–1929) – the decadent poet, translator, philosopher and literary critic. He was part of the Warsaw bohemian arts scene but also occasionally visited Kraków, mostly at the invitation of his friend Stanisław Przybyszewski. In 1899 Wyspiański drew Lange's portrait at Paon, where they mingled with the personalities who had set it up, namely 'exponents of the "naked soul" and other similar concepts – associated with the *Życie* magazine', members of the 'Sztuka' Society of Polish Artists and the City Theatre staff and associates.[18] Around this time Wyspiański, who was a regular member of Paon gatherings, conceived the idea of a portrait series of a hundred outstanding people who made up 'contemporary Kraków'. As recalled by his close friend Adam Chmiel, Wyspiański later gave up the idea due to the repetitive nature of some aspects of the composition: 'all of them wear the same cut of clothes, neckties, and collars.'[19] However, numerous works from the scheme were pinned to the walls of the café, comprising an original kaleidoscopic arrangement. Boy-Żeleński reminisced about the vicissitudes of the pictures after Paon's closure:

A few years later – Wyspiański summoned up Konrad Rakowski, a journalist and 'Paon' regular. He received him very officiously, almost severely and stated the following: that he was drawing portraits at 'Paon' in the hope of immortalising the facial features of outstanding people; however, from the perspective of a few years (... this was around 1904), he can now see that what he has retained was merely a gallery of private individuals, so he sees no point in preserving it. He is therefore asking for Rakowski to collect his portrait personally [fig.13], and to notify the other sitters in question, that they may collect their likenesses. In the event, all of them – half bemused half embarrassed – went to collect theirs ... One could not think of a more lordly way of condemning people of proving unworthy of his pencil! It reflected Wyspiański's characteristic trait – constant spurring on, constant vigilance, constant *demands* from people, the need to bring out *the most* in them, so evident in Wyspiański's letters to his friends.[20] **ML**

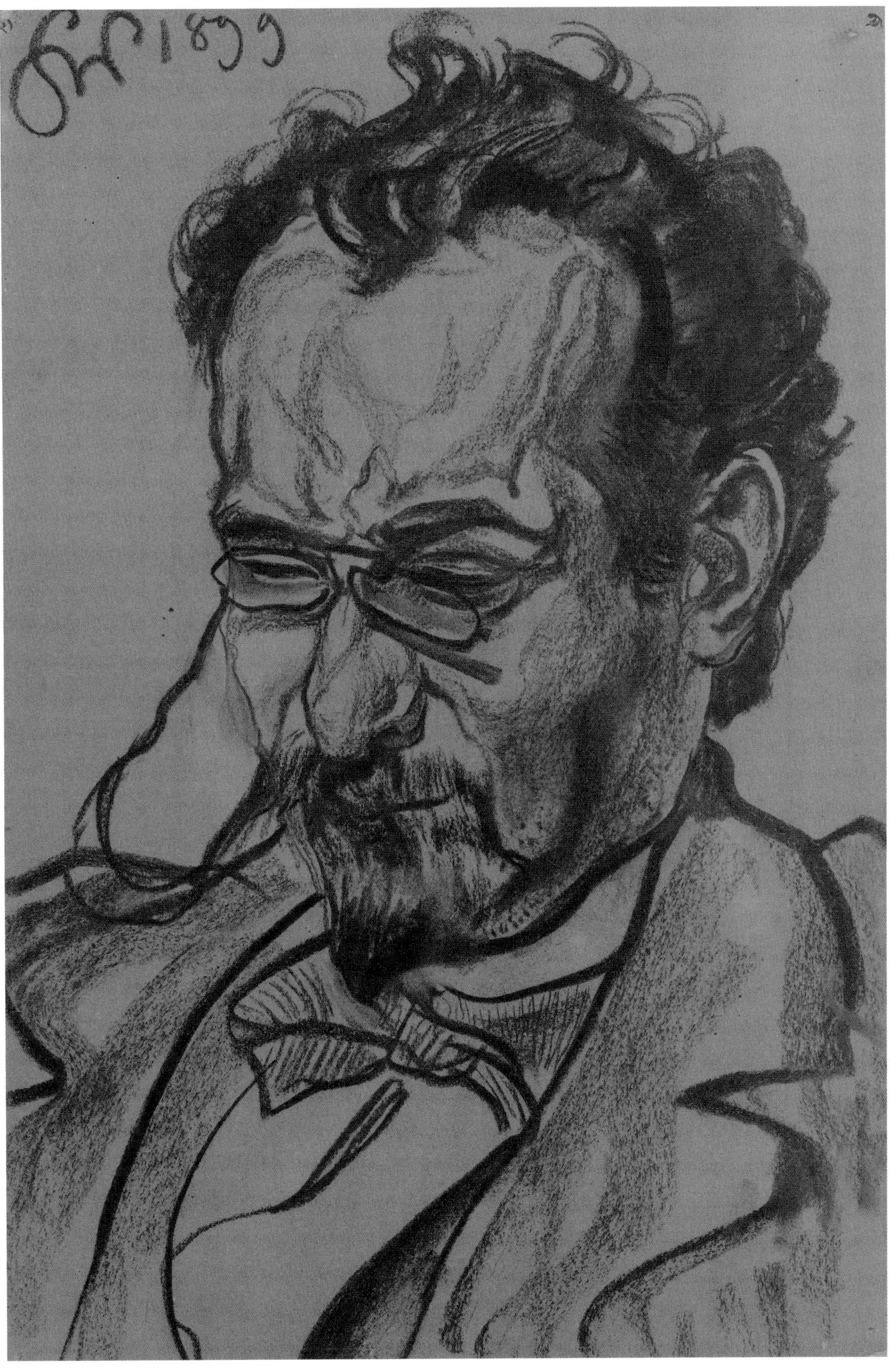
1899

JERZY ŻUŁAWSKI

1900

The sitter Jerzy Żuławski (1874–1915) was a Young Poland poet, playwright, essayist, novelist and a forerunner of Polish science-fiction. His sequence of books collectively known as *The Lunar Trilogy* (*Trylogia Księżycowa*, 1903–11), concerning an ill-fated expedition to colonise the Moon, were translated into virtually every European language except English, and exerted a huge influence on the science-fiction genre, inspiring writers such as Stanisław Lem and through him the Russian film director Andrei Tarkovsky.[21]

As a young man, Żuławski was a keen explorer of new ideas and formed part of the Cracovian bohemian artistic circle that gathered around Stanisław Przybyszewski and Stanisław Wyspiański in Kraków. All three worked for *Życie* magazine where Żuławski published his poetry and critical writings. Together with Wyspiański he shared a passion for the theatre: Wyspiański's famous play *The Wedding* (*Wesele*, 1901) inspired Żuławski to write *The Dictator* (*Dyktator,* 1903) – his work about the outbreak of the January Uprising.[22] In turn, Żuławski's *Eros and Psyche* (*Eros i Psyche*, 1904) is one of the most renowned Young Poland plays, alongside *The Wedding*.[23]

As an advocate of metaphysics in art, Żuławski aspired to give intellectual form to the decadent Symbolist concept of the 'naked soul', defining existence as a force that was both spiritual and material. Wyspiański's portrait hints at this synthesis, the writer is shown deep in thought with a faraway gaze yet appearing worldly and elegant at the same time. The subtle modelling of his face contrasts with the bold contour lines to create a compelling portrait of one of the most dynamic literary figures of the era. It comes as little surprise that this image was frequently reproduced during Żuławski's lifetime, accompanying his poems and other writings (see also fig.11).[24]

In 1910 Żuławski moved to the village of Zakopane, a hub of the Young Poland movement. His Zakopane Style house designed by Stanisław Witkiewicz, originally known as Willa (Villa) Pepita and later as Willa Łada, became a meeting place for cultural figures, such as the Expressionist artist Stanisław Ignacy Witkiewicz, known as 'Witkacy'. The Anglo-Polish anthropologist Bronisław Malinowski also visited. Żuławski was a co-founder of the Tatra Mountain Voluntary Rescue service (Tatrzańskie Ochotnicze Pogotowie Ratunkowe) and participated in search operations.

Supporting the cause of Polish independence, Żuławski volunteered for military action in the Polish Legions during the First World War; he died of typhus during the epidemic of 1915. **MS**

CAT.5
Stanisław Wyspiański
Jerzy Żuławski, 1900
Charcoal on laid paper,
430 × 490mm
National Museum in Poznań

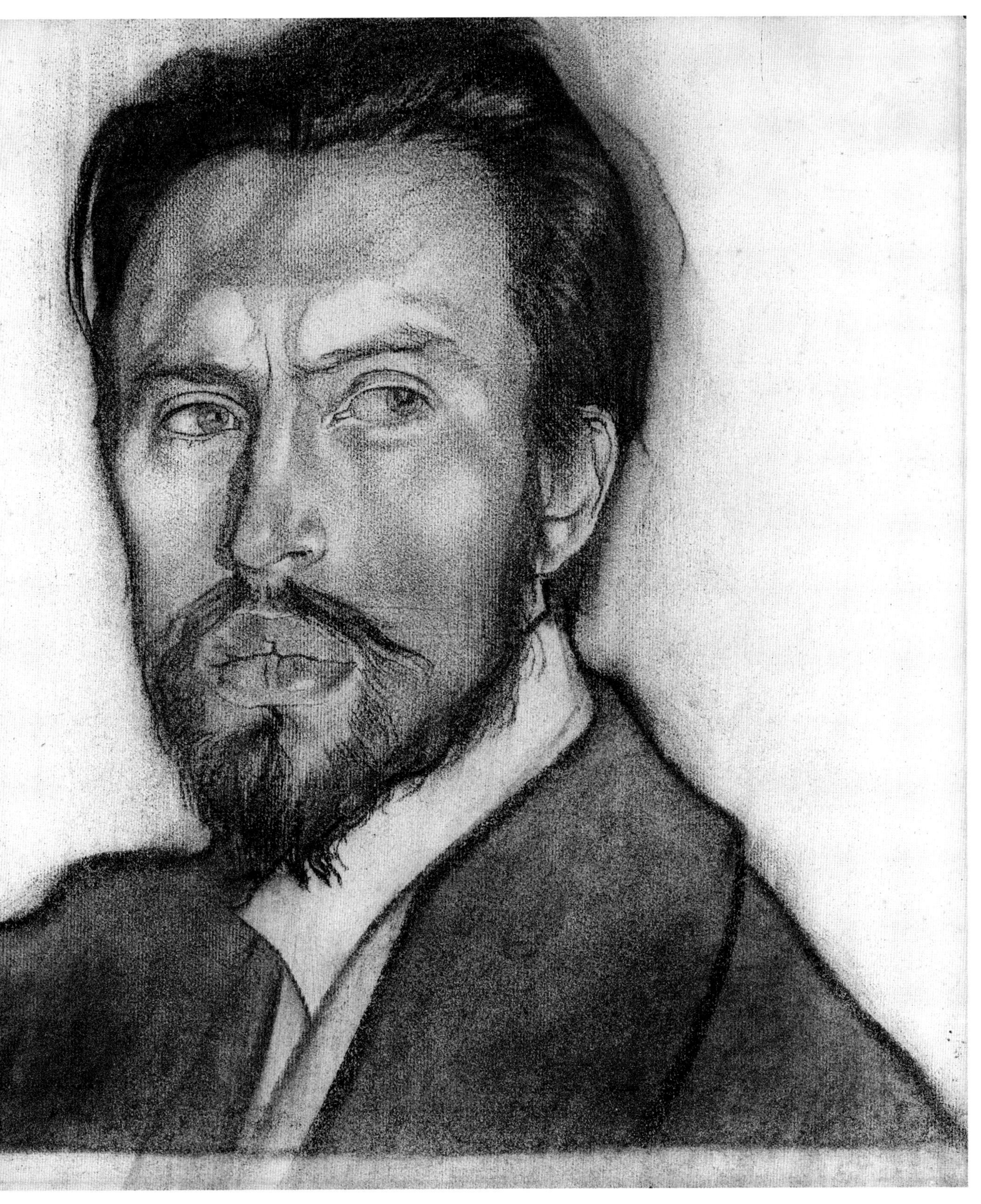

ANTONI KAMIEŃSKI

1900

Antoni Kamieński (1860–1933) was a draughtsman, graphic designer and illustrator who had studied at the Académie Julian in Paris. From 1894 until 1912 he worked for the *Illustrated Weekly* (*Tygodnik Illustrowany*) magazine in Kraków. Wyspiański's correspondence reveals that the two men met in Kraków in 1895, when Stanisław gave Antoni one of his works, holding the latter's art in high regard.[25]

This pastel may have been created as a token of gratitude for Kamieński, who had recently made a portrait drawing of Wyspiański that was reproduced in *Illustrated Weekly*.[26] It presents Kamieński's narrow face, with soft hair, trimmed beard and moustache, in a head-on perspective, very close to the picture plane, against a draped curtain. He is shown wearing a black jacket with a high collar and shearling borders, in a characteristic gesture of putting his hand inside his jacket. The likeness is typical of Wyspiański's style from this period, with its expressive distortion of the facial features and overall figure, an effect enhanced by a subdued palette, while the focus on the sitter's eyes and hands accentuates his character. It foreshadows pastel portraits by Witkacy.

Wyspiański kept the portrait due to his respect for the sitter but in 1907 sold it along with 25 other works at the Kraków Society of Friends of the Fine Arts.[27] Terminally ill and finding it difficult to work, he sought to secure funds to safeguard his family's financial future. The picture was acquired by Henryk Szarski, a well-known merchant and Kraków councillor, for 430 Austro-Hungarian kroner, a high sum compared to works sold by other artists exhibiting at the Society at this time. **ML**

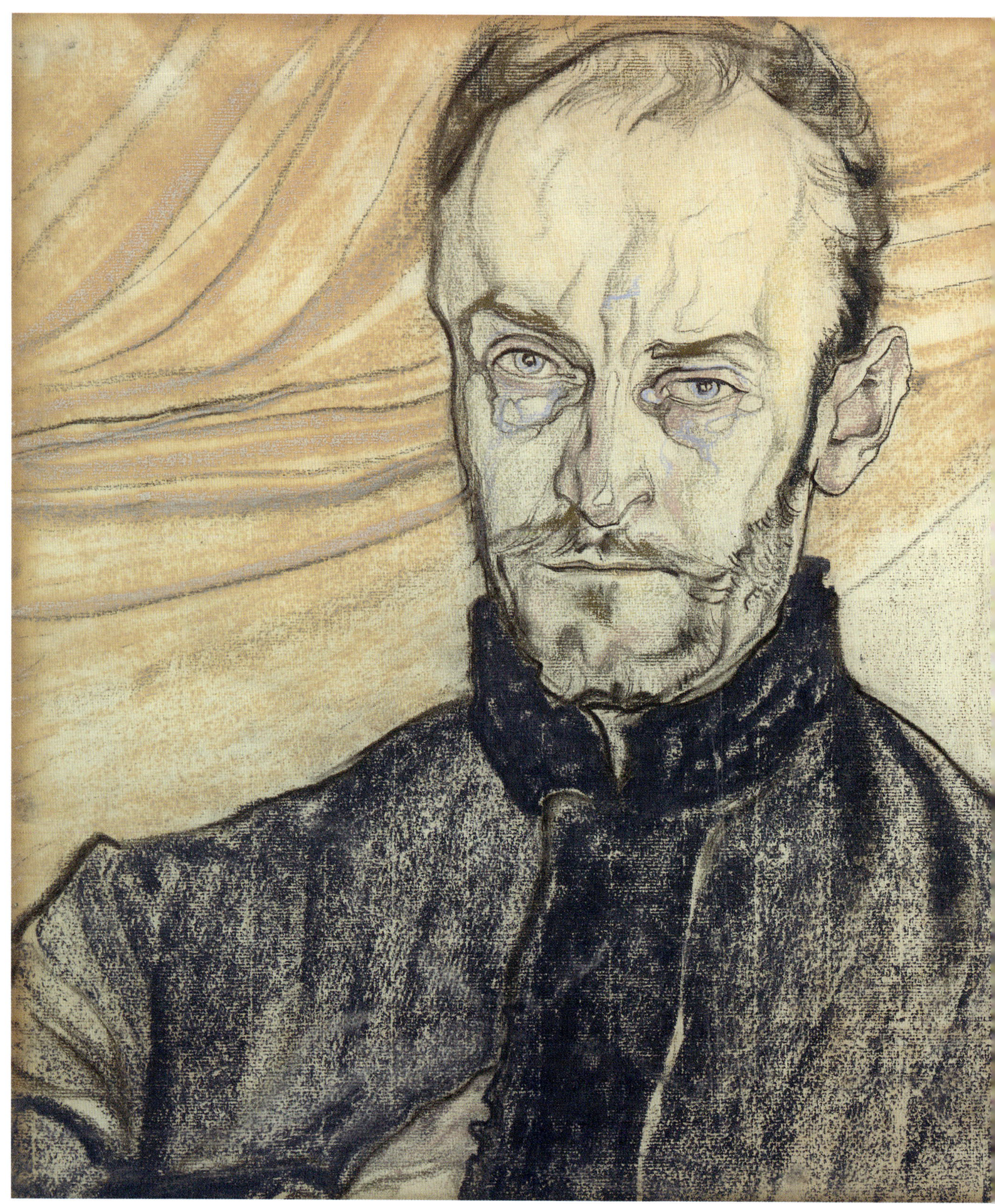

CAT.6
Stanisław Wyspiański
Antoni Kamieński, 1900
Pastel on paper,
465 × 620mm
Private Collection, on long-term loan to the National Museum in Kraków

JULIAN NOWAK

1904

Julian Ignacy Nowak (1865–1946) was a medical doctor, Professor of the
Veterinary Medicine Department at the Jagiellonian University and Chairman
of Kraków's Medical Society. In 1922 he served briefly as Prime Minister of
the new Polish Republic. Nowak was also a connoisseur and patron of art,
offering financial support to Wyspiański – who was often short of money –
by acquiring a number of his works. He also found the apartment in Ulica
Krowoderska for Wyspiański, complete with a space suited for what became
the Blue Studio.[28] It was thanks to Nowak's advocacy that Wyspiański received
the commission to design the decorative scheme for Kraków's Medical
Society with all its contents – one of his most important achievements in
the decorative arts.[29] By the inter-war period the doctor's collection had
grown to include several of Wyspiański's most significant works, not least
the stained-glass cartoon *Apollo: Copernicus's Solar System* for the Medical
Society (fig.2), the composition *Fallen Angels* related to the Franciscan
Church mural, the pastel drawing of *Polonia* based on the stained-glass design
for Lviv Cathedral (fig.3), and the oil painting *Morning at the Foot of Wawel
Hill* (also known as '*Planty Park at Dawn*').

The present portrait was created in 1904 in circumstances recalled by Nowak:

> As I was waiting for Mr Solski to depart from Wyspiański's studio – where
> they were discussing some scene – sitting there resting my elbow on
> the table and my head on my hand, suddenly Wyspiański exclaimed
> 'Please don't move, that's it – it is just right, it won't take long' – he
> grabbed hold of white card and within a quarter of an hour produced
> my portrait.[30] He said '... a portrait is a reflection of the moment, an
> artistic image of the subject's essence'. So much so that this essence
> was embodied in Wyspiański's portraits, and when Wyspiański
> approached an outstanding, wise man proposing he would portray him,
> the prospective sitter responded 'Oh, certainly not, I could not possibly
> accept so that you could expose me'.[31] **ML**

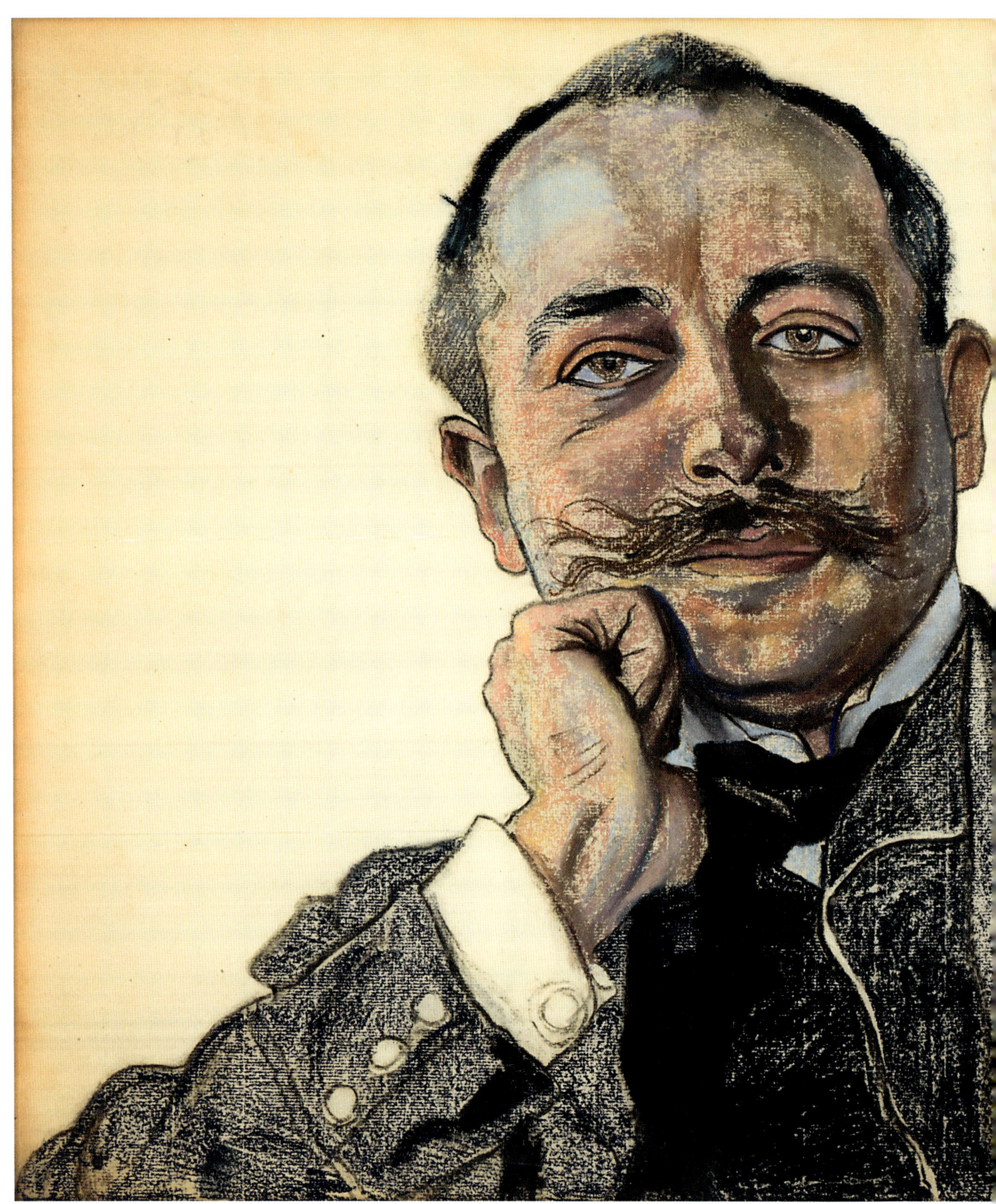

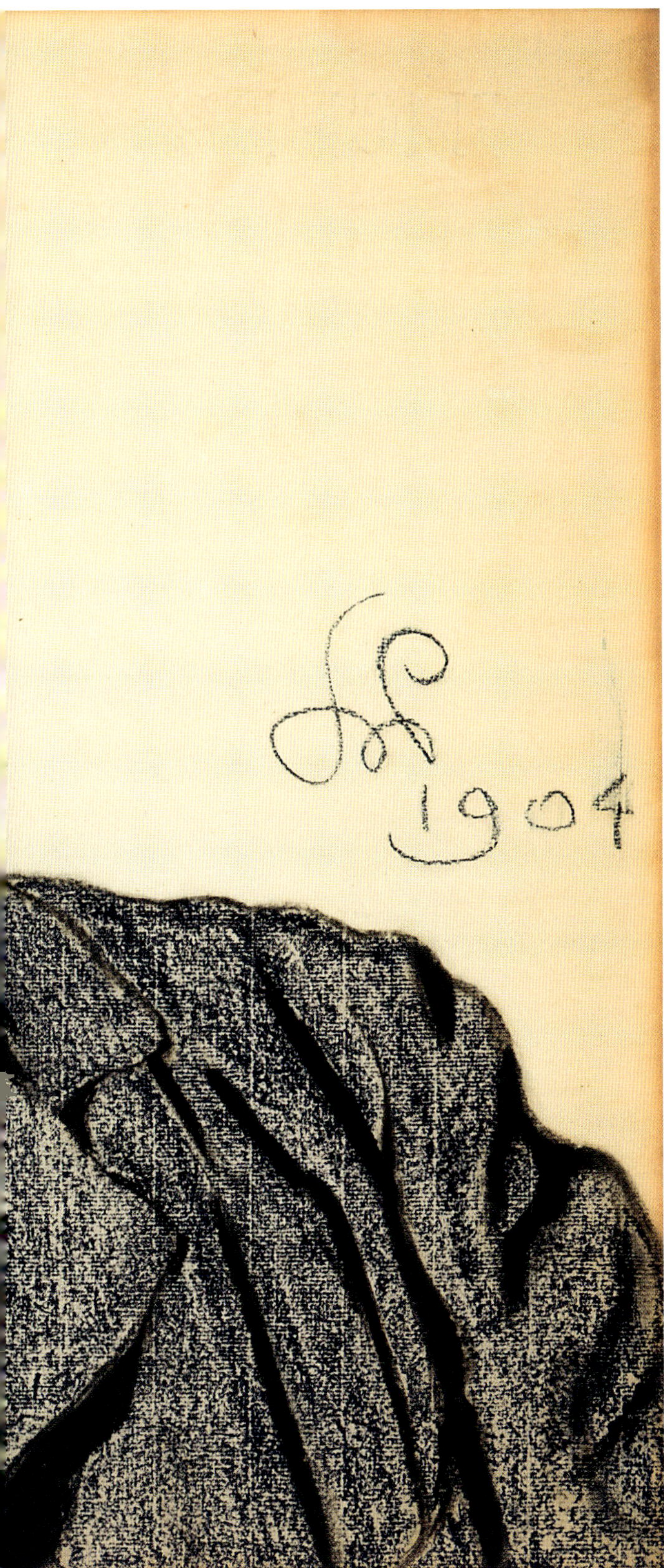

CAT.7
Stanisław Wyspiański
Julian Nowak, 1904
Pastel on paper,
470 × 615mm
Private Collection, on long-
term loan to the National
Museum in Kraków

WŁADYSŁAWA ORDON AS KRASAWICA
IN THE PLAY BOLESŁAW THE BOLD

1903

Władysława Ordon-Sosnowska (1879–1933) (née Rybicka; Sosnowska by first marriage; Feistowa by second marriage; stage name Ordon and subsequently Ordon-Sosnowska) was one of the most famous Polish actors around the turn of the century. She made her debut in 1897 with the Sosnowiec theatre troupe, and went on to perform between 1898 and 1900 in Łódź and Lviv, and from 1900 to 1909 in Kraków. From 1909 she was active in Warsaw, gaining a reputation as an interpreter of Polish contemporary drama. She appeared in Wyspiański's plays as Krasawica in *Bolesław the Bold*, the Bride in *The Wedding*, the Young One in *The Curse* and Kora in *November Night*.[32] Describing the time she worked with Wyspiański, Ordon later recalled:

> I instantly felt the radiating strength and power of the genius poet. Wyspiański took me under his wing as a young actress making my first steps, and he fuelled my development by believing in my talent and trusting my understanding of the role of Krasawica during the rehearsals at the Kraków theatre.[33]

Altogether Wyspiański made three drawings of Ordon in her stage costume for *Bolesław the Bold*: two dress designs and this pastel study of her in character, drawn on two pieces of joined paper.[34] In the play, the costumes were colour coded according to which faction the characters supported: the King's court in red, his brother's rival court, comprising primarily his opponents, in blue. The King's treacherous lover Krasawica (Polish for 'beautiful woman') – a pagan sorceress who enticed him towards violence – was a metaphysical being who did not belong to either court. Her multicoloured outfit made up of foliage and flowers underlined her connection with the natural world. Adam Chmiel, head of the Kraków City Archive, helped Wyspiański research the stage design and costumes by retrieving relevant archaeological and historical sources on Polish medieval art. In his creative process Wyspiański also drew inspiration from literature, utilising publications from his home library on Polish and Ruthenian folk art as well as on Renaissance artists. Accordingly, the costume for Krasawica was inspired by the figures in Sandro Botticelli's painting *Primavera* – the loose diaphanous drapes woven with various flowers echoing references to jasmine in the verses spoken by her in the play: 'This wreath of holy leaves I wear / First grew upon the branches there / The sacred grove, where is jasmine ... '[35]

Wyspiański made a number of striking likenesses of actors who performed in his plays, which he then presented to them as gifts. The portrait of Odon is one of the few examples that were not destroyed during the Second World War. **ML**

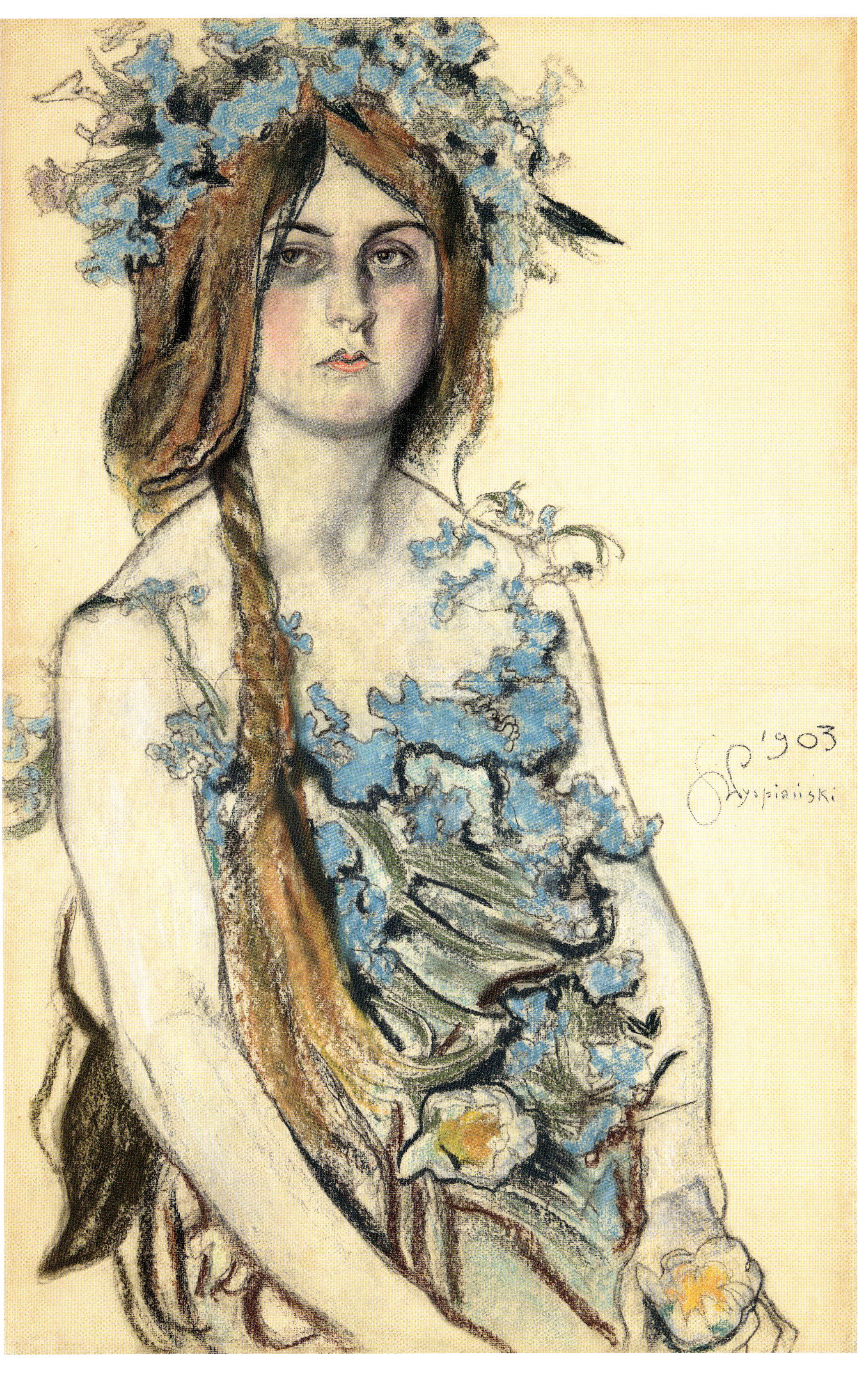
'903
Wyspiański

IRENA SOLSKA

1904

Irena Solska (1877–1958) was one of the most famous Polish actors of the early twentieth century and a muse to artists of the Young Poland movement, for whom she was the 'Egeria of symbolism, modernism, decadentism'.[36] Wyspiański most likely drew her portrait in Lviv, where she was playing the part of Savage in the stage adaptation of the tragedy *Treasure* (*Skarb*) by the Lviv poet Leopold Staff, which marked his debut as a playwright. It had its premiere at Lviv's City Theatre on 19 April 1904. On the same occasion Wyspiański made a companion portrait of Solska's husband Ludwik Solski, who was cast in the role of Guard in the same play.[37]

Although Wyspiański often drew actors in theatrical costume, he decided not to present Solska in the suit of armour she wore on stage.[38] Rather, he portrayed her in a casual gown with loose Japanese-style sleeves. Its colourful pattern is comprised of geometric forms in light shades of blue and green surrounded by black contour lines, rather like a stained-glass cartoon, and shows the influence of the Pont-Aven School. Seated in an armchair with her elbows on the armrests, her slender arms reach up to touch her fiery hair in a characteristic gesture that directs her hypnotic gaze at the viewer, rather like the women in Pre-Raphaelite paintings to which she was often compared, both in real life and with reference to her stage creations. Her beauty was specifically linked with the aesthetic of women from the paintings of Dante Gabriel Rossetti and Edward Burne-Jones.[39] In fact, Wyspiański was so struck by it that he cast her in the role of Rachela, the Jewish innkeeper's daughter in *The Wedding*, to match his verses:

> Gladly, I'll observe you – tortured
> wandering through that dreary orchard,
> like some soul astray in love –
> half-maid, half-angel, as you rub
> against a straw-protected shrub,
> like a painting by Burne-Jones –
> while I stand watching, safe and warm.[40]

Solska also appeared in a number of British plays, namely productions of Shakespeare, such as Portia in *The Merchant of Venice* (1897) and Olivia in *Twelfth Night* (1897), and later as Mrs Erlynne in Oscar Wilde's *Lady Windermere's Fan* (1906).

Before she divorced Solski in 1914, she had affairs with leading cultural figures of the day. Between 1904 and 1906 she was in a relationship with writer Jerzy Żuławski, with whom she often worked (see cat.5). He wrote the role of Psyche in his most famous play *Eros and Psyche* especially for her, which she went on to perform for two decades. Witkacy immortalised his love affair with Solska in his early novel *622 Falls of Bunga, or The Demonic Woman* (*622 upadki Bunga czyli demoniczna kobieta*), begun in 1910 but not published until 1972, largely for reputational reasons. **AS**

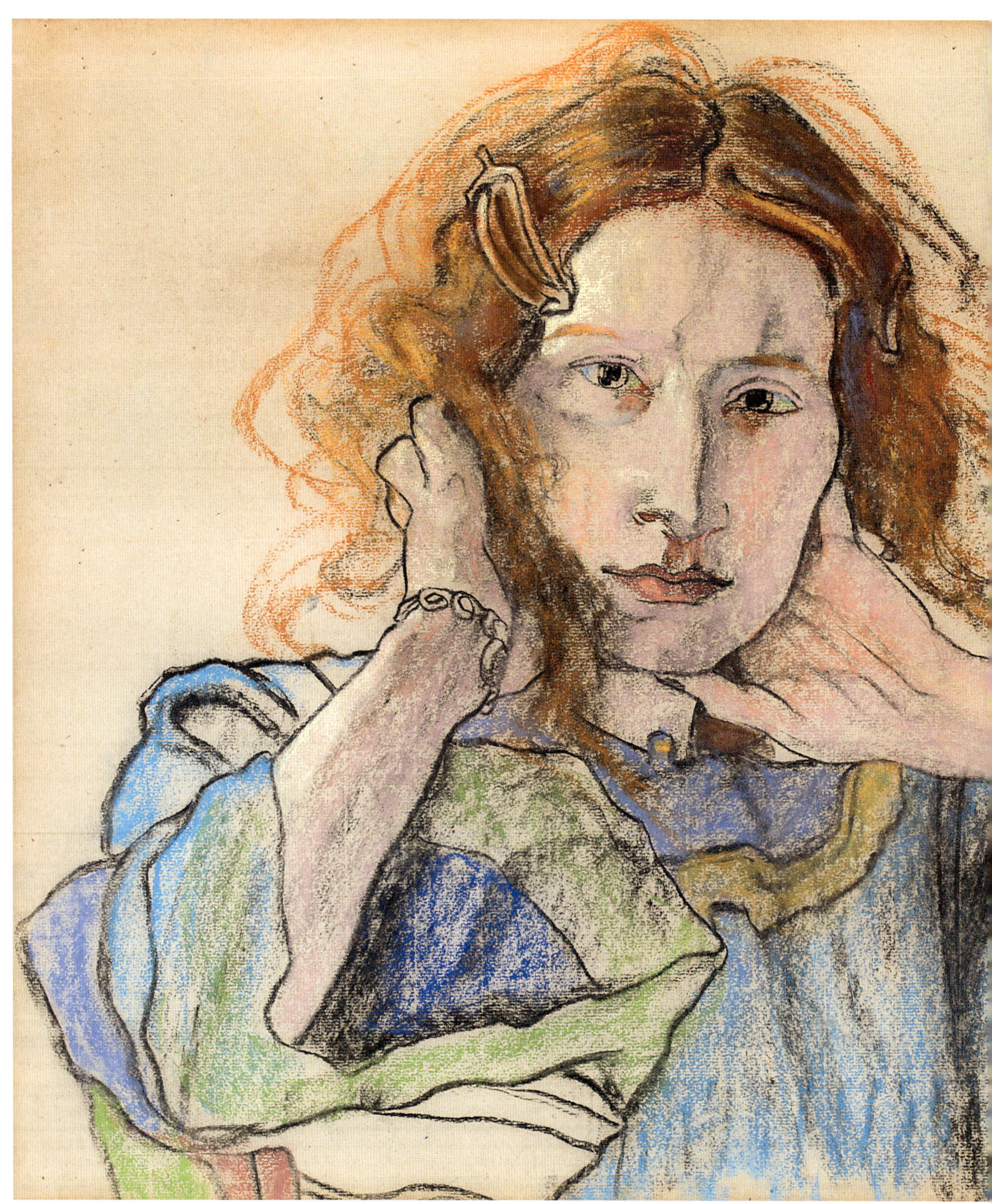

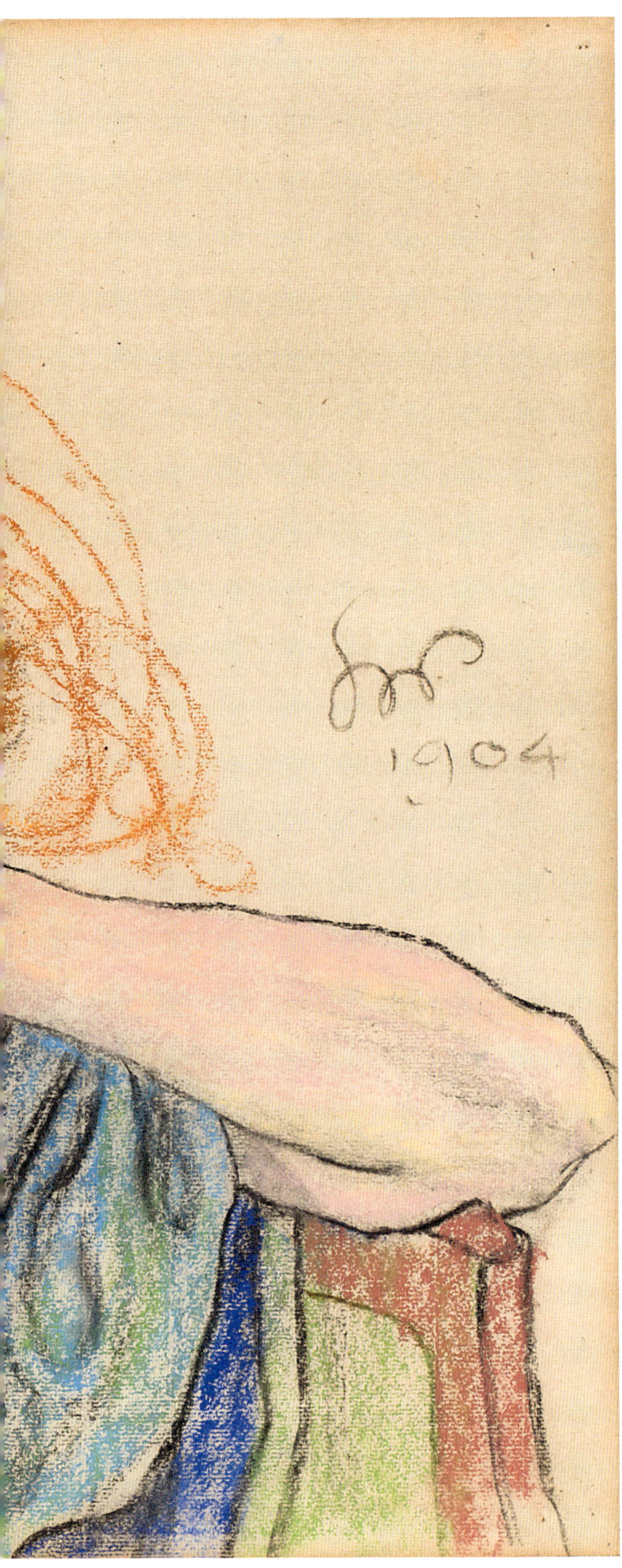

CAT.9
Stanisław Wyspiański
Irena Solska, 1904
Pastel on paper,
480 × 630mm
National Museum
in Poznań

JÓZIO FELDMAN

1905

This pastel drawing of a boy resting his chin on his hand in a melancholy gesture is a portrait of the six-year-old Józef or Józio Feldman (1899–1946). He was the son of Maria (née Kleinman) and Wilhelm Feldman, who were both part of Kraków's intellectual elite, Maria being a translator of Western literature and Wilhelm a writer and publicist who championed a new school of criticism that promoted subjectivity in perception and the importance of artistic personality. Between 1901 and 1914 Wilhelm edited the literary magazine *Criticism* (*Krytyka*), which published contributions from the most outstanding poets and writers of Young Poland. He was one of only a handful of critics of Wyspiański's work whom the artist rated. As Wyspiański's illness progressed, Feldman undertook the sale of his drawings, becoming his literary executor after his death.[41]

As a young man Wilhelm had broken with his Hasidic Jewish background to promote a Polish political identity among Galician Jews, which may explain why Józio is shown dressed in the folk costume of a Cracovian peasant, wearing a blue wool jacket with decorative edging over a white shirt.[42] From around 1900 Polish folk dress of Cracovian and Hutsul peasants, as well as Highlander shepherds from the Podhale region of the Tatra Mountains, acquired patriotic symbolism, inspiring the quest to create a distinctively Polish national costume.[43] As such, elements of original folk dress as well as outfits based on them were worn by respectable families as a manifesto of political resistance. In the case of Józio, it was probably additionally selected to signal the reconciliation of Polish and Jewish factions in the pursuit of independence, a theme also explored by Wyspiański in his play *The Wedding*.[44] Thirteen years after the portrait was completed, Józio would be a student of law; he later went on to study history, and became a professor at the Jagiellonian University, specialising in the modern history of Poland. He published on the international diplomatic history of Polish-German and Polish-British relations, notably the critical overview 'At the Root of Polish-English Relations 1788–1863' ('U podstaw stosunków polsko-angielskich 1788–1863', 1933),[45] and was a contributor to the 1941 *Cambridge History of Poland*.[46]

This pastel was first reproduced in 1908 on the occasion of the 'Sztuka' Society of Polish Artists exhibition in Vienna, where it was shown among works by other Young Poland artists. Reviews of the exhibition appeared in the Polish and French press,[47] and in *The Studio*, where it was illustrated.[48] **ML**

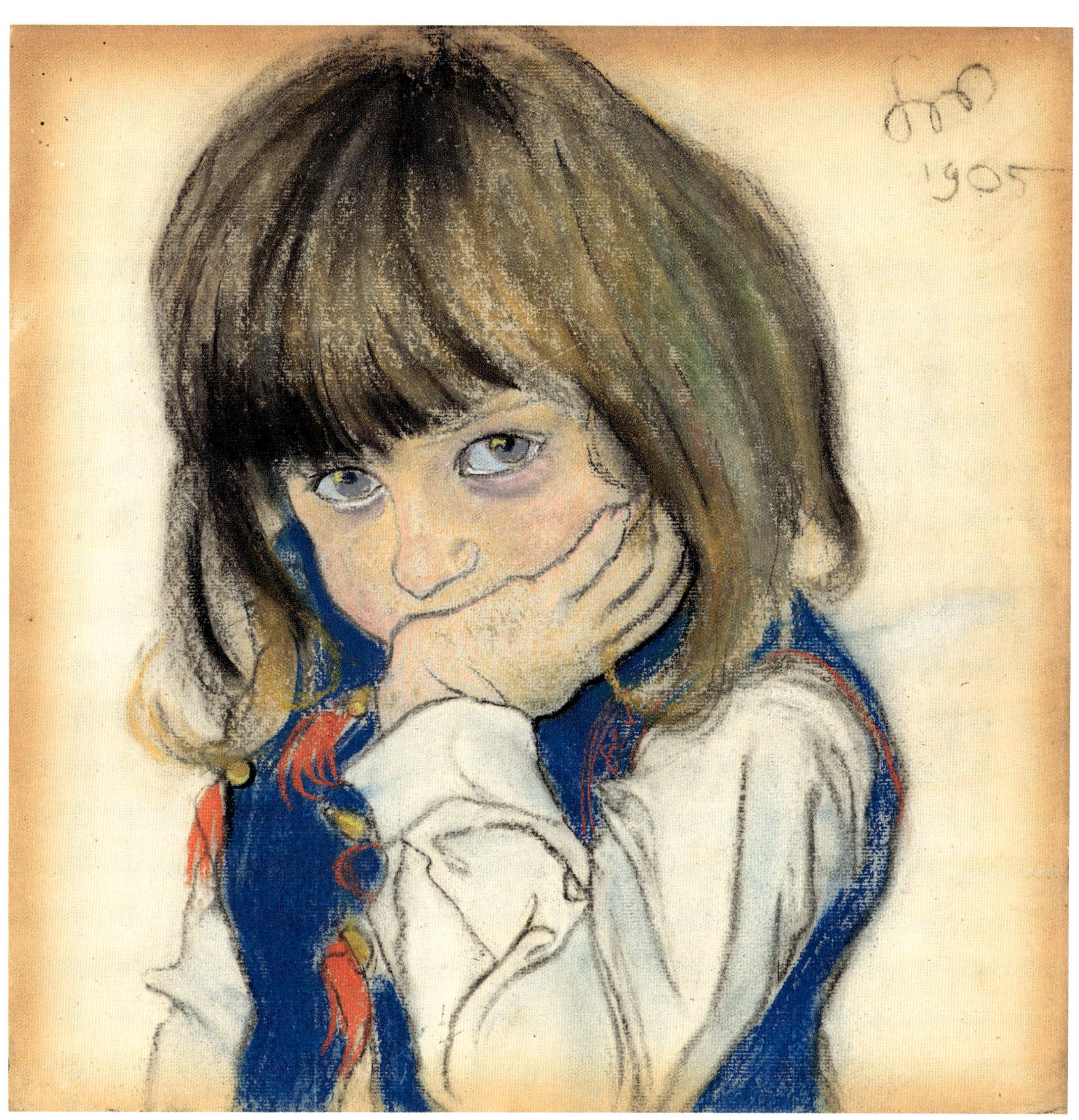

HELENKA'S HEAD

1900

Helenka, Wyspiański's only daughter, was born out of wedlock on 31 May 1895. She first sat for her father as a four-year-old after Wyspiański had moved with his wife Teodora and the children into their first family apartment at number 23 Ulica Szlak in Kraków in 1899.[49] He produced several portraits of her in various media – pastels (see also cat.12), charcoal and crayon drawings and prints. In this striking study, Helenka appears sleepy and dishevelled, as if she had just woken up and he wanted to capture her in this state. Her hair is set down swiftly in bold strokes of pastel while the colours of the face are blended to convey the suppleness of her young skin. Wyspiański also attends to Helenka's swollen glands and her apparent difficulty in breathing, signs of illness, also evident in a portrait he made of Mietek in 1901.[50]

Wyspiański was very close to his children, and his last wishes before his death revolved around safeguarding their future alongside his legacy.[51] Although his sons were to suffer considerable hardship, Helenka settled into a sheltered life of luxury. After spending almost ten years in various boarding schools following her father's death, including one in Vinzel in Switzerland, she returned to Kraków.[52] There, in 1916, she married Adam Chmurski, an engineer who was the son of the co-owner of Rząca-Chmurski, a famous Cracovian manufacturer of sparkling mineral water, with stalls across Planty Park.[53] They had two children and acted as legal guardians for Helenka's brothers as well as looking after Teodora during her final years. Helenka became the chief family representative for Wyspiański's legacy, attending commemorative events, previews of his plays and giving interviews. She died on 28 November 1971, the anniversary of her father's death.[54]

An article in *The Studio* in 1928 noted Wyspiański's 'love of children' as a recurrent subject matter that won him critical acclaim.[55] Wyspiański's portraits of his own children are honest and direct but also convey his deep affection for them. This may explain why they proved to be very popular with collectors, as was the case with this portrait, which also exists in another version, now in the National Museum in Warsaw.[56] **ML**

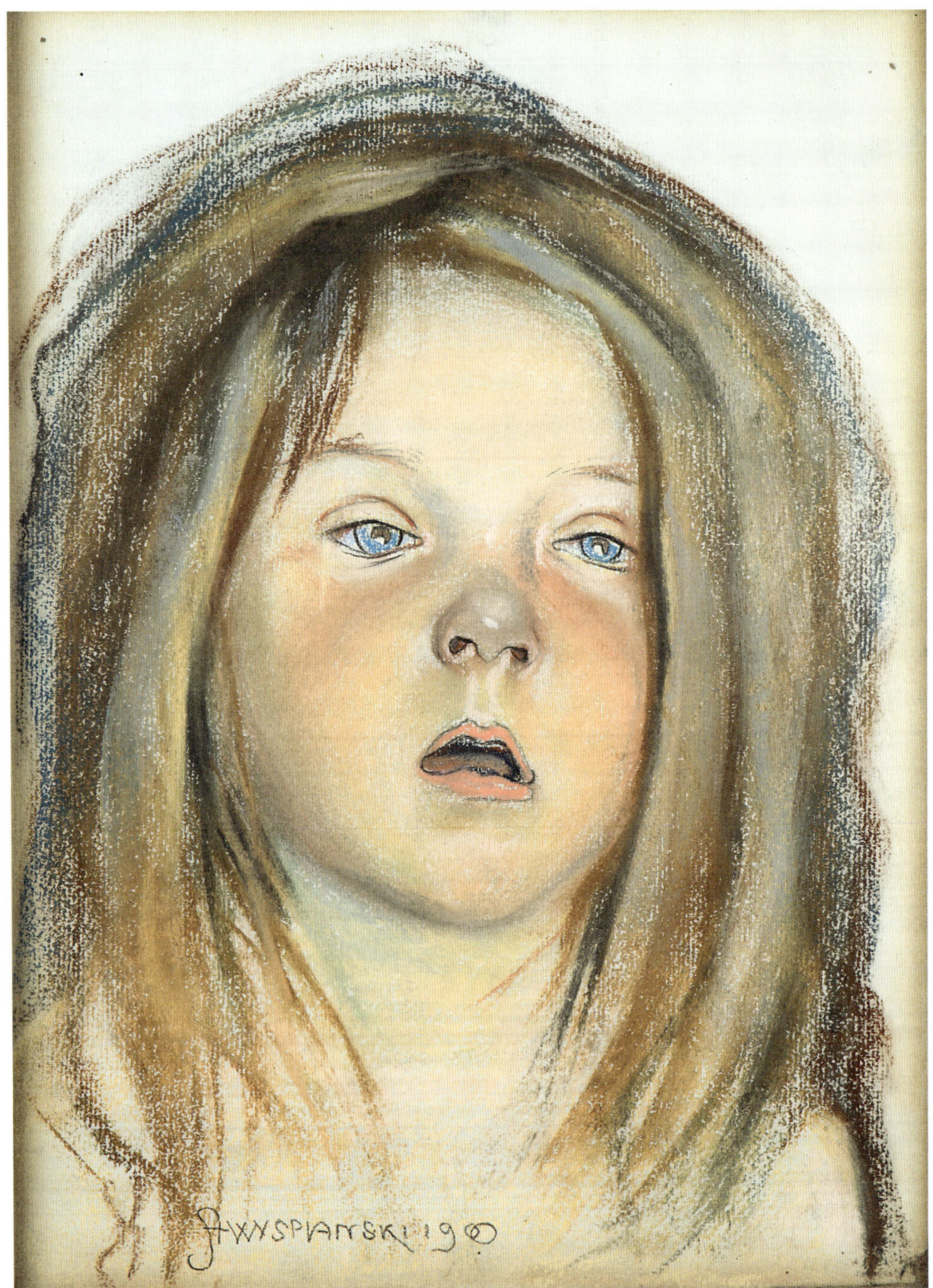

StWYSPIANSKI 1900

CAT.11
Stanisław Wyspiański
Helenka's Head, 1900
Pastel on paper,
335 × 250mm
National Museum
in Kraków

HELENKA WITH A VASE

1902

This portrait of the artist's daughter Helenka aged seven, dreamily leaning against a table and touching a jug containing forget-me-nots, is one of the most original representations of a child in Polish art.[57] Carefully observed from a vertiginous angle, the picture is filled with a lyrical, almost poetic mood. As a composition, it betrays Wyspiański's fascination with Japanese art, while the strong flat contour lines and subject matter show the influence of Paul Gauguin, whose work Wyspiański was familiar with from his time in Paris.[58]

The pastel remained at the Wyspiańskis' home until 1906 when, seeking funds to purchase a country house for his wife and children, the terminally ill artist began to sell works from his studio collection. He did so with the help of contacts, one of whom was Seweryn Böhm, Secretary of Kraków's Society of Friends of the Fine Arts.[59] It was purchased by the collector Feliks Jasieński, who subsequently donated it to the National Museum in Kraków in 1920 together with a large number of drawings and pastels. An itemised sales receipt dated 23 July 1906, complete with individual prices, lists the following pictures by Wyspiański acquired by Jasieński at the time: *Helenka's Head, Sleeping Child, Self-Portrait with Wife* and *Helenka with a Vase* – the latter priced the highest, at 800 Austro-Hungarian kroner, reflecting the artist's appreciation of its outstanding artistic merit, surpassing the other highly accomplished family portraits.[60] Another version of this work is part of the Raczyński Foundation collection at the National Museum in Poznań.[61] **ML**

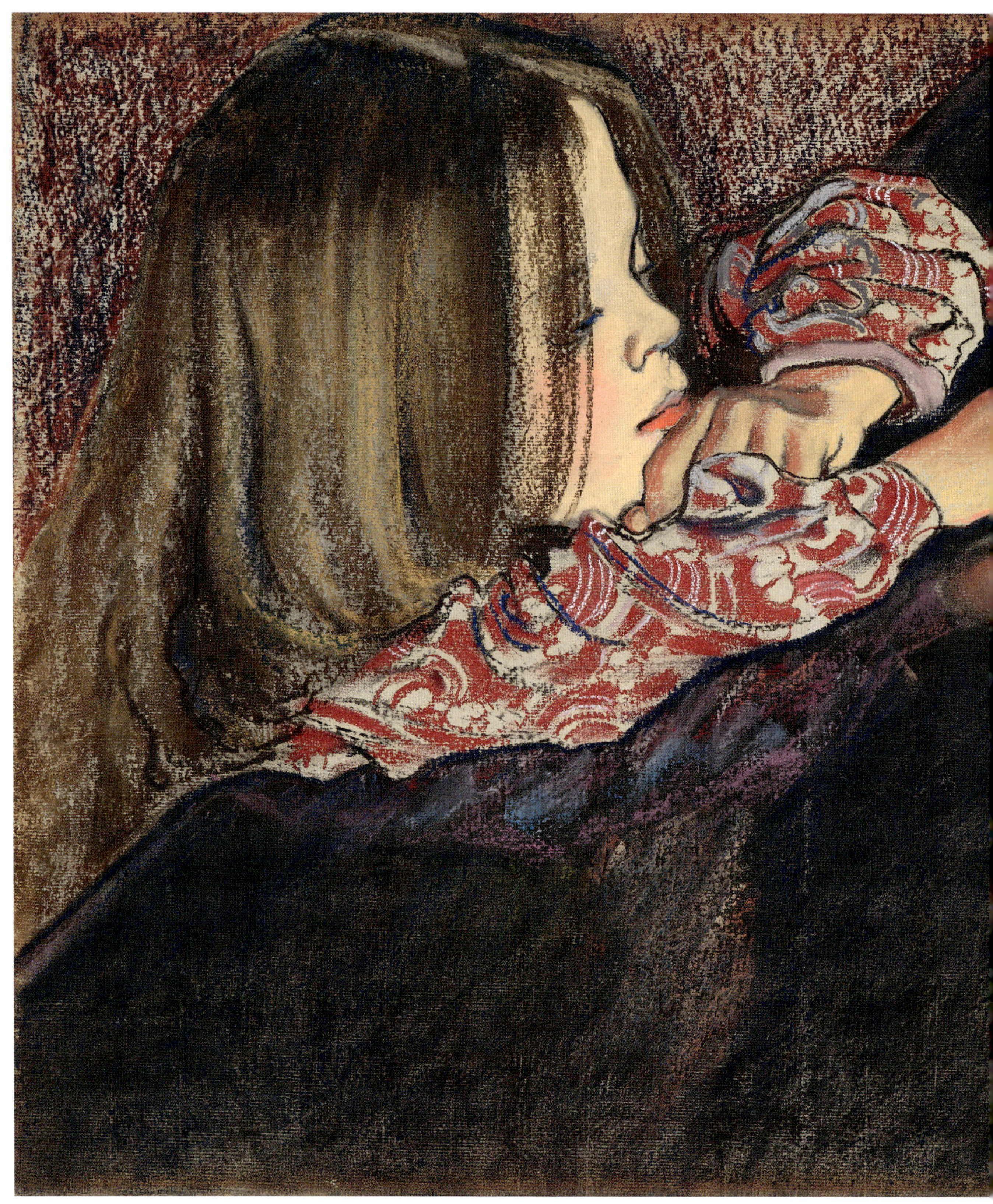

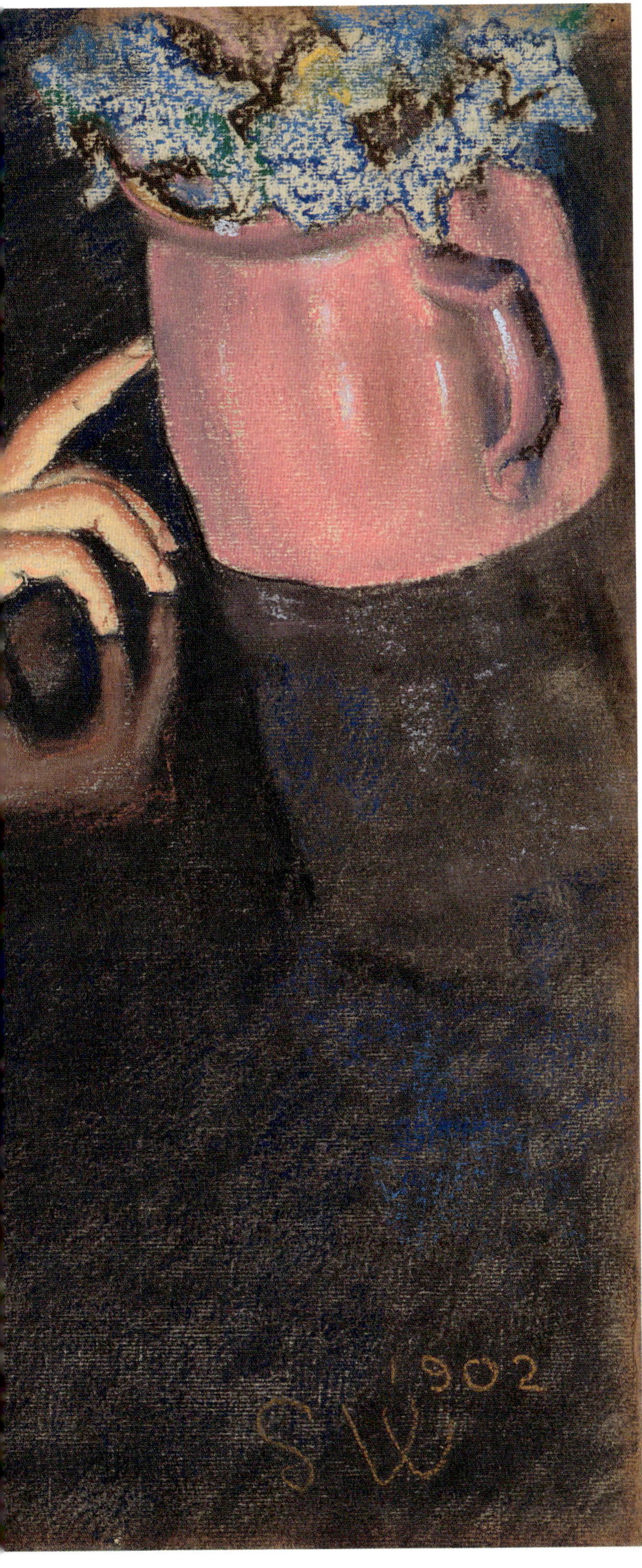

CAT.12
Stanisław Wyspiański
Helenka with a Vase, 1902
Pastel on paper,
475 × 628mm
National Museum
in Kraków

BOY WITH PISTOLS
(PORTRAIT OF TEODOR)

1902

Wyspiański's portraits of children tend to show them either asleep or in contemplation with an air of seriousness beyond their years. Among them, *Boy with Pistols* stands out, with its startling image of a child frozen in fear as he averts his gaze from three pistols laid out on the table before him. The skeletal forms of the weapons bear an intriguing resemblance to the boy's skinny fingers, indicating both the capacity of the hand to destroy life and what the child might do with the weapons were he to give in to temptation. The emotive impact of the picture revolves around this juxtaposition and is accentuated by the sober colour that hints at military culture and what might lie in future for the boy.

The child in this pastel has been identified as Teodora Pytko's eldest, illegitimate son, Teodor Tadeusz (1890–1916), whom Wyspiański adopted.[62] A thumbnail image of this work is featured in Wyspiański's sketch of a projected frieze of his family portraits, preserved at the Collegium Maius Jagiellonian University Museum (fig.17). Moreover, Teodor is depicted in a similar pose holding his bony hands up to his mouth in *Mietek and Teodor* (1902), an earlier pencil sketch the artist made of the boy with his half-brother.[63] According to oral history related by Teodora's second husband Wincent Waśka's descendants, Wyspiański tried not to favour his own children over Teodor, but the boy was less frequently depicted by the artist than his half-brothers and half-sister, who did not want to play with him.[64]

Nevertheless, perhaps on account of his being the eldest, Teodor appears to have been more attached to Wyspiański than the other children. He is said to have been challenging, possibly because of the difficulties he experienced with his mental health. Apparently, Teodor only found out that Wyspiański was not his biological father after the artist's death, which is said to have led him to drop out of school. Instead of receiving support, his legal guardian sent him to the psychiatric ward of St Lazarus Hospital in Kraków.[65] There he died aged just 25 – pneumonia was cited as the official cause on the death certificate. In this light, the drawing assumes a sinister significance. **AS**

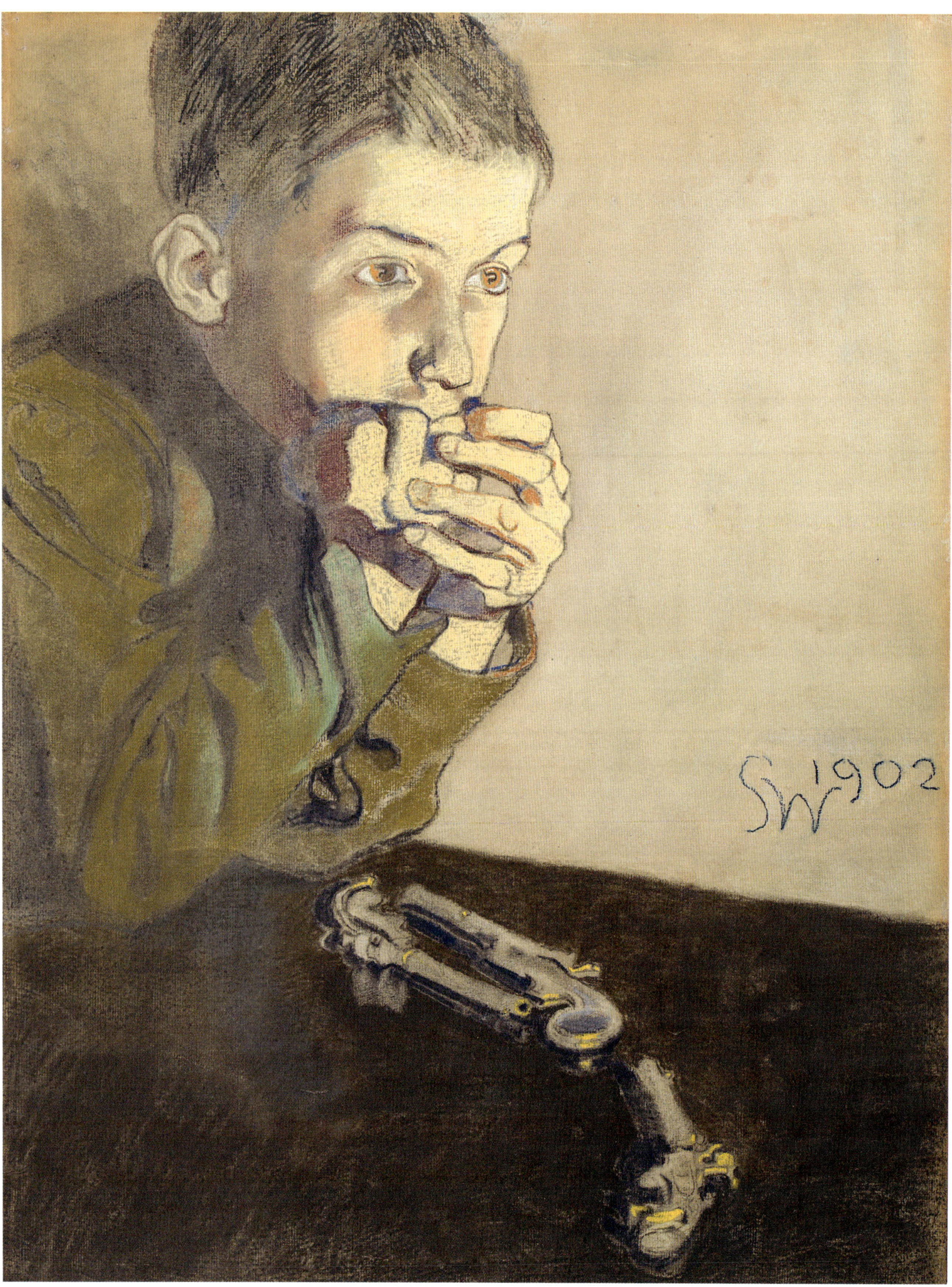

SW 1902

MIETEK RESTING ON HIS HANDS

1904

This intimate representation of Wyspiański's five-year-old son Mieczysław or
Mietek (1899–1924) leaning on a table in the 'orange-lemon' coloured nursery
in Ulica Krowoderska was one of a group of pastel drawings Wyspiański may
have intended to form a gallery of family portraits (see figs 17–21).[66] Mietek
is viewed close-up from above against a neutral backdrop in order to focus
attention on his emotional solitude. Contemporary critics admired this type
of psychological portrait as representative of the artist's practice:

> … spiritual heads and ordinary vulnerable figures, which come out from
> underneath his brush surrounded with a thick contour line … have
> the charming quality of a dream. They are mere souls, enveloped in
> discernible shapes, each characterised by a deep gaze, with an elusive
> smile, incorporeal, solely made up of expression.[67]

As a father, Wyspiański took a keen interest in his children's health, education
and first creative attempts at poetry and art. The National Museum in Kraków
holds a collection of drawings of goats, cows and horses that the artist made
to entertain his children,[68] as well as photographs of Mietek with his younger
brother Stanisław (known as Staś) drawing at their father's worktable in the
Blue Studio.[69] The Collegium Maius Jagiellonian University Museum owns a
drawing of a bird with Wyspiański's annotation 'Drawn by Mietek'.[70] The boy
was a gifted poet; in some verses he shared reminiscences of his late father,
such as: 'Play from the distant field, you the wandering winds … / Let him sing
for me like on a winter's evening / We all gathered around Father, / As our
conversations continued, / As we had happy times together … / Let him sing
for me like Father used to at the table / As he was drawing a carriage and Staszek
/ As we were all sitting there in a circle / As little Staszek made Father laugh'.[71]

Following Wyspiański's death, Mieczysław and his brother Stanisław were
sent by their legal guardian to the Jesuit Brothers' Academic and Pedagogic
College at Chyrów (now known as Khyriv), whose disciplinarian methods their
father strongly opposed during his lifetime.[72] Their education was curtailed
by the outbreak of the First World War. Mietek fought on the Italian front
but returned to complete his exams. His relationship with a Jewish girl later
caused a family feud, leading him to volunteer for the eastern front during
the Polish–Soviet War where he was taken into captivity, apparently dying of
typhus in a Russian hospital – the time and place of his death unknown.[73] **ML**

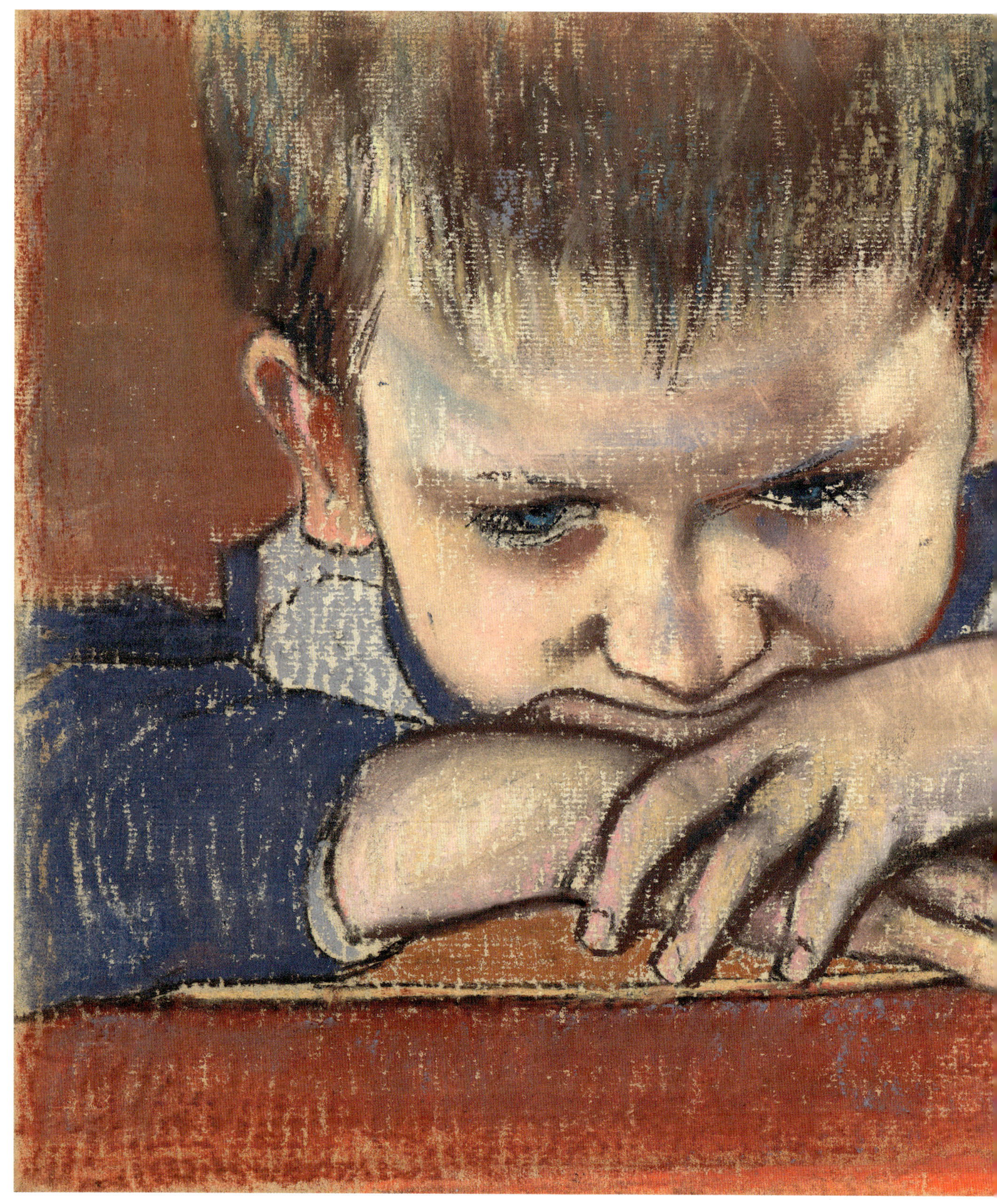

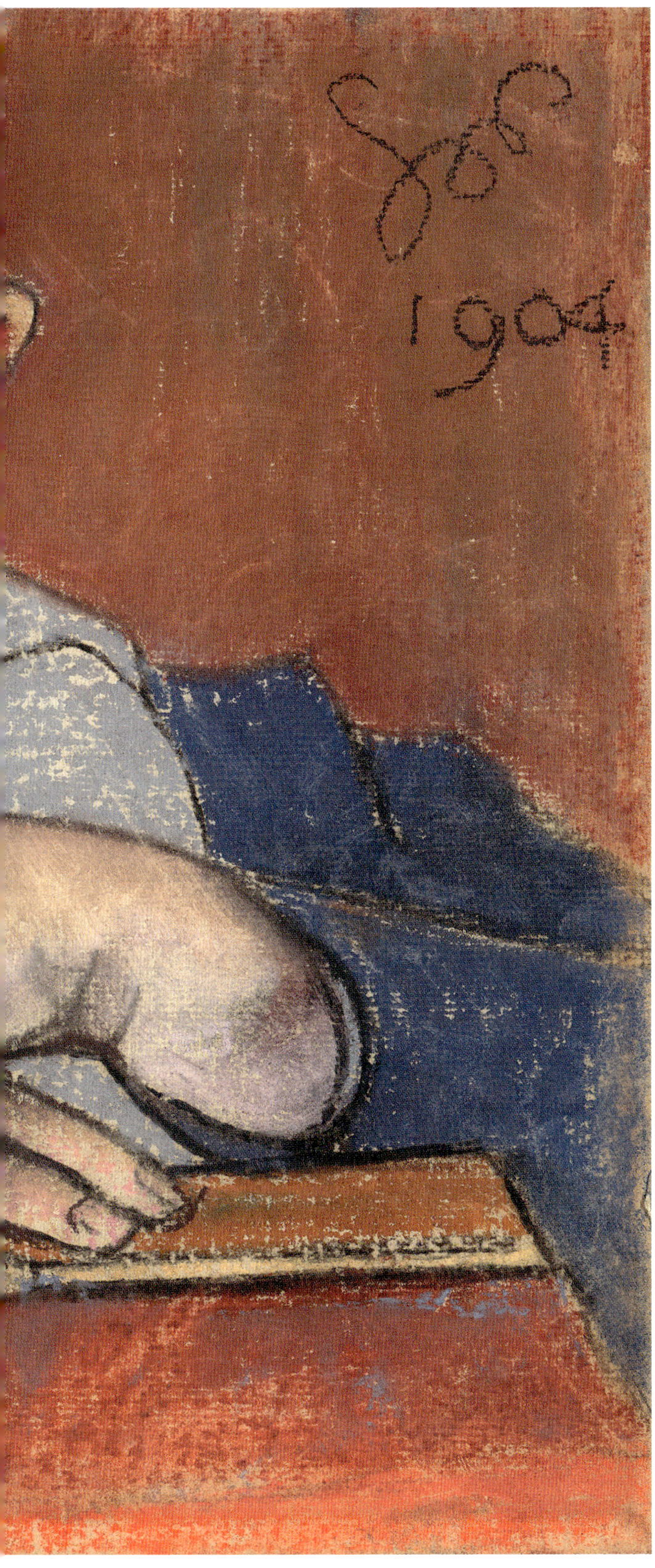

CAT.14
Stanisław Wyspiański
*Mietek Resting on
His Hands*, 1904
Pastel on paper,
approx. 240 × 323mm
National Museum
in Kraków

MATERNITY

1905

Wyspiański's pastel of his wife Teodora (1868–1957) nursing their son Staś (1901–1968) in the company of their daughter Helenka is one of the most famous portraits in Polish art, often described as a symbolic representation of fertility, new life and 'the universal mystery of maternity'.[74] Pressed close-up to the picture plane against a background of white geraniums, the bright *cloisonné*-like patterns accentuate the faces of the women as they gaze in wonder at the infant and as he looks trustingly up at his mother.

The pastel is dated 1905, at which time Staś was over three years old, not the tiny baby shown here. Based on a picture of Teodora nursing her son dating back to 1902 (fig.18),[75] Wyspiański took another composition he had started of fuchsia flowers and layered in the figures in dense pastel, using line to separate their forms as in stained glass and adapting the original fuchsia design so it doubled up as the ornamentation on Teodora's jacket.[76] He then added the double portrait of Helenka, who is shown in both profile and face on, wearing yellow ribbons and garments decorated with paisley-like patterns of his own invention.[77] That same year Wyspiański produced a *Double Portrait of Eliza Pareńska* (most likely destroyed in the Warsaw Rising of 1944).[78] Her namesake mother ran a Young Poland salon in Kraków and was Wyspiański's patron. The picture evidences the artist's interest in including multiple images of the same sitter within a portrait.[79]

Maternity is testament to Wyspiański's technical skill in drawing, modelling and compositional balance and colour, comprised here of subtly harmonised warm shades of brown, red and yellow combined with colder hues of green and white. Like his English counterpart, William Morris, Wyspiański had a passion for indigenous plants and was one of the first Polish artists to make flowers an important theme in his art. The geranium motif recurs frequently in his work and he affectionately described its leaves as 'duckling-like Cracovians' ('*kaczkowane krakowiaki*') because 'they are aligned in a row in the spirit of ducks following each other'.[80]

Maternity was first exhibited in June 1905 at Kraków's Society of Friends of the Fine Arts and enthusiastically received by the public and art connoisseurs alike. It was frequently reproduced thereafter, usually in connection with Wyspiański anniversaries. Interpretations varied – from readings that focused on the portrait's tender domestic theme, through fatalistic undertones, to appreciation of its bold Art Nouveau style, which is ironic as Wyspiański openly disassociated himself from the movement.[81] **ML**

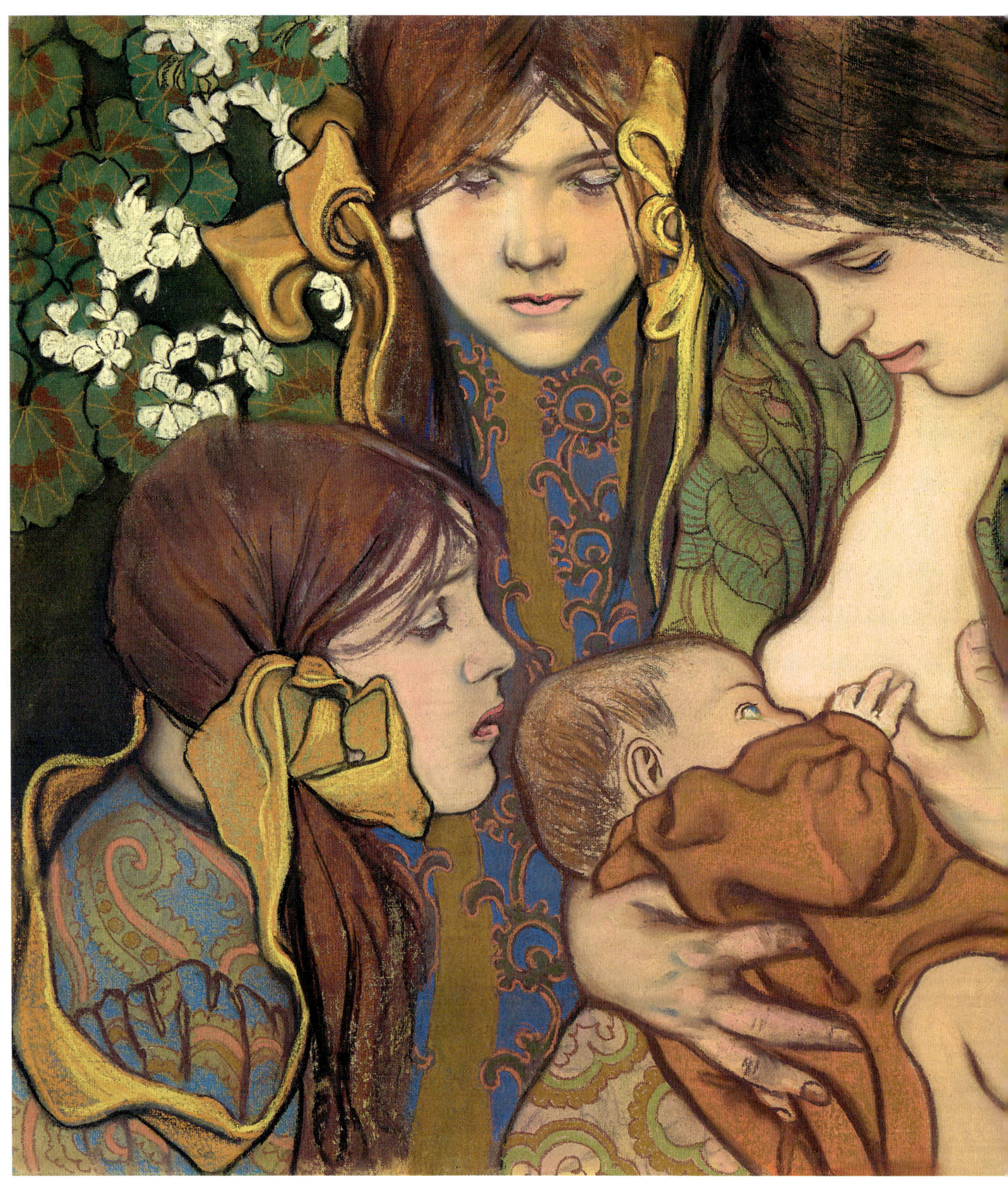

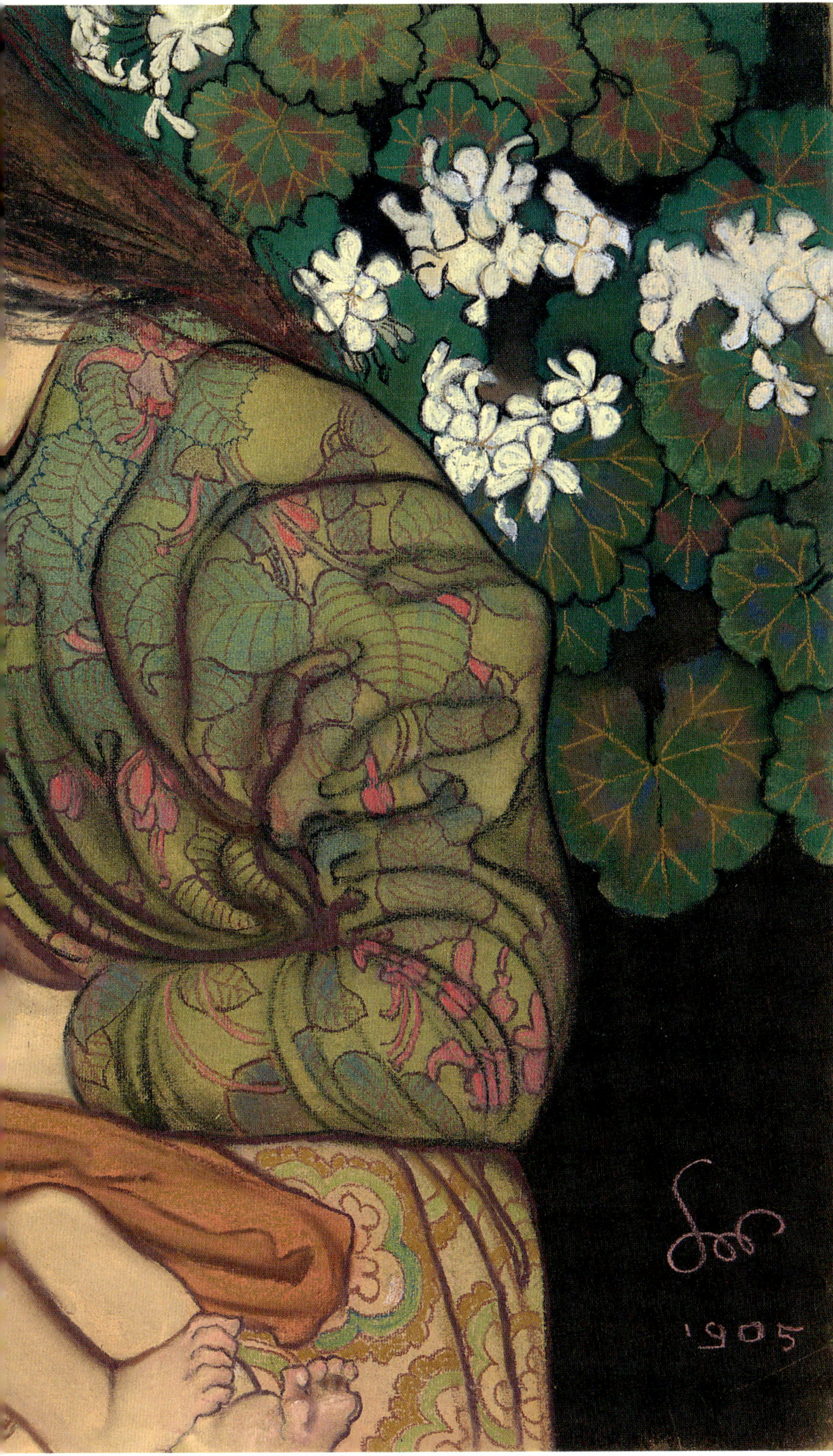

CAT.15
Stanisław Wyspiański
Maternity, 1905
Pastel on paper,
588 × 910mm
National Museum
in Kraków

SELF-PORTRAIT BEFORE DEATH

1907

Wyspiański's last self-portrait, drawn shortly before his death on 28 November 1907, is devoid of idealisation or theatricality in conveying the idea of a direct encounter with death. Drawn from a reflection in a mirror, the fall of shadow across the artist's gaunt face accentuates the dilated pupils in his deeply recessed eye sockets.[82] The Polish Nobel Prize-winning novelist Władysław Stanisław Reymont described his final meeting with Wyspiański in his reminiscences on 3 December 1907:

> I last saw him at the beginning of October, on a ripe autumnal day, golden like an ear of wheat – when the tired and empty fields covered in spider webs lay in holy dormancy ahead of new endeavours, with dying trees shedding their last bloody leaves. He was lying in bed surrounded by proofs and books. I came to visit him with Leopold Staff.[83] He received us warmly, like friends. He found it hard to sit up, he looked terrible, he resembled Piotrowin,[84] he had a hollow, blackened, and dry face, his right hand was bandaged, he only had partial command of his left hand, the voice of a stranger, indistinct, only his eyes resembled his old self, imperious and wise, full of flashes and indomitable will, the eyes of a hetman warrior. I could not speak, struck by the terror of his face. I felt that he was carrying his own corpse with much difficulty.[85]

Wyspiański's biographer Zdzisław Kępiński was moved by the power of the drawing:

> The one who proclaimed the motto 'Everything that lives must die' – the one who made the terrifying remains of royal corpses rise from their tombs – is now … looking at himself as an apparition whose decomposition has begun … In visual terms the modelling is superb – simultaneously concise and rich, it shimmers with highlights and remains flawless in all apparently sudden or uncoordinated pencil strokes – whenever I look at it I am convinced that it is the highest and the most perfect of Stanisław Wyspiański's works.[86] **ML**

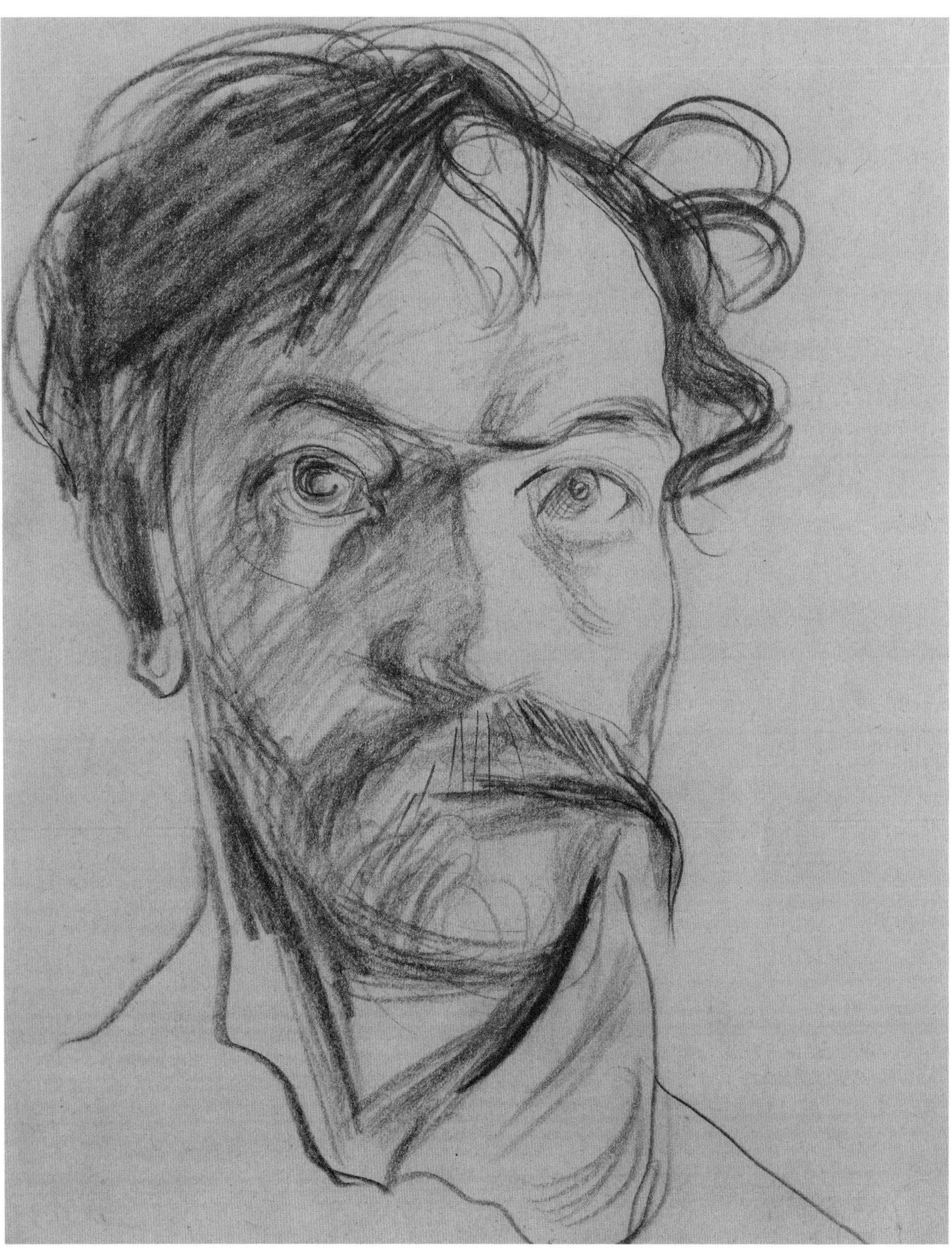

CAT.16
Stanisław Wyspiański
*Self-Portrait
before Death*, 1907
Crayon on paper,
207 × 170mm
National Museum
in Kraków

NOTES

The Life and Art of Stanisław Wyspiański
Many thanks to Magdalena Laskowska, Curator of the Wyspiański Museum (a branch of the National Museum in Kraków) for her generous help with this essay, including sharing information and archival materials on a wide spectrum of topics, not least on Wyspiański's hitherto unstudied composite portrait of 'contemporary Kraków'.

1   Mansfield 1938, unpaginated. The first Polish translation by Floryan Sobieniowski was printed in the magazine *Świat* in 1911 (no.33, p.8). Mansfield translated Wyspiański's play *The Judges* (*Sędziowie*, 1907) published for the first time in Kimber and Smith (eds) 2014.

2   Anon. 1916, p.3. See also Holme (ed.) 1906, p. xi and Levetus 1907, p.118. Amelia Sarah Levetus, *The Studio*'s Viennese correspondent, was a rare spokesperson on Wyspiański and the Young Poland movement in Britain. There was an exhibition of the 'Sztuka' Society of Polish Artists in London in 1906 (at the Imperial Royal Austrian Exhibition in Earl's Court), but Wyspiański was not featured, presumably due to terminal illness. In 1928 *The Studio* commented on Wyspiański's outstanding versatility: 'he certainly is the most original and universal artistic genius since Leonardo da Vinci' (see F.B.C. 1928, pp.90–7, p.92). For an overview of Wyspiański's design output and parallels with Morris, see Julia Griffin, 'Fellow Arts and Crafts Reformers Stanisław Wyspiański and William Morris: Parallel Lives', in Griffin and Szczerski (eds) 2020, pp.43–55.

3   For more about Young Poland, see Alison Smith, 'Preface: Young Poland and the Search for a National Style', in Griffin and Szczerski (eds) 2020, pp.9–13.

4   Both the *Polonia* stained-glass design for Lviv Cathedral (1892–4) and the *Queen of the Polish Crown* verse narrative (1893) were created in Paris. There are also pastel studies and an oil design for *Polonia*.

5   For more information about Wyspiański's links with Vienna see Wytrzens 1973; Niciński 2009; Kudelska 2015.

6   During the communist years there were Wyspiański shows in Moscow (1958), Vienna (1958) and Budapest (1978).

7   All his plays were banned under the Prussian and Russian partitions apart from *The Wedding*. For English translations see Wyspiański 1998; Wyspiański 2017; Wyspiański 2019.

8   Miodońska-Brookes (ed.) 1992, p.336.

9   Buszek 1971, p.412, quoted in Laskowska 2023a, p.155.

10   For a history and iconography of Wyspiański's Franciscan Church decorative scheme, see Magdalena Laskowska, '"Let Us Surround Ourselves With Our Own Beauty": Stanisław Wyspiański's Decorative Scheme for the Franciscan Church in Kraków', in Griffin and Szczerski (eds) 2020, pp.57–73.

11   Godyń and Laskowska 2017, pp.141–2.

12   Anna Rudzińska, '"Disappointed Love": Stanisław Wyspiański and Wawel', in Griffin and Szczerski (eds) 2020, p.77.

13   See Jan Matejko's works: painting *Inside the Tomb of King Casimir the Great* (1869, National Museum in Warsaw) and drawings of King Casimir the Great's skull and insignia (1869, National Museum in Kraków); and *Astronomer Copernicus, or Conversations with God* (1873, Jagiellonian University, Kraków); *Stańczyk* (1862, National Museum in Warsaw).

14   Jan Matejko, inaugural address to art students at the Kraków School of Fine Arts, 16 October 1882, in Treter 1939, p.84.

15   Laskowska and Skoczeń-Rąpała 2024, pp.20–1.

16   Godyń and Laskowska 2017, p.315.

17   Maszkowski 1971, pp.347–9. Thanks to Lucien Topolski for kindly translating materials from French on the subject of Madame Charlotte's crémerie.

18   SW Collected Letters (vol.III), Wyspiański to Karol Maszkowski, 2–3 February 1892, p.188, in Godyń and Laskowska 2017, p.317. For more about Wyspiański's Parisian and Cracovian influences see Godyń and Laskowska 2017, pp.311–29.

19   Chmiel 1971, p.147; Boy-Żeleński 1956, p.26. For more about the projected composite portrait of 'contemporary Kraków' scheme see Chmiel 1971, pp.146–9; Boy-Żeleński 1956, pp.24–6. For more about Paon see Małkiewicz 2004. Paon was a kind of private members' club for cultural figures created around the end of 1898 or beginning of 1899 in a single room within Ferdynand Turliński's Café Restaurant du Théâtre at Ulica Szpitalna 38. The larger establishment (open to the general public) had been in existence since 1896 and Wyspiański visited it since at least 1897.

20   Anna Rudzińska, 'Wyspiański's *Chochoły*: A Meditation on the "Straw Man" Generation', in Griffin and Szczerski (eds) 2020, pp.87–9.

21   Siedlecki 1971, p.198, in Godyń and Laskowska 2017, p.35. For

more about Wyspiański's relationship with his wife, see Godyń
and Laskowska 2017, pp.33–46.

22   Sketch of the projected family portraits arrangement,
preserved at Collegium Maius Jagiellonian University Museum
(1904, inv. no. MUJ 15681I). Information courtesy of Magdalena
Laskowska who discovered the sketch and identified
constituent portraits within it, including *Boy with Pistols* as
a portrait of Teodor.

23   SW Collected Letters (vol.IV), Wyspiański to Zygmunt Hendel,
15 March 1900, p.9.

24   Bartosiński 1971, p.274; SW Collected Letters (vol.IV), Wyspiański
to Józef Kotarbinski, 23 March 1901, pp.145–6, both cited in
Godyń and Laskowska 2017, on pp.34 and 37 respectively.

25   For more information about Solska rescuing Jewish citizens
see Kuchtówna 1980, pp. 212–7; Dołowy 2014, pp.20–2;
Grzemska 2020, pp.336–8.

26   Kępiński 1984, pp.153–4.

27   SW Collected Letters (vol.IV), Wyspiański to Adam Chmiel,
30 March 1904, pp.200–1, in Godyń and Laskowska 2017, p.327.

28   Nowak 1971, p.177, quoted in Laskowska 2023a, p.65.

29   SW Collected Letters (vol.IV), Wyspiański to Adam Chmiel,
30 March 1904, p.202, in Godyń and Laskowska 2017, p.328;
Chmiel 1971, pp.147–8.

30   Boy-Żeleński 1956, pp.25–6.

31   Laskowska 2023a, p.133. For a history and iconography of
Wyspiański's Wawel Cathedral stained-glass scheme, see Anna
Rudzińska, '"Disappointed Love": Stanisław Wyspiański and
Wawel', in Griffin and Szczerski (eds) 2020, pp.75–85.

32   Anna Rudzińska, '"Disappointed Love": Stanisław Wyspiański
and Wawel', in Griffin and Szczerski (eds) 2020, pp.80–1.

33   Ibid.

34   Ibid., pp.82–4.

35   For more about Wyspiański and flowers including *Irises* see
ibid., pp.83–4.

36   Laskowska 2023a, pp.97–9.

37   Fraciszka and Stefan Themerson, *Calling
Mr Smith*, 1943, https://archive.org/
details/1943fraciszkastephanthemersoncallingmrsmith
[accessed 21 March 2024]. The comparison between Chopin
and Wyspiański as best exponents of the 'Polish soul' was also
made in *The Studio* (F.B.C. 1928, p.96).

Portraits of the Young Poland Movement

1   For the art and history of the Young Poland movement,
see Griffin and Szczerski (eds) 2020 and Cavanaugh 2000.

2   For an analysis of Artur Górski's text and his influence on the
Young Poland artists, see Kieżun 2006. For English translations
of excerpts of the text, see Górski 2010.

3   For an overview of Stanisław Przybyszewski's views on the
human being, see Jarosz 2019.

4   Stanisław Brzozowski's work is analysed in detail in Herlth
and Świderski (eds) 2019.

5   For an account of Malczewski's life and work, see Ławniczakowa
(ed.) 1990 and Kudelska 2008.

6   For a catalogue of Boznańska's portraits, see Higersberger (ed.)
2015.

7   For a detailed account of the history of Polish psychoanalysis,
see Dybel 2020.

8   'Freud and Freudists' (*'Freudyzm i freudyści'*), published in
the widely read weekly *Prawda* (nos 2–6 and 8–9).

9   Witkiewicz's photographs are analysed in detail in
Szymanowicz 2014 and Czartoryska and Musiał (eds) 1979.
For an anthology of Witkiewicz's writings on art and theatre
plays, see Gerould (ed.) 1992.

10   For information on Leopold Gottlieb and the artists in the
Polish Legions, see Wilkosz 2014.

The Portraits

1   Architect Tadeusz Stryjeński's description in Gorzkowski (ed.)
1898, p.414.

2   Dated from December 1889 until the beginning of 1891, the
pages of the sketchbooks are in the collections of the National
Museum in Kraków, National Museum in Warsaw, National
Gallery of Art in Lviv and in private collections. For more
information, see Laskowska 2023b, p.158.

3   The Jagiellonian University's student association 'Aesthetes
Circle' Minutes Book, manuscript, entry in Wyspiański's
handwriting, 16 April [1888], Archive of the Society of Friends
of the Fine Arts (Towarzystwo Przyjaciół Sztuk Pięknych –
TPSP), Kraków.

4   For more about Feldman's relationship with Wyspiański,
see SW Collected Letters (vol.IV), pp.606–10.

5   Laskowska 2023b, p.158.

6   Hackett 1929; Jelusich and Taylor 1939.

7   Gajkowska 1972.

8   SW Collected Letters (vol.II), Wyspiański to Lucjan Rydel, 3 June 1897 p.473.

9   Czyżewski 1932, p.110.

10   Charazińska, Rudzińska and Milicer (eds) 2007, p.120: inv. no.Rys. Pol. 160341 MNW (National Museum in Warsaw).

11   For more information about this drawing, see Jarosz 2009, pp.71–83.

12   Żeleński 1929, p.16.

13   Ibid., p.15.

14   Tadeusz Boy-Żeleński recalls the origin of the name Paon (French for 'Peacock'): 'Przybyszewski was always … enchanted with particular words and their comical or mystical sound; at the time he had a predilection for words from Maeterlinck's poem "*les paons blancs, les paons nonchalants*"; it was Przybyszewski who named the little room "the nonchalant paon", which came to be known by the shortened form "Paon"' (Żeleński 1929, p.25). NB: Boy-Żeleński misquoted Maeterlinck's poem 'L'ennui' whose opening line reads 'Les paons nonchalants, les paons blancs'.

15   Żeleński 1929, p.26.

16   *'Ich liebe von ihm jede Zeile'*: Żeleński 1929, p.15.

17   Sawicka 2006, p.139.

18   B.Og. 1899, p.357.

19   Chmiel 1971, pp.146–7.

20   Żeleński 1929, p.26.

21   The first full Polish edition of the trilogy appeared in 1912 and the first English translation was not until 2020. See also Żuławski n.d.

22   Sikorowska 1980, p.39.

23   Karwacka 1962, pp.117–19.

24   Żuławski 1901.

25   SW Collected Letters (vol.I), letter of 7 December 1895, p.192.

26   *Tygodnik Illustrowany*, no.43, 1901, p.837 (front cover).

27   TPSP Report 1907, p.39.

28   Ample correspondence between the two men survives for the years 1900–5 relating to the artist's loans from the doctor as well as to Wyspiański's artistic plans and commissions, e.g. Manuscripts Department, National Museum in Kraków, File 649, vol.1, 104930, Wyspiański's letter to Nowak, 19 October 1900; File 649, vol.1, 104935, Wyspiański's letter to Nowak, 15 February 1901.

29   Gościński 2006, pp.21–2; Griffin and Szczerski (eds) 2020, pp.51–3, 150–1 and 157.

30   Nowak 1971, pp.176–7.

31   Ibid., pp.176–7.

32   Raszewski, Czachowska and Dąbrowski (eds) 1973.

33   Świerczewski 1932, p.59.

34   Drawings in the collection of the National Museum in Kraków: MNK III-r.a-2754 and MNK III-r.a-3282.

35   Wyspiański 2017, p.198. Wyspiański had a love of Old Masters and Botticelli in particular; a print of *Primavera* adorned his atelier in Paris in 1891. For more on *Primavera* in Wyspiański's Paris studio, see Laskowska 2021, pp.33–4. It served as inspiration for the portrait of his close friend the poet Lucjan Rydel with a life-sized figure of the goddess of spring in the background (1894, Museum of Kraków, Rydlówka Manor House Branch).

36   Kuchtówna 1980, p.120.

37   Letter from Irena Solska to Jerzy Żuławski, 27 April 1904 [letter no.26], in Irena Solska Collected Letters 1984, p.37. Solski's portrait in question was lost during the Second World War together with a number of his other striking portraits in stage costumes by Wyspiański. Solska's portrait was reproduced in Galis 1932, p.813.

38   Kuchtówna 1980, p.63.

39   Ibid., pp.91–2, 120–1 and 171; Szczerski and Kopszak 2006, p.10; Szczerski 2015, p.70.

40   Wyspiański 1998, p.59; Andrzej Szczerski, 'The Reception of the Pre-Raphaelites and the Arts and Crafts Movement in Poland', in Griffin and Szczerski (eds) 2020, p.29.

41   Laskowska 2023b, pp.158–9.

42   Opalski 2010.

43   See Joanna Regina Kowalska, 'Textiles', in Griffin and Szczerski (eds) 2020, pp.172–3, and Kowalska 2021, pp.144–7. Attempts to create the Polish national dress ultimately failed.

44   Nineteenth-century Poland was very multicultural, with a large Jewish diaspora in Kraków.

45   Feldman 1933.

46   Reddaway et al. (eds) 1941.

47   *Tygodnik Illustrowany*, no.12, 1908, p.228; *Gazette des beaux-arts*, no.611, 1908, p.433.

48   *The Studio*, no.187, 1908, p.72.

49   Zbijewska 1980, p.125; Śliwińska 2017, pp.243–4.

50   *Mietek's Head*, 1901, pastel on paper, National Museum
     in Kraków (inv. no.MNK III-r.a-10760).

51   Zbijewska 1980, p.145.

52   Ibid., p.149.

53   Ibid., pp.152–3.

54   Ibid., p.160.

55   F.B.C. 1928, p.92.

56   Inv. no.Rys.Pol.8697 MNW.

57   For a detailed study of this work, see Bałus 2007, pp.198–206.

58   Zdzisław Kępiński identified Paul Gauguin's *Girl in front of Still
     Life* (1889) as direct inspiration for *Helenka with a Vase* – see
     Kępiński 1984, p.158. See also Paul Gauguin, *Clovis Gauguin
     (The Sleeping Child)*, 1884, oil on canvas, 460 x 555 mm,
     Private Collection.

59   Godyń and Laskowska 2016, p.53.

60   The document in question comprises a handwritten list of
     Wyspiański's works, in Jasieński's handwriting, and receipts issued
     by S. Böhm, National Museum in Kraków Archive S 1/12, pp.133–4.

61   Inv. no.MNP FR 348.

62   Danuta Godyń and Magdalena Laskowska, *'U mnie w domu'*,
     in Godyń and Laskowska 2017, p.33, footnote 4.

63   *Mietek and Teodor*, 1902, pencil on paper, National Museum
     in Kraków (inv. no.MNK III-r.a-15790).

64   Zbijewska 1980, p.143.

65   Ibid., pp.151–2.

66   As evidenced by the sketch preserved in the Collegium Maius
     Jagiellonian University Museum collection.

67   Marrené-Morzkowska 1901, p.390.

68   Laskowska 2023b, p.303, cat.XII.41.

69   Godyń and Laskowska 2017, p.38.

70   Inv. no.MHK 2145/VIII.

71   Zbijewska 1980, p.157.

72   Ibid., p.149.

73   Ibid., p.155. Both Teodor and Staś ended up in psychiatric
     hospitals. It ended more happily for Staś – he met his wife
     there and was later released.

74   Kępiński 1984, p.146.

75   Pastel drawing entitled *Maternity* (1902) in the collection of
     the National Museum in Warsaw (inv. no.77777 MNW, fig.18).

76   For more about Wyspiański's portraits of his wife, see Bałus
     2022, pp.511–16.

77   Wyspiański recorded the origin and progress on this picture
     in his diary between 27 May and 13 June 1905: SW Diaries
     (1898–1907), pp.398–401.

78   Śliwińska 2017, p.131.

79   For more about Wyspiański's double portraits of the same
     sitter, see Bałus 2009.

80   Sztuka Catalogue 1904 – list of works exhibited at the
     'Common Room' of the Society of Friends of the Fine Arts
     headquarters in Kraków, 'Sztuka' Society of Polish Artists.

81   Mehoffer 1932, p.292: 'Characterised by its hard and black
     contour lines, his *Maternity* was equally hardened, relentless
     and fatalistic in terms of its subject matter, frightening in its
     juxtaposition of this kind of woman and girls staring at the baby.'

82   Wyka 1970, p.3.

83   Leopold Staff was an influential Young Poland poet, playwright
     and translator associated with Lviv.

84   According to the eleventh-century legend about Bishop
     Stanislaus of Szczepanów (c.1030–1079), Piotr Strzemieńczyk
     of Janiszew, known as 'Piotrowin', was resurrected by the
     Bishop in order to testify in the Bishop's trial wrongfully
     accusing him of appropriating land which he had in fact
     purchased from Piotrowin. He is typically represented as
     a skeletal figure next to Bishop Stanislaus.

85   Reymont 1971, p.457.

86   Kępiński 1984, p.150.

BIBLIOGRAPHY

Anon. 1916 Anon., 'Miscellany', *Manchester Guardian*, 1 June 1916

Bałus 2007 Wojciech Bałus, 'Dziecko-tajemnica: Stanisława Wyspiańskiego "Dziewczynka przed dzbankiem z kwiatami"', *Teksty Drugie: teoria literatury, krytyka, interpretacja*, vol.6, no.108, 2007

Bałus 2009 Wojciech Bałus, 'Do granic tożsamości: O portretach zdwojonych Stanisława Wyspiańskiego', in Anna Czabanowska-Wróbel (ed.), *Stanisław Wyspiański w labiryncie świata, myśli i sztuki* (Jagiellonian University Press, Kraków, 2009)

Bałus 2022 Wojciech Bałus, 'Stanisława Wyspiańskiego portret żony (1902) a chłopska fotografia rodzinna', in Janusz Barański, Katarzyna Maniak and Stanisława Trebunia-Staszel (eds), *Więcej niż muzeum: Szkice ofiarowane Profesorowi Janowi Święchowi* (Jagiellonian University Press, Kraków, 2022)

Bartosiński 1971 Jan Bartosiński, 'Wspomnienia o Stanisławie Wyspiańskim', in Płoszewski (ed.) 1971

Blum 1969 Helena Blum, *Stanisław Wyspiański* (Oficyna Wydawnicza Auriga, Warsaw, 1969)

B.Og 1899 B.Og., 'Kawiarnia artystyczna pod "Pawiem" w Krakowie', *Kraj*, no.51, 1899

Boy-Żeleński 1956 Tadeusz Boy-Żeleński, 'Nonszalancki Paon', *Ludzie żywi* (Państwowy Instytut Wydawniczy, Warsaw, 1956)

Buszek 1971 Antoni Buszek, 'Ze wspomnień szkolnych o Stanisławie Wyspiańskim', in Płoszewski (ed.) 1971

Cavanaugh 2000 Jan Cavanaugh, *Out Looking In: Early Modern Polish Art, 1890–1918* (University of California Press, Berkeley, CA, 2000)

Charazińska, Rudzińska and Milicer (eds) 2007 Elżbieta Charazińska, Anna Rudzińska and Ewa Milicer (eds), *Jak meteor … Stanisław Wyspiański (1869–1907): Artyście w setną rocznicę śmierci*, exh. cat. (National Museum in Warsaw, 2007)

Chmiel 1971 Adam Chmiel, 'Nieco ze wspomnień o Stanisławie Wyspiańskim (1869–1907)', in Płoszewski (ed.) 1971

Chołoniewski 1907 Antoni Chołoniewski, 'Ze wspomnień o St. Wyspiańskim', *Świat*, no.52, 28 December 1907

Czartoryska and Musiał (eds) 1979 Urszula Czartoryska and Grzegorz Musiał (eds), *St. I. Witkiewicz, Fotografie*, exh. cat. (Łódź Art Museum, 1979)

Czyżewski 1932 Tytus Czyżewski, 'Życie a sztuka w twórczości Wyspiańskiego', *Głos Plastyków*, nos 9–10, 1932

Deryng 2004 Xavier Deryng, 'Mehoffer à la crémerie de Madame Charlotte: Un artiste polonaise à Paris (1891–1896)', in Anna Zeńczak, Xavier Deryng and Marta Smolińska (eds), *Józef Mehoffer: Un Peintre Symboliste Polonais*, exh. cat. (Musée d'Orsay and 5 Continents Editions, Paris, 2004)

Dołowy 2014 Patrycja Dołowy, 'Kryjówka za Wełnę', *Gazeta Wyborcza*, no.283: *Wysokie Obcasy* supplement, no.47, 2014

Dybel 2020 Paweł Dybel, *Psychoanalysis – the Promised Land? The History of Psychoanalysis in Poland 1900–1989, Part I: The Sturm und Drang Period; Beginnings of Psychoanalysis in the Polish Lands during the Partitions 1900–1918* (Peter Lang, Bern, 2020)

F.B.C. 1928 F.B.C., 'Stanisław Wyspianski: A Great Polish Artist', *The Studio*, vol.96, 1928

Feldman 1933 Józef Feldman, 'U podstaw stosunków polsko-angielskich 1788–1863', offprint from *Polityka Narodów*, Warsaw, 1933

Gajkowska 1972 Celina Gajkowska, 'Kazimierz Lewandowski', in *Polski Słownik Biograficzny (Polish Dictionary of National Biography)*, vol.XVII/2, no.73 (Zakład Narodowy im. Ossolińskich – Wydawnictwo Polskiej Akademii Nauk, Wrocław, Warsaw, Kraków and Gdańsk, 1972)

Galis 1932 Adam Galis, '"W tragicznym teatru skłonie". O Stanisławie Wyspiańskim – jak go widzieli, słuchali, przeżywali – opowiadają wielcy aktorzy "Wesela", "Warszawianki", "Bolesława Śmiałego"', *Tygodnik Ilustrowany* (special commemorative issue on the occasion of the anniversary of Stanisław Wyspiański's death), no.50, 10 December 1932

Gaweł and Laskowska 2019 Łukasz Gaweł and Magdalena Laskowska, *Wyspiański Nieznany / Unknown Wyspiański*, exh. cat. (National Museum in Kraków, 2019)

Gerould (ed.) 1992 Daniel Gerould (ed. and trans.), *The Witkiewicz Reader* (Northwestern University Press, Evanston, 1992)

Godetzky 2022 Albert Godetzky, 'Gamins of the Studio', in Roger Diederen, Albert Godetzky and Nerina Santorius (eds), *Silent Rebels: Polish Symbolism around 1900*, exh. cat. (Kunsthalle München, Munich, 2022)

Godyń and Laskowska 2016 Danuta Godyń and Magdalena Laskowska, *Rysunki, akwarele i pastele z kolekcji Feliksa Jasieńskiego w zbiorach Muzeum Narodowego w Krakowie / Drawings, Watercolours and Pastels from Feliks Jasieński's Collection at the National Museum in Kraków* (National Museum in Kraków, 2016) (*Korpus daru Feliksa Jasieńskiego / Feliks Jasieński's Gift Catalogue Raisonné*, vol.2, part 2)

Godyń and Laskowska 2017 Danuta Godyń and Magdalena Laskowska, *Wyspiański*, exh. cat. (National Museum in Kraków, 2017)

Górski 2010 Artur Górski, 'Young Poland', in Ahmet Ersoy, Maciej Górny and Vangelis Kechriotis (eds), *Modernism: Representations of National Culture; Discourses of Collective Identity in Central and Southeast Europe 1770–1945,* Texts and Commentaries, vol.III/2 (Central European University Press, Budapest and New York, 2010), https://books.openedition.org/ceup/1100

Gorzkowski (ed.) 1898 Marian Gorzkowski (ed.), *Jan Matejko: Epoka lat dalszych, do końca życia artysty, z dziennika prowadzonego w ciągu lat siedemnastu* (Drukarnia Związkowa, Kraków, 1898)

Gościński 2006 Igor Gościński, 'Julian Nowak (1865–1946)', in Igor Gościński and Aleksander B. Skotnicki (eds), *Towarzystwo Lekarskie Krakowskie: Księga Jubileuszowa* (Krakowskie Towarzystwo Edukacyjne: Oficyna Wydawnicza AFM, commissioned by the Medical Society, Kraków, 2006)

Griffin and Szczerski (eds) 2020 Julia Griffin and Andrzej Szczerski (eds), *Young Poland: The Polish Arts and Crafts Movement, 1890–1918* (Lund Humphries, London, 2020)

Grzemska 2020 Aleksandra Grzemska, *Matki i córki: Relacje rodzinne i artystyczne w autobiografiach kobiet po 1989 roku* (Wydawnictwo Naukowe Uniwersytetu Mikołaja Kopernika, Toruń, 2020)

Hackett 1929 Francis Hackett, *Henry VIII* (Horace Liveright, New York, 1929)

Herlth and Świderski (eds) 2019 Jens Herlth and Edward M. Świderski (eds), *Stanisław Brzozowski and the Migration of Ideas: Transnational Perspectives on the Intellectual Field in Twentieth-Century Poland and Beyond* (transcript Verlag, Bielefeld, 2019)

Higersberger (ed.) 2015 Renata Higersberger (ed.), *Olga Boznańska (1865–1940)*, exh. cat. (National Museum in Warsaw, 2015)

Hoesick 1902 Ferdynand S. Hoesick, 'Wyspiański: Życie i sztuka', *Kraj*, no.1, 1902

Holme (ed.) 1906 Charles Holme (ed.), *The Art-Revival in Austria, The Studio*, Special Edition, 1906

Irena Solska Collected Letters 1984 Lidia Kuchtówna (ed.), *Listy Ireny Solskiej* (Państwowy Instytut Wydawniczy, Warsaw, 1984)

Jarosz 2009 Andrzej Jarosz, 'Melancholia Dagny Juel Przybyszewskiej. Formotwórcza i znaczeniowa rola linii w rysunku Stanisława Wyspiańskiego', in Małgorzata Okulicz-Kozaryn, Mateusz Bourkane and Michał Haake (eds), *Przemyśleć wszystko … Stanisława Wyspiańskiego modernizacja pamięci zbiorowej* (Wydawnictwo Poznańskiego Towarzystwa Przyjaciół Nauk, Poznań, 2009)

Jarosz 2019 Adam Jarosz, *Der Spiegel und die Spiegelungen: Über Geschlecht und Seele im Werk von Stanisław Przybyszewski* (Ibidem-Verlag, Stuttgart, 2019)

Jelusich and Taylor 1939 Mirko Jelusich and Eileen R. Taylor, *Oliver Cromwell* (Massie Publishing Co., London, 1939)

Juszczak 1977 Wiesław Juszczak, *Malarstwo polskie: Modernizm* (Wydawnictwa Artystyczne i Filmowe, Oficyna Wydawnicza Auriga, Warsaw, 1977)

Karwacka 1962 Helena Karwacka, 'Jerzy Żuławski (1874–1915). Szkic do monografii o pisarzu', PhD thesis, University of Łódz, 1962

Kępiński 1984 Zdzisław Kępiński, *Stanisław Wyspiański* (Krajowa Agencja Wydawnicza, Warsaw, 1984)

Kieżun 2006 Anna Kieżun, *Drogi własne: O twórczości młodopolskiej Artura Górskiego* (Wydawnictwo Uniwersytetu w Białymstoku, Białystok, 2006)

Kimber and Smith (eds) Gerri Kimber and Angela Smith (eds), *The Poetry and Critical Writings of Katherine Mansfield*, vol.3 (Edinburgh University Press, Edinburgh, 2014)

Koller 1933 Jerzy Koller, 'Nieznany autoportret Wyspiańskiego', *Tęcza: Ilustrowane pismo miesięczne*, vol.7, no.2, 1933

Kowalska 2021 Joanna Regina Kowalska, 'National Styles in Polish Fashion', in Andrzej Szczerski (ed.), *Polskie Style Narodowe / Polish National Styles, 1890–1918*, exh. cat. (National Museum in Kraków, 2021)

Kuchtówna 1980 Lidia Kuchtówna, *Irena Solska* (Państwowy Instytut Wydawniczy, Warsaw, 1980)

Kudelska 2008 Dorota Kudelska, *Dukt pisma i pędzla: Biografia intelektualna Jacka Malczewskiego* (Wydawnictwo KUL, Lublin, 2008)

Kudelska 2015 Dorota Kudelska, 'Między Secesją a Hagenbundem – artyści polscy w Wiedniu 1898–1914', *Pamiętnik Sztuk Pięknych*, no.10, 2015

Laskowska 2021 Magdalena Laskowska, '"Cudze zbiory": Zespół luźnych reprodukcji, kart książkowych, wycinków oraz fotografii ze spuścizny po Stanisławie Wyspiańskim w kolekcji Muzeum Narodowego w Krakowie', in Agnieszka Gronek (ed.), *O miejsce książki w historii sztuki*, Part III: *Sztuka książki około 1900: W 150 rocznicę urodzin Stanisława Wyspiańskiego* (Wydawnictwo Księgarnia Akademicka, Kraków, 2022)

Laskowska 2023a Magdalena Laskowska, *Stanisław Wyspiański* (Bosz, Olszanica, 2023)

Laskowska 2023b Magdalena Laskowska, *Wyspiański: Szkicowniki i rysunki w zbiorach Muzeum Narodowego w Krakowie* (National Museum in Kraków, 2023)

Laskowska and Skoczeń-Rąpała 2019 Magdalena Laskowska and Łucja Skoczeń-Rąpała, *Wyspiański: Posłowie,* exh. cat. (National Museum in Kraków, 2019)

Laskowska and Skoczeń-Rąpała 2024 Magdalena Laskowska and Łucja Skoczeń-Rąpała, *Wyspiański: Studya z natury: Pokaz nieznanych dzieł Stanisława Wyspiańskiego ze zbiorów Ziyada Raoofa / Studies from Nature: Presentation of Unknown Works by Stanisław Wyspiański from the Ziyad Raoof Collection,* exh. cat. (National Museum in Kraków, 2024)

Ławniczakowa (ed.) 1990 Agnieszka Ławniczakowa (ed.), *Malczewski: A Vision of Poland*, exh. cat. (Barbican Art Gallery, London, in partnership with the National Museum in Poznań, 1990)

Ławniczakowa 1996 Agnieszka Ławniczakowa, catalogue entry, in *Fin de siècle in Polen: Poolse schilderkunst 1890–1918 uit de collectie van het Nationaal Museum Poznań*, exh. cat. (Waanders Uitgevers, Zwolle, 1996)

Levetus 1907 Amelia Sarah Levetus, 'Notes on Some Polish Artists of To-Day', *The Studio*, vol.XLI, 1907

Łoch and Trześnikowski 2011 Eugenia Łoch and Dariusz Trześnikowski, *Zasługi Jerzego Żuławskiego i jego rodu dla literatury i kultury XX wieku* (Wydawnictwo UMCS, Lublin, 2011)

Małkiewicz 2004 Barbara Małkiewicz, '"Paon" – Pierwsza kawiarnia artystyczna Młodej Polski', *Rozprawy Muzeum Narodowego w Krakowie: Seria Nowa*, vol.II, 2004

Mansfeld 1969 Bogusław Mansfeld, *Stanisław Wyspiański: Próba interpretacji programu artystycznego* (National Museum in Poznań, 1969)

Mansfield 1938 Katherine Mansfield, 'To Stanislaw Wyspianski' (Privately printed for Bertram Rota by The Favil Press, London, 1938), unpaginated

Marrené-Morzkowska 1901 Waleria Marrené-Morzkowska, 'Stanisław Wyspiański (I)', *Echo Muzyczne, Teatralne i Artystyczne*, no.8, 1901

Maszkowski 1971 Karol Maszkowski, 'U Madame Charlotte (1894 r.)', in Płoszewski (ed.) 1971

Mehoffer 1932 Józef Mehoffer, 'Wyspiański – zjawisko', *Sztuki Piękne*, 1932, no.11

Mehoffer Diaries Jadwiga Puciata-Pawłowska (ed. and annotated), *Józef Mehoffer: Dziennik* (Wydawnictwo Literackie, Kraków, 1975)

Miodońska-Brookes (ed.) 1992 Ewa Miodońska-Brookes (ed.), *Feliks Jasieński i jego Manggha, Excerpts from Writings in Polish and English* (Universitas, Kraków 1992)

Niciński 2009 Konrad Niciński, 'Wyspiański na wystawach Secesji w zwierciadle wiedeńskiej krytyki', in Małgorzata Okulicz-Kozaryn, Mateusz Bourkane and Michał Haake (eds), *Przemyśleć wszystko ...*

Stanisława Wyspiańskiego modernizacja wyobraźni zbiorowej (Wydawnictwo Poznańskiego Towarzystwa Przyjaciół Nauk, Poznań, 2009)

Nowak 1971 Julian Nowak, 'Wspomnienia o Wyspiańskim', in Płoszewski (ed.) 1971

Opalski 2010 Magda Opalski, 'Feldman, Wilhelm', *YIVO Encyclopedia of Jews in Eastern Europe*, 6 August 2010, https://yivoencyclopedia.org/article.aspx/Feldman_Wilhelm [accessed 10 May 2024]

Płoszewski 1971 Leon Płoszewski, 'Komentarz', in Płoszewski (ed.) 1971

Płoszewski (ed.) 1971 Leon Płoszewski (ed.), *Wyspiański w oczach współczesnych*, vol.I (Wydawnictwo Literackie, Kraków, 1971)

Przybyszewski 1899 Stanisław Przybyszewski, *Nad morzem* (Gebethner, Kraków, 1899)

Przybyszewski, Żuk-Skarszewski and Świerz 1925 Stanisław Przybyszewski, Tadeusz Żuk-Skarszewski and Stanisław Świerz, *Stanisław Wyspiański (1869–1907): Dzieła malarskie* (Instytut Wydawniczy 'Biblioteka Polska', Warsaw and Bydgoszcz, 1925)

Puchalski 1963 Gustaw Puchalski, *Stanisław Wyspiański. Twórczość plastyczna 5. Karykatury* (Wydawnictwo Literackie, Kraków, 1963)

Raszewski, Czachowska and Dąbrowski (eds) 1973 Zbigniew Raszewski, Jadwiga Czachowska and Stanisław Dąbrowski (eds), *Słownik Biograficzny Teatru Polskiego 1765–1965* (PWN, Warsaw, 1973)

Reddaway et al. (eds) 1941 W. F. Reddaway, J. H. Penson, O. Halecki and R. Dyboski (eds), *The Cambridge History of Poland: From Augustus II to Pilsudski (1697–1935)* (Cambridge University Press, Cambridge, 1941)

Reymont 1971 Władysław Stanisław Reymont, 'Ostatnie odwiedziny u Wyspiańskiego', in Płoszewski (ed.) 1971

Romanowska 2015 Marta Romanowska, *Stanisław Wyspiański* (Ożarów Mazowiecki, Kraków, 2015)

Sawicka 2006 Agnieszka Sawicka, *Dagny Juel Przybyszewska: Fakty i legendy* (słowo/obraz terytoria, Gdańsk, 2006)

Siedlecki 1971 Michał Siedlecki, 'Wspomnienia o Wyspiańskim i Reymoncie', in Płoszewski (ed.) 1971

Sikorowska 1980 Barbara Sikorowska, 'Poglądy filozoficzno-estetyczne Jerzego Żuławskiego a niektóre aspekty jego twórczości dramatycznej', in Jan Nowakowski (ed.), *Rocznik Naukowo-Dydaktyczny*, issue 72: *Prace historyczno-literackie*, vol.VII, (Wydawnictwo Naukowe Wyższej Szkoły Pedagogicznej w Krakowie, Kraków, 1980)

Skalska (ed.) 2019 Agnieszka Skalska (ed.), *Choroba jako źródło sztuki*, exh. cat. (National Museum in Poznań, 2019)

Skrudlik 1911 Mieczysław Skrudlik, 'Portrety własne Stanisława Wyspiańskiego', *Krytyka, miesięcznik poświęcony sprawom społecznym, nauce i sztuce.*, vol.32, 1911, p.324

Śliwińska 2017 Monika Śliwińska, *Stanisław Wyspiański: Dopóki starczy życia* (Iskry, Warsaw, 2017)

Smith (ed.) 2009 Alison Smith (ed.), *Symbolist Art in Poland: Poland and Britain c.1900*, exh. cat. (Tate Publishing, London, 2009)

Stankiewiczowa 1971 Janina Stankiewiczowa, 'Krótkie notatki, jakie zebrałam z pobytu, wychowania i wykształcenia Stanisława Wyspiańskiego w naszym domu od 1874 r. po 1907', in Płoszewski (ed.) 1971

SW Collected Letters (vol.I) Maria Rydlowa (ed.), *Listy Stanisława Wyspiańskiego do Józefa Mehoffera, Henryka Opieńskiego i Tadeusza Stryjeńskiego*, 'Listy zebrane' series, vol.I (Wydawnictwo Literackie, Kraków, 1994)

SW Collected Letters (vol.II) Maria Rydlowa and Leon Płoszewski (eds), *Listy Stanisława Wyspiańskiego do Lucjana Rydla*, 'Listy zebrane' series, vol.II, (Wydawnictwo Literackie, Kraków, 1979)

SW Collected Letters (vol.III) Maria Rydlowa (ed.), *Listy Stanisława Wyspiańskiego do Karola Maszkowskiego*, 'Listy zebrane' series, vol.III (Wydawnictwo Literackie, Kraków, 1997)

SW Collected Letters (vol.IV) Maria Rydlowa (ed.), *Listy Stanisława Wyspiańskiego różne – do wielu adresatów*, 'Listy zebrane' series, vol.IV (Wydawnictwo Literackie, Kraków, 1998)

SW Collected Works Leon Płoszewski (ed.), *Stanisław Wyspiański: Dzieła zebrane*, 16 vols (Wydawnictwo Literackie, Kraków, 1958–95)

SW Diary 1904 *Raptularz z 1904 r.,* in Maria Rydlowa (ed.), *Listy Stanisława Wyspiańskiego różne – do wielu adresatów,* 'Listy zebrane' series, vol.IV, pp.370–82 (Wydawnictwo Literackie, Kraków, 1998)

SW Diary 1905 *Raptularz z 1905 r.,* in Maria Rydlowa (ed.), *Listy Stanisława Wyspiańskiego różne – do wielu adresatów,* 'Listy zebrane' series, vol.IV, pp.383–413 (Wydawnictwo Literackie, Kraków, 1998)

SW Diaries (1898–1907) *Raptularze,* in Maria Rydlowa (ed.), *Listy Stanisława Wyspiańskiego różne – do wielu adresatów,* 'Listy zebrane' series, vol.IV, pp.370–413 (Wydawnictwo Literackie, Kraków, 1998)

SW Chronology (1890–98) Maria Stokowa (ed.), *Kalendarz życia i twórczości 1 marca 1890 – ostatnie dni marca 1898 Stanisława Wyspiańskiego* (Wydawnictwo Literackie, Kraków, 1982) (SW Collected Works, vol.16/II)

SW Chronology (1898–1907) Alina Doboszewska (ed.), *Kalendarz życia i twórczości 26 marca 1898 – grudzień 1907 Stanisława Wyspiańskiego* (Wydawnictwo Literackie, Kraków, 1995) (SW Collected Works, vol.16/III)

Sztuka Catalogue 1904 *Spis dzieł pomieszczonych w budynku Towarzystwa Przyjaciół Szt: Pięknych w świetlicy 2-ej, Towarzystwo Artystów Polskich Sztuka z Siedzibą w Krakowie,* designed and compiled by Stanisław Wyspiański, exh. cat. (Towarzystwo Artystów Polskich Sztuka, Kraków, 1904)

Świątek 1977 Henryk Świątek, 'Krakowskie mieszkania i pracownie Stanisława Wyspiańskiego', *Krzysztofory: Zeszyty naukowe Muzeum Historycznego Miasta Krakowa,* vol.4 (Muzeum Historyczne Miasta Krakowa, Kraków, 1977)

Świerczewski 1932 Eugenjusz Świerczewski, 'Rozmowy z aktorami: Co mówią: Solski, Solska i Ordon-Sosnowska', in *Wyspiańskiemu Teatr Krakowski 1907–1932* (Zakłady Graficzne Styl, Kraków, 1932)

Szczerski 2015 Andrzej Szczerski, *Views of Albion: The Reception of British Art and Design in Central Europe, 1890–1918* (Peter Lang, Oxford, 2015) (originally published in Polish in 2002)

Szczerski and Kopszak 2006 Andrzej Szczerski and Piotr Kopszak, *Śladami Prerafaelitów: Artyści polscy i sztuka brytyjska na przełomie XIX i XX wieku,* exh. cat. (Muzeum Pałac w Wilanowie, Warsaw, 2006)

Szydłowski 1930 Tadeusz Szydłowski, *Stanisław Wyspiański* (Gebethner i Wolff, Warsaw, 1930)

Szymanowicz 2014 Maciej Szymanowicz, 'In the Private Sphere: The Photographic Work of Stanisław Ignacy Witkiewicz', in Mitra Abbaspour, Lee Ann Daffner, Maria Morris Hambourg (eds), *Object:Photo; Modern Photographs: The Thomas Walther Collection 1909–1949,* exh. cat. (Museum of Modern Art, New York, 2014)

TPSP Catalogue 1906 *Katalog wystawy Towarzystwa Przyjaciół Sztuk Pięknych w Krakowie we wrześniu 1906 roku,* exh. cat. (Towarzystwo Przyjaciół Sztuk Pięknych, Kraków, 1906)

TPSP Report 1905 *Sprawozdanie Dyrekcyi Towarzystwa Sztuk Pięknych w Krakowie z czynności za rok 1905, Spis dzieł sztuki wystawionych w ciągu 1905 roku na wystawie nieustającej* (Towarzystwo Przyjaciół Sztuk Pięknych, Kraków, 1906)

TPSP Report 1907 *Sprawozdanie Dyrekcyi Towarzystwa Sztuk Pięknych w Krakowie z czynności za rok 1907* (Towarzystwo Przyjaciół Sztuk Pięknych, Kraków, 1908)

Treter 1939 Mieczysław Treter, *Matejko: Osobowość artysty, twórczość, forma i styl* (Książnica Atlas, Lviv and Warsaw, 1939)

Wilkosz 2014 Piotr Wilkosz, *Legiony Polskie 1914–1918: wystawa w stulecie wybuchu Wielkiej Wojny i Czynu Legionowego / Polish Legions 1914–1918: Exhibition on the Centenary of the Outbreak of the Great War and the Legions,* exh. cat. (National Museum in Kraków, 2014)

Wójcik 2007 Agata Wójcik, 'Stanisław Wyspiański w paryskiej Académie Colarossi', *Krzysztofory: Zeszyty naukowe Muzeum Historycznego Miasta Krakowa,* vol.25 (Muzeum Historyczne Miasta Krakowa, Kraków, 2007)

Wyka 1970 Kazimierz Wyka, 'Mam ten dar bowiem: patrzę się inaczej', *Życie Literackie,* no. 941, 7 February 1970

Wyspiański 1910 Stanisław Wyspiański, *Pisma Pośmiertne, II: Wiersze – Fragmenty Dramatyczne – Uwagi* (Wilhelm Feldman, Kraków, 1910)

Wyspiański 1962 Stanisław Wyspiański, *Bolesław Śmiały, Legenda II, Skałka* (Wydawnictwo Literackie, Kraków, 1962) (SW Collected Works, vol.6)

Wyspiański 1998 Stanisław Wyspiański, *The Wedding* [1901], trans. Noel Clark (Oberon Books, London, 1998)

Wyspiański 2017 Stanisław Wyspiański, *Acropolis: The Wawel Plays*, trans. and ed. Charles S. Kraszewski (Glagoslav Publications, London, 2017)

Wyspiański 2019 Wyspiański, Stanisław, *The Hamlet Study and The Death of Ophelia*, trans. Barbara Bogoczek and Tony Howard (Shakespeare's Globe, London, 2019)

Wytrzens 1973 Günther Wytrzens, 'Wiedeń w życiu i twórczości Stanisława Wyspiańskiego', *Pamiętnik Literacki*, vol.64, no.2, 1973

Zbijewska 1980 Krystyna Zbijewska, *Orzeł w kurniku: Z życia Stanisława Wyspiańskiego* (Państwowy Instytut Wydawniczy, Warsaw, 1980)

Żeleński 1929 Tadeusz Żeleński (Boy), *Ludzie żywi* (Wydawnictwo J. Mortkowicza: Towarzystwo Wydawnicze w Warszawie, Warsaw and Kraków, 1929)

Żuławski 1901 Jerzy Żuławski, *Poezje I* (Księgarnia D.E. Friedleina, Kraków, 1901)

Żuławski n.d. Adam Żuławski, 'The origins of Polish Sci-Fi & the legacy of Jerzy Żuławski', *Culture.pl*, undated, https://culture.pl/en/feature/the-origins-of-polish-sci-fi-the-legacy-of-jerzy-zulawski [accessed 14 September 2024]

CONTRIBUTORS

Dr Alison Smith is Director of Collections and Research at the Wallace Collection, London, and formerly Chief Curator at the National Portrait Gallery. Previously published works include: *Charles III: The Making of a King* (National Portrait Gallery, 2023), *Edward Burne-Jones* (Tate Publishing, 2018), *Reflections: Van Eyck and the Pre-Raphaelites* (Yale University Press, 2017).

Dr Julia Griffin is an art historian and museum curator with a dual research specialism in British and Polish art. She co-curated and co-edited *Young Poland: The Polish Arts and Crafts Movement, 1890–1918* (Lund Humphries Publishers Ltd, 2020), joint winner of the Association for Art History's 2022 Curatorial Prize. She has also published on William Morris and Dante Gabriel Rossetti, including contributions to *The Cambridge Companion to William Morris* (2024) and the *Routledge Companion to William Morris* (2021).

Prof Andrzej Szczerski is the Director of the National Museum in Kraków and a Professor in the Institute of Art History at the Jagiellonian University. He has authored publications and curated exhibitions on 19th–20th century art, architecture and design. In 2021, he co-curated *Young Poland: The Polish Arts and Crafts Movement, 1890–1918* at the William Morris Gallery in London.

Magdalena Laskowska is an art historian and Curator of Drawings and Watercolours at the National Museum in Kraków, including responsibility for the works of Stanisław Wyspiański at the Wyspiański Museum. She was co-curator of the recent exhibitions *Stanisław Wyspiański* (2017–18) and *Unknown Wyspiański* (2019) and has published extensively on the artist's life and work.

Dr Agnieszka Skalska is Curator of Polish Art from the eighteenth century to 1945 at the National Museum in Poznań. She has researched the art of Olga Boznańska, Katarzyna Kobro and Maria Nicz-Borowiakowa, and curated exhibitions on 19th and 20th-century art, including *Choroba jako źródło sztuki* (2019) and *Awangardzistka. Maria Nicz-Borowiakowa 1896–1944* (2022; co-curator).

Maria Skrzypczak-Latzke trained as an art historian at the Adam Mickiewicz University in Poznań. Since 2018 she has worked in the Prints and Drawings Department at the National Museum in Poznań. She specialises in eighteenth- and nineteenth-century Polish drawing. She has published academic articles in journals including *Studia Muzealne*.

PICTURE CREDITS

The National Portrait Gallery would like to thank the copyright holders for granting permission to reproduce works illustrated in this book. Every effort has been made to contact the holders of copyright material and any omissions will be corrected in future editions if the publisher is notified in writing.

pp.2, 21 (all), 23, 33, 34, 35, 38–9, 46–7, 55, 59   Digital collections of the National Museum in Warsaw.

pp.9, 14 (right)   Franciscan Friary, Kraków. Photo: Tomasz Markowski/NMK Digitization Studio.

pp.11, 12, 15, 54, 56   National Museum in Kraków. Photo: NMK Digitization Studio.

pp.14 (left), 36, 68, 72–3, 81, 88–9 , 97, 112–13, 105   National Museum in Kraków. Photo: Bartosz Cygan/NMK Digitization Studio.

p.17   Ziyad Raoof Collection. Courtesy of the Ziyad Raoof Collection.

p.19   National Museum in Kraków. Photo: Patryk Jezierski/NMK Digitization Studio.

p.20   Wilhelm Feldman, *Polish literature 1880–1904* (*Piśmiennictwo polskie 1880–1904*), vol.2 (H. Altenberg Publishing, Lviv, 1905). Collection: National Library of Poland.

p.25   Andrzej Szoka (Museum of Kraków) © All rights reserved.

pp.26, 120–1, 124–5, 128   National Museum in Kraków. Photo: Bartosz Cygan, Mateusz Szczypiński, Piotr Idem /NMK Digitization Studio.

p.28 (below right)   Collections of the Silesian Museum in Katowice. Photo: Rafał Wyrwich.

p.28 (above)   Collegium Maius, Jagiellonian University Museum. Image courtesy of Magdalena Laskowska.

p.28 (below left)   National Museum in Warsaw Collection.

p.29 (below)   © 2024 Muzeum Sztuki w Łodzi.

pp.29 (above), 45   The Raczyński Foundation at the National Museum in Poznań.

pp.30 (left and right)   Museum of Kraków.

p.42   Munchmuseet, Oslo. Photo: Munchmuseet/Juri Kobayashi.

p.49   Muzeum Ziemi Tarnowskiej.

p.51   National Museum in Kraków. Photo: Karol Kowalik /NMK Digitization Studio.

pp, 53, 108   National Museum in Kraków. Photo: Jakub Płoszaj, Karol Kowalik/NMK Digitization Studio.

p.58   The Collection of the Museum of Opole Silesia.

p.60   Muzeum Tatrzańskie in Zakopane.

pp.62, 92–3   National Museum in Kraków. Photo: Paweł Czernicki/ NMK Digitization Studio.

pp.64–5, 84–5, 100–1, 116   National Museum in Poznań.

pp.76–7   Collection of Krzysztof Musiał, on loan to the National Museum in Warsaw. Photo: Agra Art auction house.

DIRECTOR'S ACKNOWLEDGEMENTS

This display and publication are significant in being the first in the UK devoted to the portraits made by Stanisław Wyspiański, an artist little known in Britain but a legendary figure in Poland. A one-man Polish renaissance, Wyspiański was active across many disciplines, especially theatre and design, which may explain why his portraits have been eclipsed by the more public-facing side of his achievement. Drawn swiftly in bold, gestural strokes of pastel, the portraits cast a dramatic light on the hopes and aspirations of a generation of people who lived through a pivotal moment in Poland's history, in the era leading up to independence in 1918. Some went on to play key roles in the future of the country while several died young in the years that culminated in the tragedy of the Second World War.

I am grateful to Alison Smith, former Chief Curator at the National Portrait Gallery, now Director of Collections and Research at the Wallace Collection, for proposing the idea in collaboration with co-curator Professor Andrzej Szczerski, Director of the National Museum in Kraków. This project has been developed in partnership with both the National Museum in Kraków and the National Museum in Poznań, and I would like to thank Andrzej Szczerski and Tomasz Łęcki, Director of the National Museum in Poznań, for supporting the project with major loans from their respective collections, as well as Krzysztof Musiał for the important loan from his collection. Further thanks are due to the contributors to the catalogue: Magdalena Laskowska, Agnieszka Skalska, Maria Skrzypczak-Latzke and especially to Julia Griffin who brought great expertise to the subject as well translating the Polish texts into English.

The exhibition has been supported with generous funding from the Polish Ministry of Culture and National Heritage as well as the Polish Cultural Institute, as part of the British Council's UK/Poland Cultural Season 2025. We are extremely grateful to both organizations for their help and dedication in helping to see the project through to realisation.

Victoria Siddall
Director, National Portrait Gallery

CURATOR'S ACKNOWLEDGEMENTS

I would like to acknowledge all those who have been involved in helping introduce Wyspiański to audiences in Britain. Special thanks are due to Marta de Zuniga, former Director of the Polish Cultural Institute for her enthusiasm and commitment in promoting the project, supported by Natalia Puchalska, former Head of Education, Literature and Communications, and Paulina Latham, Head of Visual Arts and Music. Professor Andrzej Szczerski has been a wonderful collaborator and I would like to thank him and his team at the National Museum in Kraków: Magdalena Laskowska, Katarzyna Pawłowska, Aleksandra Kłaput, Damian Sularz, Anna Kowalczyk, Łucja Skoczeń-Rąpała, Katarzyna Stolarz and Agata Ralska. At the National Museum in Poznań, I am grateful to Tomasz Łęcki, Agnieszka Skalska, Maria Skrzypczak-Latzke, Grażyna Hałasa, Martyna Łukasiewicz as well as Julia Juskowiak and Alicja Serafin. Further thanks to Ewa Leszczyńska, Ewelina Radecka and Małgorzata Palka and to Ziyad Raoof for his warm hospitality. Thanks also to Lucien Topolski, Natalia Bahlawan, Anna Jóźwik and Anna Bednarek. Finally, I am grateful to Julia Griffin and Abigail Grater for their scrupulous attention to detail and to Nicholas Tromans for his support throughout.

Many colleagues at the National Portrait Gallery have been involved in the development and implementation of this project: Denise Vogelsang, Poppy Andrews and Anna Pharoah have been a consistent support in Communications and Development, as has Melanie Pilbrow in International Partnerships, together with Sarah Tinsley. Yasmin Anwer and Katherine Robson have been diligent in overseeing loans and transportation. Taylor Bentley has steered this publication through each stage of production supported by Kara Green, Jemma Jacobs, Priti Kothary, Katie Anderson and designer Peter Dawson. I would like to extend my thanks to the Art Handling and Conservation teams for the installation of the display and to Charlotte Bolland for keeping an attentive curatorial eye on the project, as well as Andrea Easey and Jude Simmons for overseeing design and interpretation.

Alison Smith
Director of Collections and Research, The Wallace Collection

Published in Great Britain by National Portrait Gallery Publications
National Portrait Gallery
St Martin's Place
London WC2H 0HE

Published to accompany the display:
Stanisław Wyspiański Portraits
National Portrait Gallery, London
27 March – 13 July 2025

This display has been made possible as a result of the Government Indemnity Scheme.
The National Portrait Gallery, London, would like to thank HM Government for providing
indemnity and the Department for Culture, Media and Sport and Arts Council England
for arranging the indemnity.

Every purchase supports the National Portrait Gallery, London. For a complete catalogue
of current publications, please visit our website at www.npg.org.uk/publications

The project 'Portraits of Stanisław Wyspiański at the National Portrait Gallery in London' under
the 'Inspiring Culture' Programme is realised in cooperation with the National Portrait Gallery
and the Polish Cultural Institute in London.

Co-financed by the Minister of Culture and National Heritage under the 'Inspiring Culture' Programme

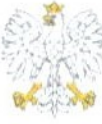

Ministry of Culture and National Heritage
Republic of Poland

Co-organisers of the exhibition:

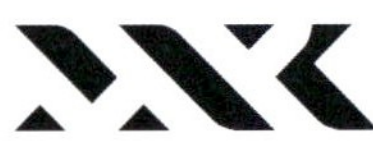

Muzeum
Narodowe
w Krakowie

NATIONAL
PORTRAIT
GALLERY

Exhibition Partner:

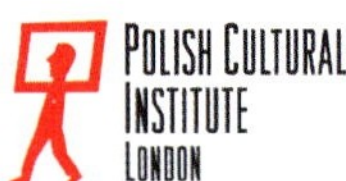

ISBN 978-1-85514-579-5

A catalogue record for this book is available from the British Library

10 9 8 7 6 5 4 3 2 1

Printed and bound in Italy by Printer Trento
Reproduction by DL Imaging

FRONT COVER:
Stanisław Wyspiański
Irena Solska, 1904
Pastel on paper,
480 × 630mm
National Museum
in Poznań
(see p.100)

BACK COVER:
Stanisław Wyspiański
Józio Feldman, 1905
Pastel on paper,
380 × 380mm
National Museum
in Kraków
(see p.105)

Director of Commercial and Operations: Anna Starling
Senior Publishing Manager: Kara Green
Project Editor: Taylor Bentley
Picture Research: Katie Anderson
Production Manager: Priti Kothary
Publishing Assistant: Jemma Jacobs
Copy Editors: Abigail Grater and Lizzy Silverton
Proofreader: Lizzy Silverton
Design: Peter Dawson, Ronja Rønning, www.gradedesign.com

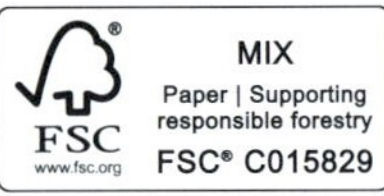